THE IDENTITY OF YEATS

THE IDENTITY

OF

YEATS

BY

RICHARD ELLMANN

OXFORD UNIVERSITY PRESS

NEW YORK

TO MARY

First published by Oxford University Press, New York, 1954
Second edition published as an Oxford University Press paperback, 1964
printing, last digit: 10 9 8 7 6 5
Printed in the United States of America

CONTENTS

PREFACE TO THE SECOND EDITION

WHEN we think of Yeats's mind in concentration, brooding upon silence, as he said, 'like a long-legged fly upon a stream,' we may well hesitate to clatter in armed with our new-fangled muskets — our readers' guides and commentaries, our iconographies and identities — and to aim them at that noble quarry. The danger was brought home to me when the editor of a continental encyclopedia invited me to write an article about Yeats. Being understandably fearful of American caprices, he supplied me with detailed instructions on how to proceed. I should be sure to show Yeats as a late Pre-Raphaelite, as a member of the Rhymers' Club and of the *Savoy* group, as a symbolist in the school of Mallarmé, as a leader in the revival of William Blake, as a participant in the Celtic Renaissance. I should make clear that he was a friend of Oscar Wilde, of Madame Blavatsky, of Lady Gregory, of the magician MacGregor Mathers, of Ezra Pound. I should demonstrate the effect upon Yeats of other arts. The prescription was intimidating, and as I tried to follow it my misgivings increased. Was Yeats really a jack-of-all-movements? Did he putter about in the past? Was he an other-people's-friend? And while the encyclopedist was German, I have an uneasy feeling that I have not been blameless in helping to establish the kind of criticism of Yeats which made this detailed assignment a logical outcome. But I will not incriminate only myself. Yeats is in some present peril everywhere of being swallowed up by the great whale of literary history. We must do what we can to help him out of that indiscriminate belly.

To be told that what looks new is really old, that every step forwards is a step backwards, is hard on trail blazers, and Yeats was impatient enough with those of us who edit and annotate lines young men tossing in their beds rhymed out in love's despair. We need not, however, repudiate editing or annotating; Yeats comforts us elsewhere when he says that 'truth flourishes where the student's lamp has shone.' But to read the literature on Yeats is to come to feel that the search for his sources and analogues has become disproportionate, and that a tendency is growing to turn all that marvellously innovative poetry into a resumé of what other people have written. An inspired resumé, of course, but still a resumé. Sometimes the resumé includes what other people have painted or carved, too. A few years ago, for example, G. D. P. Allt and T. R. Henn suggested that Yeats's poem, 'Leda and the Swan,' grew out of a painting of this subject by Michelangelo and possibly also out of a drawing of Jupiter and Ganymede by the same artist. Later Giorgio Melchiori, developing these hints in an important book, reproduced three copies of Michelangelo's lost picture, the drawing too, a picture of Leda and the swan by a follower of Leonardo and one by Gustave Moreau, and then a Hellenistic statue of the same subject. Seven in all. But the conclusion to which a study of these works of art brings one is that Yeats has done something different from any; not only are his graphic details at variance (none of them show the bird's beak holding the nape of Leda's neck), but the whole intellectual weight is distinct.

In Michelangelo what is expressed is the suave perfection of the union of human and divine. Under the pressure of Christian doctrine, there is no irony recognized in this union. Yeats has a different object, as he makes clear at once:

> A sudden blow, the great wings beating still
> Above the staggering girl . . .

For Yeats the significance of this mating is that it is not tender or easy; the bird, filled with divine power and knowledge, is still the brute blood of the air. The incongruities are glossed over by Michelangelo, in Yeats they are heightened. The sense of disproportion, of shock, of rape, is captured in those phrases which describe the blow, the flapping of huge wings, the strange dark webs, the catching of the helpless Leda. She is dazed and overcome, not cajoled, and the god, once the sexual crisis is past, lets her drop from his indifferent beak. I do not mean that Yeats is a naturalist as Michelangelo is an idealist; both of these positions are too easy.

Rather what Yeats does is to let both views of the subject coalesce, to see them with double sight, and this is why his poem is modern as Michelangelo's painting is not. Mr. Melchiori shows intelligently how fond Yeats was of the personality of Michelangelo, but whether fond or not, Yeats belongs to a different persuasion from the Renaissance.

The issue of a pictorial source for 'Leda and the Swan' was drawn more sharply last summer, when Charles Madge published in *The Times Literary Supplement* a reproduction of a Greek bas-relief which Yeats probably saw in the British Museum. This carving is much more convincing than Mr. Henn's or Mr. Melchiori's examples; in it the details are in fact the same as in the first part of the poem. The resemblance is too close for coincidence. The only question is, what does it prove? Mr. Melchiori wrote a letter to the editor conceding that this illustration was more apt than his own, but declaring that it confirmed his theory that visual imagery had priority for Yeats. But does it? Priority has become an offensive word, and it is not an easy thing to determine. Presumably Yeats knew from his reading who Leda was before he saw the bas-relief at the British Museum. Is it not hopeless to attempt to determine through which sense a poet is most deeply affected? For example, if we were to grant that the bas-relief helped Yeats to frame the octave of the sonnet, what inspired the next three lines?

> A shudder in the loins engenders there
> The broken wall, the burning roof and tower,
> And Agamemnon dead.

There is nothing in the bas-relief to suggest these after-effects of the coupling. Is it useful to speculate on how Yeats conceived of the image of burning? Did he see a fire, hear the crackling of flames, smell burn, scorch his hand, taste something that was too hot? Or did he remember Marlowe's description of 'flaming Jupiter' when he appeared not to Leda but 'to hapless Semele'? Or Rossetti's refrain of 'Tall Troy's on fire.' Even if we determined beyond doubt that he had seen a picture of a fire, or a bas-relief of it, or read a poem, we could still not explain the tele-

scoping of historical events in those lines. Or the stages of the
sexual violation which are probably implied in the series of images
— the broken wall, the burning roof and tower, and Agamemnon
dead. It is conceivable that he found these out by personal experience, and that the suggested relation of sexual stages to historical
events came as an ironic echo of the octave from his own mind, not
someone else's. And if we admit this possibility, we can ask more
peremptorily what is the use of trying to isolate creative motivation. The only effect is to minimize the role of the poet in shaping
his impressions.

We can go farther and say that, given this bas-relief, Yeats's
poem does not necessarily emerge from it. He uses its details in so
far as they are convenient, but his emphasis is not the Greek artist's
either. For the Greek the rape of Leda by the swan was apparently
a magnificent variety of sexual assault; he was interested in its
minute physical oddities; the god and the woman receive his equal
attention. In Yeats, however, the interest is centred on the mortal
woman, on the psychological implications for her and, by exten-
sion, for us. We watch Leda's reactions, not the god's. And Yeats
goes beyond the strangely assorted pair to meditate on the destruc-
tiveness of sexual passion, on its power to upheave the world. At
the end of the poem, he exclaims in bewilderment at the disparity
between gods and men, between the minds as well as the bodies of
Zeus and Leda. The generating theme of the poem is a feeling he
had from childhood, of the tantalizing imperfection of human life;
his own experience told him that power and knowledge could never
exist together, that to acquire one was to lose the other. All Yeats's
poetry embodies this theme. Leda and the swan are only one of
many embodiments of it in his verse. When we study that verse we
put source after source behind us until we are in the poet's mind,
not in the British Museum.

If painters and sculptors have not provided us with enough
analogues, we have all been unable to resist comparing Yeats with
William Blake. Two books have been written to elicit these
similarities. Certainly Yeats had a passion for Blake, and certainly
he spent three years from 1889 to 1892 strenuously editing and

commenting on the Prophetic Books. It is tempting to relate Blake's Four Zoas to Yeats's Four Faculties, and I have done so elsewhere in this book. Even if connections can be made, however, is it not time to emphasize the disconnections instead? When we think of Blake, we think of a mind of almost unprecedented assertiveness. When we think of Yeats, we think of a force of almost unprecedented modulation. Blake, as Yeats himself tells us, 'beat upon the wall / Till truth obeyed his call.' Yeats is rather a great cat in his dealings with truth than a beater upon walls. Blake condemns the world of the five senses, Yeats gives it substantial acceptance. Blake is determined that England should become heaven, Yeats is not sure that even Ireland will achieve this goal. Blake impresses us by his initial and unswerving conviction, Yeats by his serpentine struggle towards bold declaration. Blake commits himself to his own system and spends most of his creative years elaborating it in special terms. Yeats remains ambiguous about his symbology, lodges it in prose, and never uses its special terms in his verse unless they have accepted as well as eccentrically personal meanings. Finally, Yeats wrote an explanation of Blake, a favour that Blake, who hated explanations, would never have done for Yeats.

Since Yeats is not Blake, perhaps he is Mallarmé. Graham Hough, a critic I respect too much not to wish to disagree with, contends in a recent book that the early Yeats at least belongs to the French symbolists. 'Symbolism', Mr. Hough points out, 'moves in the direction of an impassable gulf. . . . For the symbolist poet there is no question of describing an experience; the moment of illumination only occurs in its embodiment in some particular artistic form. There is no question of relating it to the experience of a lifetime, for it is unique, it exists in the poem alone.' And he finds in the early Yeats the symbolist doctrine full-blown, though contaminated a little by a non-literary occultism. The fact that it is contaminated at all should warn us. I cannot concede to Mr. Hough that even in the early Yeats there is any desire for an autonomous art, separated from life and experience by an impassable gulf. We have been taught so often that we live in a degenerate age, that the audience has become obtuse and sterile, that writers have detached themselves from it perforce, that we are almost embarrassed when we bethink ourselves of the sizeable number of our best writers who are not alienated, not isolated, not even inaccessible. Yeats's early dream was not to live in an ivory tower, but on an Irish island, not in unnature, but in nature, not in a place he had never seen, but in a place he had known as a child. If there was anything that he shied away from it was the separation of his art from his life, of his work from his audience. Consider all those interrelations he set up between himself and his public by founding Irish literary societies in London and Dublin, by attaching his affections to a woman who was an Irish nationalist, by writing poems which should be Irish, local, amorous. All these poems confirm an intention to stay on earth, however much he may hint at the existence of another world.

When Yeats seriously contemplates leaving the observable world, he customarily points out what a mistake it would be. For example, in one of his earliest poems, 'The Seeker,' the hero is so enraptured by the pursuit of an other-worldly ideal that he cannot fight in battle, and men say his heart has been stolen by the spirits. At last, after a lifetime of unheroic behaviour and tenacious searching, he reaches the visionary figure he has sought. But she is no image of transcendent beauty, instead she is a 'bearded witch,' and when asked her name replies, 'Men call me infamy.' Yeats suppressed this object-lesson for symbolists about the danger of isolating experience from an ideal, but its theme is common to many poems he retained.

In 'Fergus and the Druid' Fergus begs the gift of other-worldly wisdom; receiving it, he is appalled and laments,

> But now I have grown nothing, knowing all.
> Ah! Druid, Druid, how great webs of sorrow
> Lay hidden in the small slate-coloured thing!

So far from yielding to another world of the spirit, Yeats in his verse is always demonstrating that we had better cling to this one. In the poem which he put at the beginning of his second volume of verse, 'To the Rose upon the Rood of Time,' he acknowledges his fear that he may do what Mallarmé perhaps wished to, and 'learn to chaunt a tongue men do not know.' Yeats testifies to his determination to keep in touch with common things, with the weak worm, the field mouse, with 'heavy mortal hopes that toil and pass.' He acknowledges the call of isolation, but affirms that he will resist it. His next volume, *The Wind among the Reeds*, also begins with an appeal from the other world, this time from the Sidhe who call, 'Away, come away.' We listen to their musical voices without obeying. Occasionally someone is taken away, like the child the fairies steal in *The Land of Heart's Desire*, but the fairies are baleful and predatory here. In Yeats's later poetry the same struggle is portrayed: it becomes the theme of such poems as 'Vacillation' and 'A Dialogue of Self and Soul,' but while the poet tries to play fair, the dialogue, and his vacillation, have always the same resolution. To follow the soul into another world is to give up one's heart and self, and worst of all for a poet, to give up one's tongue, for in the presence of that unblemished world our tongue's a stone, in the simplicity of fire we are struck dumb. The poet is committed to this world by his profession as well as by his temperament.

How different all this sounds from Mallarmé for whom the artist treats experience as gingerly and probingly as a detective looking for the incomprehensible crime which appearances cover up. Mallarmé constitutes the poet a specialist in reality, a detective writing for detectives. What can be said in the open is not worth saying. Mallarmé's acknowledged image of the poet is the awesome magus who evokes by words an intangible reality. But this is a French magus more than an Irish one. Yeats, who knew magic at first hand as Mallarmé did not, took a homelier view of it. One thinks of his experiments in putting certain substances under his pillow to see what effect his dreams might have upon them, or they upon his dreams. And for Yeats the incantatory word is not something achieved by exclusion of much of the mind; it is achieved by a spiritual struggle of the whole being, of which the poetic imagination forms a part, and it is inside, not outside, the stress of experience. Unassumingly, too, Yeats does not talk of the magician as a manufacturer but an importer; his images are not created new but come from the Great Memory, a kind of collective imagination. In Mallarmé the attempt is to separate the poem from all that is not poem, to abolish the poet, to free an object originally palpable so that it becomes impalpable. All real bouquets render up their fragrance to form an essence they do not themselves possess.

In Yeats, the emphasis is on the tangibility of the images which the artist cleans and perfects, and on the struggle to clean and perfect them. The poet is not ostracized from his poem, he is its all-important inhabitant. The act of creation itself is curiously democratic for Yeats, comparable to other forms of intense endeavour, so that the poet can represent his work as human too. He must write with such airs that one believes he has a sword upstairs. The desire to see Mallarmé in Yeats has encouraged a misconception of some of his best poems. His pursuit of images is held to be an escape from experience, when the images are rather focuses of experience. In 'The Circus Animals' Desertion', Yeats at first seems to take another view, as when he says,

> Players and painted stage took all my love,
> And not those things that they were emblems of,

but even here the word 'emblems' recalls to us the dependent character of the images. And his conclusion recognizes firmly the dependence of art upon life:

> Those masterful images because complete
> Grew in pure mind, but out of what began?
> A mound of refuse or the sweepings of a street,
> Old kettles, old bottles, and a broken can,
> Old iron, old bones, old rags, that raving slut
> Who keeps the till. Now that my ladder's gone,
> I must lie down where all the ladders start
> In the foul rag-and-boneshop of the heart.

An excellent critic interprets these lines to mean that Yeats is in despair at the idea of lying down in his heart, at being 'left to live merely, when living is most difficult, life having been used up in another cause.' But this is reading Yeats's words without considering their intonation. While the poet is disgusted for the moment with his own heart, he is well aware that this heart has engendered all his images. He pleads necessity for what he does by desire; he *wants*, in short, to lie down in the foul rag-and-boneshop of the heart. For, as he says in 'Two Songs from a Play,'

> Whatever flames upon the night
> Man's own resinous heart has fed,

and in 'Vacillation,'

> From man's blood-sodden heart are sprung
> Those branches of the night and day
> Where the gaudy moon is hung.

At the end of the poem 'Byzantium,' Yeats, having described the miraculous creations which are produced in art, suddenly recalls the flood of time from which they come, and sees the time-world as made up of passionate images too:

> Those images that yet
> Fresh images beget,
> That dolphin-torn, that gong-tormented sea.

We have been asked to believe that these lines express Yeats's revulsion from the welter of experience, when clearly they imply that even from the vantage point of Byzantium that welter is fascinating.

So I do not think we can describe Yeats as alienated or even as aloof, either from his own experience or from other people's. From childhood on he is delighted with the life of peasants, with Irish life. Mallarmé, always straining to avoid space and time, would find Irish nationalism an absurdity, as perhaps it is, though Yeats did not think so. Yeats even wrote his poem, 'To Ireland in the Coming Times,' to establish his rightful place once and for all as Ireland, his claim to be counted one with the Irish poets Davis, Mangan, Ferguson. And at the end of his life he wrote a poem to make sure that his body after death should be Irish too:

> Under bare Ben Bulben's head
> In Drumcliff churchyard Yeats is laid.

Yet I do not find it very helpful either to consider Yeats, as some would do, one of a group of Irish poets who freshened up Celtic legends. Yeats could be and wanted to be provincial, but he could also be cosmopolitan. When he wrote *A Vision*, he forgot he was an Irishman. And while he calls the fairies by their Irish name of the Sidhe, I suspect that they too are internationalists. His later versions of preternatural beings are, except in the play *The Dreaming of the Bones*, indifferent to race althought they retain their interest in families and in individuals. Irishness is an essential quality, but a secondary one.

Perhaps then we should pursue another direction by seeing Yeats as a follower of the occult tradition or, as it has been renamed by one critic, the Platonic tradition. But here too his allegiance is doubtful. If we try to think of him as a Platonist we have to remember he wrote a poem to say, 'Those Platonists are a curse, . . . God's fire upon the wane,' and another in which he said, 'I cry in Plato's teeth.' If we mean by Platonism the later followers of Plato, we have to remember that Yeats also wrote, 'I mock Plotinus' thought,' and that he buffeted Plotinus as well as Plato about in several poems. At moments his theories seem to coincide with Plato's, as in that heroic defense of a woman's primping, 'Before the World Was Made.' In a way she agrees that this world is a copy of a more Platonic one, but the real theme is her deliberate energy in attempting to override human imperfection. Plato's philosophy is used only to the extent that it can be made Yeatsian, the extent to which the bodiless can be bodied.

If we ally Yeats with the occultists who followed in secret a metaphysical tradition, we will find him asserting his independence of them too. There is danger in connecting him too closely with either MacGregor Mathers or Madame Blavatsky, for he quarrelled and broke with both of them. Insofar as occultism is cloistered and moralistic — and most magicians are tediously moralistic or immoralistic — Yeats stands apart from them. Insofar as they hope to alter the phenomenal world, Yeats is very sceptical. The phenomenal world is not so easily dismissed, or at least not for long. Insofar as they hold converse with spirits and win from them preternatural powers, Yeats is only sporadically credulous and then for his own reasons. Fundamentally he is like Queen Edain in 'The Two Kings,' who rejects the advances of an immortal lover so as to stay with her mortal one. We long for immortal essences but when they accost us we resist. The poet, firm among the five senses, imagines their perfection, not their abandonment. He tolerates the ideal only when it is covered with what Yeats calls 'casual flesh.'

In seeking to emphasize the degree to which Yeats is unlike Michelangelo or Plato or Blavatsky or Mallarmé or Blake, I have the ulterior motive of offering another view. What is the mental atmosphere that makes Yeats's poems so individualistic? We might try to establish first the outer borders of his mind, with the initial admission that, as Yeats said, these are constantly shifting; and then its inner qualities. The intimation that seems to have been with him from his earliest days is that life as we generally experience it is incomplete, but that at moments it appears to transcend itself and yield moments of completeness or near-completeness, moments when, as he says half-humorously in the poem 'There,' 'all the barrel-hoops are knit, . . . all the serpent-tails are bit.' In his early work Yeats conceives of the boundary line between the worlds of completeness and incompleteness as twilit, in his later work it is lit by lightning. Whether the light is blurred or stark there are strange crossings-over.

The trespassers come from both directions, from this world to that, from that world to this. The fairies or Sidhe would like to translate us, to possess us, to catch us in nets of dreams, to tempt us, to remind us of what we lack and they have, and sometimes they succeed. More often they only manage to make us miserable. Something about the world of generation saddens them, as if the separation of worlds were difficult for them, too, to bear and caused them suffering. In middle life Yeats discards the fairies (as he already had given up the Rose), and begins to call the denizens of the other world antiselves or simply ghosts; in his later work they are usually spirits in his verse, daimons in his prose. Under their changed names, they continue to busy themselves about us.

Some readers of Yeats are put off by this metaphysical popula-
tion, and by his related interest in all sorts of extrasensory perception. Could Yeats really have believed in these things? they ask.
But to ask this question is to show that one is several generations
in time behind Yeats, who asked with more point whether the
word *belief* belonged to our age at all. Elsewhere in this book are
listed all the locutions which Yeats used to avoid the term 'believe,' and it can be said that nothing is further from his mind than
simple credence. The word *God* he generally skirted with the same
dexterity. It is puzzling to read a recent interpretation of the poem,
'Mohini Chatterjee,' where there is the line, 'I asked if I should
pray.' The critic says, Yeats asks if he should pray to God; but
Yeats doesn't mention God, and it is not at all certain that he is
addressing himself to that early authority. He may be invoking his
deeper self, or some daimon or group of daimons, or some indeterminate object, or he may be meditating with an even vaguer
audience, praying to no one and to nothing, just praying. Occasionally Yeats does make use in his verse of supernatural machinery
or of preternatural machinery, but always without precise or
credal commitment.

He needs this machinery because of his conviction, as I have
indicated, that there is a conceivable life which is better than
human life in that it is complete, undiminished, unimpairable. Let
us call this the daimonic world. In relation to the daimons we are
mere abstracts. Yeats astonishes us by the bluntness with which he
makes clear the defects of our own world. But having made clear
its limitations, he suddenly enters upon its defence. It has pain, it
has struggle, it has tragedy, elements denied to the daimons. Seen
from their point of view, life always fails. Yet it does not fail
utterly, for man can imagine their state even if he cannot participate
in it. And the capacity to imagine is redemptive; man, in a frenzy
at being limited, overthrows much of that limitation. He defiantly
asserts his imagined self against futility, and to imagine heroism
is to become a hero.

And now we are led from a comparison of worlds to one of
people. Man, according to Yeats's view, is a being who is always

endeavouring to construct by fiction what he lacks in fact. Born
incomplete, he conceives of completeness and to that extent
attains it. We outfling ourselves upon the universe, people the
desert with our fertile images. The hero does this unconsciously,
the artist consciously, but all men do it in their degree. The dead
bone upon the shore in 'Three Things' sings still of human love.
Space and time are unreal, Yeats sometimes concedes to the
philosophers, but he says they are marvellously unreal; they, and
life and death, heaven and hell, day and night, are human images
imposed like form upon the void. Yeats looks at two withered old
women, Eva Gore-Booth and Constance Markiewicz, and writes
of them,

> The light of evening, Lissadell,
> Great windows open to the south,
> Two girls in silk kimonos, both
> Beautiful, one a gazelle.

The girls in the gazebo of the country-house are summoned up by
the poet as more real than the decrepit women; if the great gazebo
of the world is false, it must be true as well. It is true when it
conforms, as at moments it does, to our image of perfection.

But the mind has another glory besides its power to create: it can
also destroy. Man lowers his plumb-line into the darkness and
establishes measurement, form, number, intellect. But he has
hardly established all these before he casts the line away, as if
every imaginative construct could only momentarily satisfy his
creative need and must then be demolished. 'What's the meaning
of all song?' Yeats asks in 'Vacillation,' and replies, 'Let all things
pass away.' His most powerful statement of this kind is in the
poem called 'Meru,' where the hermits on the Indian mountain sum
up in themselves this dissatisfaction with every human fabrication.
They are Asiatic hermits, but Yeats recognizes that every mind has
an Asiatic aspect which would destroy the shows of this world —
shows which he associates with Europe. We live in 'manifold illusion'; and, as Yeats puts it in another poem, 'mirror on mirror
mirrored is all the show.' Having put on our finery we take it off

again. We strip the masks we have created for ourselves. We descend into our own abyss; if we cannot burn up the gazebo, we scornfully aspire to do so. The urge to destruction, like the urge to creation, is a defiance of limits; we transcend ourselves by refusing to accept completely anything that is human, and then indomitably we begin fabricating again. As Yeats says in 'Lapis Lazuli,'

> All things fall and are built again,
> And those that build them again are gay.

If we try to relate Yeats's poems more narrowly to the contrast between daimons and men on the one hand, and between man and his limitations on the other, I think we will see that each such contrast gains its force from a confrontation of passive acceptance with energetic defiance. It would be so easy to grant, as any objective witness would, that the poet's daughter should not associate with a man who has the worst of all bad names. When he admonishes her, however, she replies unanswerably: 'But his hair is beautiful, / Cold as the March wind his eyes.' In a greater poem, it would be so easy to concede that Maud Gonne had behaved badly towards Yeats; but the sense of 'No Second Troy' is that this aspect of her life is of no consequence, and the important thing is that she has tried to live by the high laws of imagination. The poet is always faced with a commonsense solution, as by a sort of minimum wage, and always chooses to take nothing rather than take that. If Maud Gonne's energies were destructive, that was because she lived in a world of outworn images and had to destroy them. The pacific soul, which Yeats contrasts in his later verse with the military self, always offers a conventional way to heaven, and the self always rejects it, preferring the turmoil of this world, with its desperate search for words and images, to an easy and dumb-striking heaven. Every poem establishes alternatives to indicate only one choice is worth making, and that the agonized, unremunerative, heroic one.

These are not Yeats's ideas or beliefs; they are the mental atmosphere in which he lived, or if that term sounds too climatic, they are the seethings, the agitations of his mind which he learned to control and direct. His symbolism has to be understood not as a borrowing from Mallarmé, but as the only way in which he could express himself. 'I have no speech but symbol,' he wrote. His symbols are condensations of his theme that all struggle is futile except the struggle with futility, his recognition of the problem of the empty cornucopia, the crowded void. Each symbol is a kind of revolving disc, like Yeats's wheel or moon with their dark and light phases in *A Vision*. We can compare the tower in the poem of that name with the one in 'The Black Tower'; in the first it is intellectual aspiration, in the second it is the insubstantiality of that aspiration. The image of the tree also has its two sides, not only in the poem, 'The Two Trees,' but when it emerges as an epitome of unity in 'Among School Children' and then as an image of decay in 'the old thorn tree' of 'A Man Young and Old.' The dance is frantic, purposeless destruction in 'Nineteen Hundred and Nineteen,' while in 'Among School Children' it is composed perfection. 'The Peacock' is a symbol of the lavishing imagination, while in another poem, 'Nineteen Hundred and Nineteen,' when the mad Lady Kyteller brings the blind Robert Artisson peacock feathers, it seems some image of beauty gone hollow.

Not only are the symbols double-natured in different poems; they usually take on shifting implications within the same poem, as if they were being slowly revolved. The ancestral houses described in 'Meditations in Time of Civil War' summon up glory only to remind us of its transience. In 'Two Songs from a Play,' the staring virgin brings her divine child to begin a new cycle of time, as if it were the only cycle, yet the muses know that there are many cycles, that this has all been done before and will be done again. The pomp of the new god is contrasted with images of darkness and nullity; as Yeats says in one of his finest images of the doubling involved in all identity, 'The painter's brush consumes his dreams.' 'Only an aching heart,' he declares ('Meditations in Time of Civil War'), 'conceives a changeless work of art.' 'The Tower' that dominates the countryside has ruin in its history; on the other hand, 'The Black Tower,' so ruined as to be indefensible, finds defenders. The great-rooted blossomer is the tree in its springtime only, the perfection of dancing is achieved only momentarily before the turmoil of the greenroom begins again. Yeats is fond of showing how ambiguous the word *dream* itself is, since it is at once something brilliantly imagined, and something delusive, real and unreal, 'flowers' ('I pray that I ever be weaving') and 'cold snows' ('Meditations'). But all his key words share in this property; youth is strength and folly, old age is wisdom and debility. Images of substance are always on the verge of nothingness, narrowly balanced: 'The boughs have withered because I have told them my dreams.' 'Through all the lying days of my youth / I swayed my leaves and flowers in the sun; / Now I may wither into the truth.' Even art participates in this double-nature. For though all-powerful in its own realm, that realm is balanced uneasily between this world and the daimonic one. If it became daimonic it would be ethereal, insubstantial; if it became human, it would be helpless. Yeats summarizes this condition of art in 'Byzantium' where he writes of those artistic fires of Byzantine forges that they are

> Dying into a dance,
> An agony of trance,
> An agony of flame that cannot singe a sleeve.

In art the fires are all-powerful, but in life they have no effect at all. The same mediation is evident in 'Sailing to Byzantium,' where the bird is at once more than human in its golden perfection, and less than human in its toylike character; out of generation, it yet must sing of generation, of what is past, passing, or to come, irrevocably dependent upon the nature which it affects to spurn.

Not only do the symbols turn like wheels, but the intellectual or thematic content of each poem balances two meanings contingent upon each other. The poem 'Friends,' for example, begins with two orthodox examples of friendship, Lady Gregory and Mrs. Shakespear, and then takes up Maud Gonne who is totally unfriendly. The secret of the poem is that she has unconsciously given him more than the others gave consciously, that she did so because she represented a more fundamental energy. In 'The Magi' Yeats plays upon the standard picture of the magi dazzled by Christ's

miraculous birth, and perplexes them with his human death. In
'The Second Coming' he accepts the title from Christianity but
represents the new god as destructive rather than benign, a
monster rather than a lamb. In 'The Cold Heaven' a hideous afterlife, where injustice prevails, confronts the naked soul in search of
paradise. Or, to take a lighter example, there is his short poem
with the long title, 'On Hearing That the Students of Our New
University Have Joined the Agitation against Immoral Literature,'

> Where, where but here have Pride and Truth
> That long to give themselves for wage,
> To shake their wicked sides at youth
> Restraining reckless middle-age?

The poem's subtlety derives from its conceiving of Pride and
Truth not as draped Grecian caryatids but as middle-aged prosti-
tutes. Yet the denigration is mocking, as if he would remind us how
lofty a wage pride and truth really demand.

I sometimes think that we could try to codify the laws that
govern the complexities of Yeats's poetry. Every poem offers
alternative positions. While the choice between them may surprise
us, we can be sure it will be based upon a preference for what is
imprudent, reckless, contrary to fact, but that in so choosing the
poet does not act out of folly but out of understandable passion.
The alternative is never completely overwhelmed, but remains like
the other side of the moon, or, to use another of Yeats's images,
like some imprisoned animal, ready to burst out again with its
message of common sense or of renunciation of the world. The
basic choice of the poem is reflected in the symbols, which either
contain the same alternatives or at any rate imply them, as day
implies night. The poem ends not in a considered conclusion, but
in a kind of breathlessness, a break-through from the domain of
caution and calculation to that of imprudence and imagination; the
poem gathers its strength from putting down one view with
another, from saying, against the utmost opposition, what must
be said.

Usually the poems take one of two directions: either they are visionary, concerned with matters of prophecy, of the relations of the time-world and daimonic timelessness, or they are concerned with human enterprise, the relations of people with each other or with their own secret hopes and ambitions. In the visionary poems such as 'Leda and the Swan' or 'The Second Coming,' Yeats is concerned to intermesh the divine world with the animal, to show the world of time as centaurlike, beautiful and monstrous, aspiring and deformed. In the poems which deal with artists or with heroes or with other men, he wishes also to show how brute fact may be transmogrified, how we can sacrifice ourselves, in the only form of religious practice he sanctions, to our imagined selves which offer far higher standards than anything offered by social convention. If we must suffer, it is better to create the world in which we suffer, and this is what heroes do spontaneously, artists do consciously, and all men do in their degree.

To represent his themes Yeats originally tried to dislodge conventional attitudes by a slow rhythm which would attenuate sense and draw it onwards, as it were, into new possibilities. Sense would make way like some equerry before the sovereign spirit. Gradually he substituted for this rhythm of longing and fascination a rhythm of conquest. Like Jupiter, the daimons penetrate our world by shock, and we in turn surprise them by sudden incursions, as when, in an ordinary shop, our bodies of a sudden blaze. We do not hope to intermingle but to encroach upon each other. The language of this struggle needs to be vigorous, for it must bring us beyond statement, to the central agitation of the mind, where mission and futility brother each other, where as in the sun destruction and creation go on at once. The mind is a rage, not a warehouse. And while Michelangelo and Blake and Mallarmé and the rest may be tutelary spirits on the perimeter of this consciousness, at its centre we see only and supremely Yeats.

The new edition of this book is slightly altered here and there, but most of what was published almost ten years ago seems to me not yet discredited. In *The Identity of Yeats* I attempted to display the patterns of Yeats's poetry as in my earlier book, *Yeats: The*

Man and the Masks, I tried to understand his life. A biography must necessarily emphasize beginnings, efforts, forays, while a critical work can dwell upon accomplishments.

By the title I meant to express two purposes: the book would search for Yeats's essential mode of transforming experience, and it would insist also upon the integrity of his work, no matter in what period of his life it was composed. For the first, the preceding pages of this preface may serve as a summary of my conception. The second may now require a brief explanation. After Yeats died his critics, necessarily younger, were inclined to dismiss his early work as aberrant, and to exalt his later work as an entirely different thing. In seeking to extract his identity, I had to notice that the early work was also daring and skilful, that it was based upon a symbology and a group of never deserted themes, that its attitudes were complicated and its rhythms intricate. The change from 'The White Birds' (1892) to 'Sailing to Byzantium' (1926) is substantial; the later poem's superiority is obvious and need not be laboured. But they have in common that in both a bird images perfection, and that in both the world of time, while much disparaged, is only partially surrendered. That the later bird is easier to visualize, though equally ideal, is important, but the resemblance is none the less striking. Or we could take Yeats's prose, in his early life so graciously understated, in his later life so defiantly overstated. We do not need to be reminded that statements are altered by the mildness or force with which they are expressed, but we will not glibly call one modern and the other something else.

On evidence of such continuity it was possible to name in a unified way the stages of Yeats's development, and to clarify many poems, early and late, which appeared to offer difficulties. I hope the book may still serve these modest aims.

R. E.

NORTHWESTERN UNIVERSITY
June 13, 1963

PREFACE

I MUST mention with gratitude the names of a few friends. Mrs. W. B. Yeats has very kindly permitted my extensive use of unpublished material and of quotations from published works. Edwin Honig, John V. Kelleher, Charles Feidelson, Jr., and my brother, Erwin B. Ellmann, have made searching criticisms of various drafts of the manuscript. Allan Wade called my attention to a number of inaccuracies. Frank O'Connor, Harry Levin, John L. Sweeney, Norman Pearson, H. M. Magee, and Ellsworth Mason have helped me in many ways. Roger Manvell lent me the valuable tables of Yeats's revisions which he had compiled. The libraries of Yale University, the University of Chicago, and the University of Buffalo have allowed me to quote from certain manuscripts ; Jens Nyholm, Librarian of Northwestern University, acquired a valuable Yeats document on my behalf ; and Dr. R. J. Hayes, Director of the National Library of Ireland, has been constantly obliging. One chapter of this book has appeared in the *Kenyon Review*. Macmillan & Company, Ltd., of London, and the Macmillan Company of New York, have authorized my quotations of material from their editions. I wish to thank the Guggenheim Foundation, Harvard University, and Northwestern University for enabling me to write this book.

R. E.

Evanston, Illinois
January 27, 1953

INTRODUCTION

EXPLORERS come to a new land full of dreams of their private Cathays, and their first reactions to it depend upon how well it can be accommodated to their hopes. Only gradually do they begin to separate what is there from what is not, and to chart the true country.

Having all Yeats's poems before us is itself a guide to reading them. The oldest, written in the eighties and nineties of the last century, and the newest, written up to two days before his death in 1939, take on a different complexion. The first seem less remote and spiritual, the last less exclusively sensual. There are seasonal changes, but no earthquakes or tidal waves. His themes and symbols are fixed in youth, and then renewed with increasing vigour and directness to the end of his life.

This continuity is the more surprising because it does not strike the reader at once, as does the continuity of other poets like Wallace Stevens, E. E. Cummings, and T. S. Eliot. Changes in diction are likely to blind us to the constancy of themes. The substitution of one symbol for another is likely to conceal their equivalence. Yeats's powerful creative energy deceives us into thinking that its movement is spasmodic rather than regular.

The more one reads Yeats, the more his works appear to rotate in a few orbits. Again and again we are obliged to ask the same questions he asked. He was greatly concerned, for example, over the relations of his themes to his beliefs, especially because from the very beginning he adopted attitudes in different poems which seemingly conflicted with one another. This diversity, which he perhaps hit upon intuitively, he came to defend rationally in ways that most modern poets have left unexpressed. He displayed and interpreted the direction in which poetry was to go.

How the poet's statements and affirmations relate to his symbols was another issue that Yeats found crucial. Symbols, after all, may be simply traditional metaphors used with special emphasis, but they may also be conduits to a world of Platonic forms. The poet may use them as counters for his fancy to disport with, or imply through them a scale of values and a metaphysic. What, for example, does the cross mean to a man who is not a Christian? Yeats persistently returned to this subject until it no longer tormented him.

Themes and symbols in Yeats are questions of execution as well as of content, and style, with which he was so deeply concerned, was a question of content as well as of execution. Changes in rhythm, vocabulary, and syntax were substantive. Style, he considered, was the self-conquest of the writer who was not a man of action. Altering a word like 'dream' to 'image' or 'curd-pale' to 'climbing' involved the whole man. Stages of stylistic development were stages of personal development.

Beyond theme, symbol, and style is the general pattern or framework of Yeats's verse, in which each of these participates. Every poem embodies a schematization, conscious as well as unconscious, of his way of living and seeing; and all his poems form a larger scheme which we can watch in the process of evolving. The stature of his work, which seems to tower over that of his contemporaries, comes largely from this ultimate adhesion of part to part to form a whole.

In weighing Yeats's work from these points of view, criticism finds its justification in the sentence of Spinoza, 'The intellectual love of a thing consists in the understanding of its perfections'. Spread out in full panoply, Yeats's poetry best reveals his originality and genius.

At the outset some first principles may be arrived at. Yeats's work, so strongly individualized, remains difficult to classify. It has been described as magical or occult poetry, but both terms must be rejected. The case for occultism is simple and tempting. He undoubtedly had a lifelong interest in the subject, beginning with Theosophy in the 'eighties, continuing with magical invocation in the 'nineties, and proceeding to spiritualism and automatic writing in later life. These activities have understandably made everyone uneasy. It would be more comfortable if the outstanding poet of our time had hobnobbed with, say, Thomas Henry Huxley, instead of Helena Petrovna Blavatksy, Samuel Liddell MacGregor Mathers, a medium in Soho, or Shri Purohit Swami. But he has not obliged us, and a number of critics have therefore attacked him for failing to attach himself to a more decent and gentlemanly creed.

Yeats lent some support to the charge when, as a young man, he wrote John O'Leary that occultism, to which he gave the wider name of 'the mystical life', was the centre of his work and bore to it the same relation that Godwin's philosophy held to the work of Shelley. But occultism is a big centre, a much bigger one, in fact, than is generally acknowledged. Along with spells and spooks from every culture, it has managed to assimilate many of the leading philosophical notions of eastern and western thought. To identify it with hocus-pocus alone is evidence of a socially acceptable common sense but not of acquaintance with the subject. Yeats found in occultism, and in mysticism generally, a point of view which had the virtue of warring with accepted beliefs, and of warring enthusiastically and authoritatively. He wanted to secure proof that experimental science was limited in its results, in an age when science made extravagant claims; he wanted evidence that an ideal world existed, in an age which was fairly complacent about the benefits of actuality; he wanted to show that the current faith in reason and in logic ignored a far more important human faculty, the imagination. And, in his endeavour to construct a symbolism, he went where symbols had always been the usual mode of expression.

Predilections of this sort made him not a mystic or an occultist but one of what he called 'the last romantics'. In so referring to himself, however, he was writing ironically, equating the word with all defenders of 'traditional sanctity and loveliness', and would no doubt have said that the first romantics were

Homer and Sophocles. He might have called himself 'the last Quixote' or 'the last traditionalist' or even 'the last poet' with about the same significance. Following T. E. Hulme, we may take romanticism to be 'the view which regards man as a well, a reservoir full of possibilities', and classicism to be the view 'which regards him as a very finite and fixed creature'. Yeats is a romantic, but with compunctions. He admires imagination and individualism and excess and the golden future as much as Blake did, but he also at times evinces a strong strain of awareness that man's possibilities may not be limitless. He is unexpectedly interested in determinism ; he insists on stateliness, courtliness, control, and orderliness as criteria for judging past, present, and future. His nature is not Wordsworthian, his heroes are not Byronic, his emotional expression is not Shelleyan. His outlook is, in fact, close at points to what Hulme describes as classicism : 'In the classical attitude you never seem to swing right along to the infinite nothing. If you say an extravagant thing which does exceed the limits inside which you know man to be fastened, yet there is always conveyed in some way at the end an impression of yourself standing outside it, and not quite believing it, or consciously putting it forward as a flourish. You never go blindly into an atmosphere more than the truth, an atmosphere too rarefied for man to breathe for long. You are always faithful to the conception of a limit.' Considered in the light of Hulme's statement, what seems at times in Yeats's poetry to be romantic extravagance needs always to be read twice for its possible backspin.

It was as an Irish poet that he aspired to become known, and now that he is dead the category seems more fully established and distinguished from the state of being an English poet. Yeats's Irishism is of a special kind. Like Joyce's prose, his poetry makes use of national and local borders only to transcend them. He is Irish ; he is also anti-Irish in an Irish way ; and his interest in Irishmen is always subordinated to an interest in men. His method of treating his Irish background and subject-matter is therefore exceedingly complex. Ireland is his symbol

for the world, and he is caught between estrangement and love
for both.

His work finds its real centre in the imagination, which is
both sensual and spiritual, with no other aim than the creation
of images as lusty as itself. At its most extreme he asserts that
the imagination creates its own world. There is also the reverse
of this medal, an acknowledgment that the world should be the
creation of the imagination but is not. These two conceptions
underlie Yeats's early work as well as his late, and bring the
'far-off, most secret, and inviolate Rose' and Crazy Jane's ideal
of a love which shall be 'sole' and 'whole' into the same web.

To voice these conceptions Yeats created three principal
dramatic roles. The first, that of the seer, presents the power of
the imagination and the comparative frailty of experience most
strikingly. The seer has little or no personality of his own ; he
is often at pains to declare that his images are not remembered
from experience but imaginatively inspired. He reports on
moments of crisis when the tension between the ideal and the
actual is greatest, as when the swan descends to Leda or the
dreadful beast of the second coming slouches towards Bethlehem.
Not many of the poems present so momentous a view, but those
that do lend a prophetic firmness to the whole.

More often the protagonist of the poems takes the parts of
victim and assessor. As the frustrated, unsuccessful lover of the
early verse, as the hounded public figure of the middle period,
as the time-struck, age-worn old man of the later work, he has
always something of the scapegoat about him. The scapegoat's
sacrifice is not, however, an empty one. To abandon himself to
a hopeless passion and all its attendant suffering has the fruitful
result of glorifying the beloved and, by implication, the perfect
concord which his imagination conceives but cannot proffer.
The lover's failure becomes symbolic of the defect of all life.
To give up easy comfort and calm for the dangerous losing
battle with vulgarity and prudery, as the protagonist and his
friends do in Yeats's middle period, has the virtue of perpetuating
those qualities which are imaginatively sacred, such as courage,

freedom from abstract restraints, and creative force. To struggle against 'dull decrepitude' and death enables the speaker to defend life to its bitter end.

So, although at each stage he is victimized, the victimization is only half the story, the other half being the endowment of the situation with heroic consequence. If he takes 'all the blame out of all sense and reason', as in 'The Cold Heaven', or thirsts 'for accusation', as in 'Parnell's Funeral', it is because such sacrifices are parts of rituals through which they are transcended. The speaker is himself transcended; one forgets his plight to regard the qualities represented in it. That is why the poems, although in them he constantly talks about himself, rarely seem self-preoccupied.

The agent of transcendence is the assessor, standing at once inside and outside his own experience. He is perpetually evaluating, weighing in a scale ('A Friend's Illness'), balancing ('An Irish Airman Foresees His Death'), counting his good and bad ('Friends'), turning all he has said and done into a question until he stays awake night after night ('The Man and the Echo'). The assessment is conducted passionately, and disregards conventional morality to arrive at only those decisions which the imagination can accept because they are positive, imprudent, and dignified, never mean or narrow. A poet has a miller's thumb, and his scales operate in an unusual way. A consideration of wrongs done him does not lead to heaping insult upon his enemies, but to a secret, proud exultation, as in 'To a Friend Whose Work Has Come to Nothing', that he can escape the limitations of petty enmity.

Because the assessment is made in particular and personal terms, arising directly from some incident or development of the poet's life, the poems rarely seem didactic. When they do, their message is almost invariably iconoclastic. The protagonist flaunts his heterodoxy as superior to the impartial conclusions of abstract logic and to the traditional formulations of Puritan morality. So he inculcates an arrant subjectivism in several poems in part because any other theory reduces man's stature as against a monopolistic God's, or life's stature as against an overwhelming heaven's or against the state of nothingness. Or he frightens the bourgeois by having Crazy Jane announce that

> . . . Love has pitched his mansion in
> The place of excrement,

or makes Tom O'Roughley say, in defiance of sentimental mourning,

> 'And if my dearest friend were dead
> I'd dance a measure on his grave.'

Many of his most direct statements of this sort go into the mouths of fools and madmen, who speak as if they desired no audience for their unconventional wisdom but themselves.

Frequently the assessment takes the form of establishing differences. There are the mob and the poet, trade and art, various states of the soul ascending from confusion to unity of being. The table of differences serves much the same function as the conception of degree in the Elizabethan age; that is, it establishes differences only to bring all into a pattern. As Yeats noted in a manuscript book when he was twenty-one, 'Talent perceives differences, Genius unity'. If he contrasts the natural world with a more ideal or supernatural one, it is to conclude that 'Natural and supernatural with the self-same ring are wed'. His work can be read as a concerted effort to bring such contrasting elements as man and divinity, man and woman, man and external nature, man and his ideal, into a single circle. His sages, wrapt in their perfect sphere, must whirl down from eternity as he rises from time to meet them, and other spirits descend for 'desecration and the lover's night'; his heaven is never remote or ineffable. Against the spirit of anarchy Yeats offers his own conception of degree. When he declares that his 'medieval knees lack health until they bend', he longs for no idol but for a principle of organization in which reverence and a sense of the fitness and orderliness of things will be possible.

But his organization of the world is never placid. It is enlivened by a keen sense of tension. He upset the Indian

Abinash Bose, who came to see him in 1937, when he replied
to Bose's request for a message to India : 'Let 100,000 men of
one side meet the other. That is my message to India.' He
then, as Bose describes the scene, 'strode swiftly across the room,
took up Sato's sword, and unsheathed it dramatically and shouted,
"Conflict, more conflict"'. The message sounds savage enough,
but can serve more purpose if we put aside the histrionics which
made Yeats for the moment oblivious to India and politics and
everything but his momentary dramatic role. It had its origin
in a view of the world as almost incessant strife between opposites,
and in a similar view of the poem. He wrote Ethel Mannin late
in life, 'I find my peace by pitting my sole nature against something and the greater the tension the greater my self-knowledge'.
What came easy could not be trusted. In explaining to Dorothy
Wellesley how he wrote a poem addressed to her, he said, 'We
have all something within ourselves to batter down and get our
power from this fighting. I have never "produced" a play in
verse without showing the actors that the passion of the verse
comes from the fact that the speakers are holding down violence
or madness — "down Hysterica passio". All depends on the
completeness of the holding down, on the stirring of the beast
underneath.'

     This determination and resistance are everywhere visible in
Yeats's writings. 'Summer and Spring' is a useful illustration
because in it the processes of composition and thought show
through. The poem opens single-mindedly enough :

> We sat under an old thorn-tree
> And talked away the night,
> Told all that had been said or done
> Since first we saw the light,
> And when we talked of growing up
> Knew that we'd halved a soul
> And fell the one in t'other's arms
> That we might make it whole . . .

But love cannot come to rest so easily in a Yeats poem ; it has to
be fortified by opposition, provided here by one Peter :

> Then Peter had a murdering look,
> For it seemed that he and she
> Had spoken of their childish days
> Under that very tree.

Now Peter, having supplied the sourness to make love sweet, is dropped from sight, and we are left with the image of young love which grows out of his misery :

> O what a bursting out there was,
> And what a blossoming,
> When we had all the summer-time
> And she had all the spring !

The speaker brazenly takes for granted that his listeners will share in his satisfaction at the thwarting of Peter, but he does so in the name of love and, if he wins us, it is by reducing Peter's hatred to the status of a catalyst. The rivalry of the two young men cements the successful lover's happiness. If this conclusion seems cruel, Yeats will tell us that love is compounded of cruelty as well as sweetness.

So, in his greater poem, 'A Dialogue of Self and Soul', he sets earthly against heavenly glory ; the soul at first appears to have all blessedness as its exclusive preserve, and offers it with the confidence that the self has nothing so good. But at the height of the rivalry the self realizes it has a blessedness of its own, a secular blessedness ; this discovery is called forth by the heat of battle, and enables the self to triumph :

> I am content to follow to its source
> Every event in action or in thought ;
> Measure the lot ; forgive myself the lot !
> When such as I cast out remorse
> So great a sweetness flows into the breast
> We must laugh and we must sing,
> We are blest by everything,
> Everything we look upon is blest.

Self and soul are not reconciled, but their opposition has generated in the victorious self a new knowledge and a new strength.

The opposition is often less overt; sometimes Yeats creates it by neglecting one side while he overstates the other. This is the method of 'All Things Can Tempt Me':

> All things can tempt me from this craft of verse:
> One time it was a woman's face, or worse —
> The seeming needs of my fool-driven land;
> Now nothing but comes readier to the hand
> Than this accustomed toil. When I was young,
> I had not given a penny for a song
> Did not the poet sing it with such airs
> That one believed he had a sword upstairs;
> Yet would be now, could I but have my wish,
> Colder and dumber and deafer than a fish.

The poet, as a young man, had believed that poetry should be written by a man of action; but now he would like nothing better than to isolate himself from action so as to devote himself wholeheartedly to his art. But in choosing a fish for his model he betrays the absurdity of his own wish; he is not renouncing action, but only impatient with it. For if he were really colder and dumber and deafer than a fish, he would not be a writer at all. So the fascination and necessity of action are implied in their seeming rejection. Yeats's desire to be turned into a beautiful but mechanical bird in 'Sailing to Byzantium' is also a wish which qualifies itself by its very excess; half of the poet's mind rejects the escape from life for which the other half longs.

Seeing life as made up of such stresses, Yeats naturally looks about for events and personages where the tension is greatest. He is addicted to analysing his friends as men torn between different aspects of character; Wilde, for example, seemed to him a frustrated man of action. All kinds of relations, whether between man and woman, man and God, man and fate, or man and death, involve to Yeats's mind some admixture of enmity and love.

This perpetual conflict, with victories so Pyrrhic that the poet is compelled to return again and again to the field of battle, makes his world chequered and dense. His lifelong occupation with tragic drama is understandable as a consequence, for life is an endless competition between the imaginative hero and the raw material of his experience, the experience being necessary to bring out the heroic qualities to the full. The hero is one who sacrifices nothing of the ideal he has imagined for himself ; death can do nothing but confirm his integrity.

Such are the lineaments that mark Yeats's work from first to last. They lend a strange excitement to it, as if it had all been written for an emergency, and to the search for what lie behind it, the choice among literary directions, the development of theme, symbol, style, and pattern.

CHAPTER II

THE SEARCH FOR LIMITS

'Art has, I believe, always gained in intensity by limitation.'
YEATS, 'Speech to the British Association', September 4, 1908

I. BECOMING IRISH

IN 1889 Yeats, then twenty-four years old, gave some fatherly advice to an aspiring poet. He wrote to her : 'You will find it a good thing to make verses on Irish legends and places and so forth. It helps originality — and makes one's verses sincere, and gives one less numerous competitors — Besides one should love best what is nearest and most interwoven with one's life.'

This blend of practicality and sentiment is reassuring when found in a young poet, to whom the dangers of being either too sincere or too scheming are about equal. Yeats had obviously considered his literary nationality from different points of view. The 'numerous competitors' whom he had in mind were Browning, Swinburne, Tennyson, Rossetti, and Morris ; they were a heavy weight for any poet to hope to counterpoise, even though the deaths of Rossetti in 1882, of Browning in 1889, and especially of Tennyson in 1892 suggested that their poetic age was coming to an end. On the other hand, an Irish poet competing only with his own countrymen had a good chance to make a name for himself ; Ferguson, Allingham, Mangan, and Thomas Davis had clearly left much to be done.

Not, however, that Yeats had an exaggerated esteem for even the major Victorian poets. At home his father had acutely disparaged them, objecting to Rossetti's sensuality as a substitute for passion, to Swinburne's unawareness of common experience, to Browning's obtrusive attachment to his own beliefs, to Tennyson's generalizations about the state of the world. A too exclusive concern with feelings, or a too rigorous adherence to ideas, were equally taboo in the Yeats household, where they were held to be 'something other than human life'. Of all the Victorian poets, the one whom Yeats particularly admired was William Morris, whom he knew personally. But, while he profited from Morris's example, he was careful to make his own poetry stand apart.

To begin with, it was deliberately Irish. The Victorians gave little conscious thought to literature as a vehicle of nationality. We can be sure that Yeats was deliberate because his verse had no reference to Ireland until he was twenty, by which time he had been writing steadily for about three years. Until then he 'preferred to all other countries Arcadia and the India of romance, but presently I convinced myself . . . that I should never go for the scenery of a poem to any country but my own'. His decision is usually attributed to the influence of old John O'Leary, the Fenian hero, who returned to Dublin from a twenty years' exile in 1885, and immediately gathered around him a group of young writers. Certainly O'Leary was important in turning Yeats in an Irish direction. He encouraged his disciples — Yeats, Katharine Tynan, Douglas Hyde, and others — to borrow his many books on Irish subjects, and he could talk to them about the Young Ireland poet-revolutionaries of forty years before, around whom a legendary aura already lay, because he had known them personally. In 1888 he helped his friends to finance and publish a book whose title, *Poems and Ballads of Young Ireland*, suggests the continuity which they felt between their efforts and those of their predecessors, the poets of 1848. He was also able to print their contributions regularly in a small weekly review, the *Gael*, the literary section of which he controlled. When Yeats took to editing Irish books himself, beginning with *Fairy and Folk Tales of the Irish Peasantry* in 1888, *Stories from Carleton* in 1889, and *Representative Irish Tales* in 1890, O'Leary gave him many useful suggestions as to what to include.

Their points of view were not, however, identical. Yeats learned from O'Leary, as from Morris, only the lessons he chose to have him teach. O'Leary, a sincere but limited man, saw the problem of the poet chiefly as patriotic : poets born in Ireland should be Irish poets, and help to develop what the Young Ireland writers had called 'the spirit of the nation'. Yeats was patriotic too, and agreed that poetry could serve this function, although he disliked sentimental nationalism. But he also saw the problem as literary. He had evidently begun to realize that the eclecticism of the Victorians, which led them to set their poems in Asia Minor or Timbuctoo, had become an affectation, and that freshness lay in avoiding the exotic in favour of familiar scenes. His early work he now thought misdirected : on the one hand he had produced the Byronic melodrama and unconvincing passionateness of *Mosada*, and on the other the pretty pictures of *The Island of Statues*. To produce poetry of 'insight and knowledge', as he told Katharine Tynan he wished to do, he would need more significant decoration, more sincere passion. For this purpose he would 'call the Muses home'.

His letters of 1890 reveal how seriously he took his new attitude. 'All poetry', he writes, 'should have a local habitation when at all possible.' 'We should make poems on the familiar landscapes we love, not the strange and glittering ones we wonder at.' By landscape Yeats meant more than a collection of inanimate natural objects. As soon as locality became important to him, he sought out all the imaginative connections with places that he could find. Local customs, local characters, local songs and stories, local expressions gave the landscape its 'look' more than sun or moon did. If he wrote about Howth, Wicklow, or Sligo, he would write also about Howth's crazy woman, Moll Magee, about the old Wicklow peasant who told him, 'The fret [doom] lies on me', or expand the three lines of a local song about 'the salley [willow] gardens' which an old woman at Ballisodare near Sligo sang to him. He made a number of ballads to embody this kind of material, for, like many modern artists, he assumed that the more primitive a person or an expression, the more certain to be universal. Beyond adhering to this law of fructifying barbarism, he had a further motive. Through the ballad he hoped, as Scott, Wordsworth, and Coleridge had hoped a century earlier, to rescue himself from current poetic diction as from current poetic subjects. For that diction, like Arcadian scenery, lacked personal ties, and without these he could not take full possession of his subjects. He wanted a personal, specialized, local language to go with his local setting.

The effect of his new interests was visible in all that he wrote. One of his letters to O'Leary in 1890 set forth this agenda : 'I am taking a few days, having finished Carleton [his edition of Carleton's stories], at my play the "Countess [Kathleen]". When that is done I mean to write a series of Irish ballads — folk-tales from Sligo set into rhyme and things out of history and so forth. You will like the "Countess", it's Irish right through.' It was, in fact, founded on what Yeats assumed incorrectly (as he soon admitted) to be a west of Ireland folk-tale. He also altered his earlier work to give it a more Irish air. The lines in his Moorish play, *Mosada*, which in 1886 had read :

> He brings to mind
> That song I've made — ['t]is of a Russian tale
> Of Holy Peter of the Burning Gate :
> A saint of Russia in a vision saw
> A stranger new arisen wait
> By the doors of Peter's gate . . .

were by 1889 revised to make the Russian tale 'an Irish tale', and 'a saint of Russia' 'a saint of Munster'. His prose underwent a similar process of naturalization. He wrote to Katharine Tynan in 1891 that he would like her to review the newly published *John Sherman* as an Irish novel, because he had written it to suit that description and aspired to become known as an Irish novelist.

[The ultimate purpose of Yeats's use of nationality in his verse was, paradoxically, to enable him to transcend it.] An article that he wrote on September 2, 1888, makes this intention precise :

To the greater poets everything they see has its relation to the national life, and through that to the universal and divine life : nothing is an isolated artistic moment; there is a unity everywhere; everything fulfils a purpose that is not its own; the hailstone is a journeyman of God; the grass blade carries the universe upon its point. But to this universalism, this seeing of unity everywhere, you can only attain through what is near you, your nation, or, if you be no traveller, your village and the cobwebs on your walls. You can no more have the greatest poetry without a nation than religion without symbols. One can only reach out to the universe with a gloved hand — that glove is one's nation, the only thing one knows even a little of.

Here Yeats diverges further from Victorian poetic practice, for he writes, even at this early date, as a symbolist. The poet, he declares, works with a series of concentric circles; he begins, like Stephen Dedalus, with his home, his village, and his nation, and ends with the universe. Every detail in one circle has its correspondence in the next. Like Blake, Yeats sees the universe upon the point of a grass blade before him. His principle is to encompass an area of thoroughly known objects, always with a view to their ulterior symbolic significance. By drawing his native landscape inside him, he has at hand a group of symbols to which he feels related by personal experience and, because of legendary and historical associations, by the experience of his race. In choosing a glove as his metaphor, Yeats suggests both that the group of associations has to be consciously assembled, and that the universe cannot be approached without the clothing of familiar symbols.

Such symbolism had more to invigorate it than scenery and folk-tales, which were, after all, still comparatively raw. There was in Ireland also a developed literature, of power and beauty, which until the middle of the nineteenth century had remained almost unknown in Europe because of a lack of translations from the Irish. This literature consisted of sagas, prose stories, and poems, some of them written as early as the eighth century, some as late as the eighteenth century, which gave literary, mythological, and historical associations to every part of Ireland. Yeats was born at a fortunate moment. From the early 1840's Celtic scholars were in a fever of translation. The Celtic Archaeological

Society and the Ossianic Society were formed for the express purpose of making texts available in Irish and English, and the labours of O'Curry and O'Donovan and others made it possible for Yeats, who did not know Irish, to read his national literature.

He was not the first to experiment with this new collection of literary materials. Standish O'Grady wrote a series of books in archaistic prose, and Sir Samuel Ferguson made dull but finished verse based on ancient Irish tales. Neither of these predecessors affected Yeats deeply, although he paid handsome tributes to both of them. They proved only that the literature was malleable, and encouraged Yeats to think that he might do for Ireland what Hugo with his *Légende des siècles* had done for France. In his first prolonged test of the Celtic materials, *The Wanderings of Oisin*, on which he laboured from 1886 to 1888, Yeats went beyond O'Grady and Ferguson in developing a way of handling the old stories.

When approaching a tale of great antiquity, Yeats's method was to assume that its shape was not accidental but reflected, even if imperfectly, a hidden and significant scheme. Every detail was like the blade of grass : the poet's task was to determine its concentric circles of significance. By uncovering these he could make the myth apply to his own time as well as the past, for the basic wisdom of the race which it contained must be for ever applicable. Myths in which no such significance appeared, or which could not easily fall into an impressive pattern, were to be rejected for poetic treatment. The principal dangers for the poet lay in slavishness to the letter of the story, or excessive freedom with the spirit. So Yeats wrote warning letters to his friends Katharine Tynan and 'Fiona Macleod', who seemed to epitomize in their work the defect and excess of the resurrection of dead myths. He said to the former, 'I am not very fond of retrospective art. I do not think that pleasure we get from old methods of looking at things — methods we have long given up ourselves — belongs to the best literature. . . . I do not mean that we should not go to the old ballads and poems for inspiration, but we should search them for new methods of expressing ourselves.' To the latter he wrote that her myths were too mannered, that they should 'stand out clearly, as something objective, as something well born and independent', and not 'seem subjective, an inner way of looking at things assumed by a single mind'. They must be given 'independent life'. To avoid mere eccentricity the artist was to conceive of himself as a representative figure, to identify himself with all men, or with Ireland, or with some traditional personage. In this way the correspondences of old legends with modern life could be established, and so, as Yeats proposed, a dead mythology might be changed to a living one.

The Wanderings of Oisin becomes a more interesting poem if Yeats's intentions in it are recognized. He read translations of Michael Comyn's poem, *The Lay of Oisin in Tir na nOg*, and found in Oisin's journey to 'the country of the young' an *exemplum*, as he later remarked, of the rise and fall of all life. Consciously or unconsciously, he asked himself what relation the myth had to himself, to his nation, and to the world. In searching for the relation he realized he would have to reshape the story to clarify its meaning. His most drastic modification of Comyn's account was turning the country of the young into three islands; he claimed for this the support of a tradition among the Irish peasantry, but the interpretation of the islands was his own. They are islands of dancing, of victory, and of forgetfulness. On the personal level, they represent Yeats's idyllic boyhood at Sligo, his subsequent fights with the English boys in West Kensington because he was Irish, and his daydreaming adolescence on Howth. But these three stages in his life had wider implications, for they paralleled the periods of childhood, of aggressive maturity, and of senility in the lives of all men. Conceptually, they stood for three intermingled aspects of life which he isolated for separate portrayal, 'vain gaiety, vain battle, vain repose'. He did not forget to connect the myth with his nation : the chained lady whom Oisin has to liberate in the second island bears a strong resemblance to Ireland in English chains, and Oisin's 'battles never done' suggest the never-ending

Irish struggle for independence. Yeats wove his poem into web of symbolic cross-reference.

Within his main plan come several minor tableaux, each of which reinforces some aspect of the myth. For example, Oisin twice sees a hound following a hornless deer, and a phantom boy following a girl with an apple. Comyn had not explained what they represented, but Yeats saw in them symbols of 'eternal pursuit' and eternal unfulfilment. He added two symbolic statues, one of which regards the stars and the other the waves, and in sending Oisin between them suggests that the hero must seek his way between the ideal and actual worlds. The scenery is made sympathetic ; that is, in the idyllic first island nature is perfectly self-sufficient, the dew-drops there listening only to the sound of their own dropping ; in the second island the rocks and stormy surf suggest the struggles to be undergone ; while the still trees and pouring dew of the third island harmonize with the quiescence of this phase of life. Every natural detail has its appropriate mental correspondence.

The result is a poem which, within the framework of the Irish legend, reaches towards a more complex meaning. Yeats felt at liberty to transplant and graft one legend upon another, or within reasonable bounds to invent his own variations. He elicited implications that were latent in the earlier text, or inserted implications consistent enough for it to sustain. Assuming the same authority that Comyn and the nameless writers of Ossianic poetry had, he took old elements and reworked them into a design which belonged to him as well as to tradition, and yet was neither too personal nor too detached.

The poem is not, however, perfectly fused ; sometimes the symbols and the narrative diverge from one another. So Oisin, who is living a heroic life with the Fenians, is induced to leave Ireland behind and go to the three islands. But the three islands, instead of being a refuge from life, are a symbolical representation of it. Oisin's nostalgia for the life he has left behind him is therefore inconsistent. Similarly, a powerful contrast which Yeats draws in the poem between Oisin and Patrick, as repre-

pagan and Christian Ireland, seems irrelevant to the
ait of life in the three islands. Yeats had not de-
in the full panoply of his resources for working
.n. The technique for which T. S. Eliot has praised him,
ot manipulating 'a continuous parallel between contemporaneity
and antiquity', was not yet sure-handed. But neither could the
wanderings of Oisin be considered random wanderings ; they
were rather a prearranged tour of a rich and fairly well-governed
symbolical land.

II. ARTISTIC DISCIPLINE

By becoming an Irish poet Yeats chose an art which would
intensify the significance of a restricted area. For this intensification he needed rigorous discipline, and one means of securing it
was to borrow for his poetry effects which had been achieved not
by other poets but by practitioners of other arts. We cannot
tell the precise degree of deliberateness in Yeats's borrowings,
but they occur throughout the whole of his literary career
and can hardly have been accidental. A painter's son, and a
painter *manqué* himself, Yeats naturally cultivated certain pictorial
and sculptural effects. Among his earliest poems was one which
attempted to restate in words a painting by Nettleship ; and
among his latest was one, 'News for the Delphic Oracle',
modelled in part from a cast at the Victoria and Albert Museum.
He went to other arts more self-consciously : to the drama
because it required lifelike passions at a time when he feared to
be too ethereal ; to the sung lyric because its strong rhythms and
generalized sentiments precluded a private art ; to the dance,
which united an abstract, stylized, and symbolic pattern with
visible action, because he needed an impersonal element in his
work. Another art, however, probably supplied him with the
primary model for his poetry of the late 'eighties and the 'nineties.
There is a series of signs pointing to it. One comes in a late
book, *Dramatis Personae*, where he refers deprecatingly to his
early play, *The Countess Cathleen* (1892), as 'a piece of tapestry'.

That play, in turn, makes mention of a tapestry on which is woven the legend of *Oisin*, Yeats's most ambitious work before the *Countess* :

> See you where Oisin and young Niam ride
> Wrapt in each other's arms, and where the Finians
> Follow their hounds along the fields of tapestry. . . .

The word recurs in a description of *The Shadowy Waters* (1899), where, Yeats declared a few years after its publication, his 'endeavour was to create for a few people who love symbol, a play that will be more a ritual than a play, and leave upon the mind an impression like that of tapestry where the forms only half-reveal themselves amid the shadowy folds'. These associations of his three most imposing early subjects with tapestry are reinforced in his writings from 1885 to 1900 by an image-cluster of words like 'weave', 'entwine', and 'enwind'.

On one level Yeats may have been encouraged to develop a poetry analogical in some of its methods to tapestry by his frequent visits to the house of William Morris from 1888 to 1890, since Morris was deeply involved in reviving the dead art of tapestry-making, and was doing his best work at that time. Yeats's sisters helped May Morris to execute designs furnished by Morris, Burne-Jones, and others. But an interest in tapestry antedated Yeats's friendship with Morris. He apparently thought of tapestry as an art of great intricacy and rather limited means ; looking for boundaries for his imagination, he may unconsciously have imitated the way that the artists he knew cut out excited rhythms, strong passions, and unexpected developments, in favour of a decorum and continuity of rhythm and feeling. He would devise an alternative to vulnerable intimacy, with the forms of life imbedded in pattern and beauty. It offered a texture suited to his intention of binding the world together.

The example of the weaver's art probably helped Yeats, as the musical analogy of *Four Quartets* helped Eliot, to specialize and intensify his means and attitudes in the same way that he had localized his setting and subject-matter. Granted that his heroes and heroines were to be of Irish blood, how should they look and act? The answer was that they should look and act like figures in a Morris tapestry, static, statuesque, and exalted. They should have the air not of acting but of re-enacting, as if they were characters in some ancient drama or ritual. He gave them names that were traditional, like Mongan and Aedh, or that sounded traditional without being so, like Robartes and Hanrahan. Their movements should be slow and sacramental :

> Fasten your hair with a golden pin,
> And bind up every wandering tress. . . .
>
> I went out to the hazel wood,
> Because a fire was in my head,
> And cut and peeled a hazel wand,
> And hooked a berry to a thread. . . .
>
> I bring you with reverent hands
> The books of my numberless dreams. . . .

Even the fairy host that rides by from Knocknarea rushes slowly enough so that its individual members, like Caolte and Niamh, can be distinguished. Their energy is never unseemly, their movements began before the beginning of time. The fact that the first line of 'The Lake Isle of Innisfree', 'I will arise and go now, and go to Innisfree', echoes the New Testament ('I will arise and go unto my father') is symptomatic of the traditional, almost religious stateliness of this verse. Yeats's ideal is not the man who works out, like Robinson Crusoe, new ways of dealing with new problems, but rather the man who, like an actor in the Japanese *Noh*, tries to perpetuate a style and role which have been handed down through the generations.

The tapestry analogy manifests itself in various ways. Each of Yeats's early books is unified in tone, and each has the form of a series of related panels. He groups the details in each poem, as a rule, around a single image, such as an old woman, a lovely lady, or fairies on horseback. Grammatical devices enable him to secure an especially close texture. The conjunction 'and', inserted with abnormal, almost Biblical frequency, binds clauses and phrases together and helps to increase the intertwined effect by providing a chain of reactions to every verb. Long compound predicates follow short subject clauses, and by an elastic punctuation Yeats contrives to make most of the short poems in *The Wind Among the Reeds* only one sentence long.

The concatenation of attitudes and words is carried out both from stanza to stanza and from poem to poem. He firmly restricted the temper of *The Wind Among the Reeds* to a desire to escape from love's misery and from an imperfect world, and a wistful aspiration towards a more ideal state of things. A small number of words is repeated again and again, as if the poet wished to confine himself to a small nook of the language. So he portrays his lady steadily as pallid :

Pale brows, still hands and dim hair. . . .

For that pale breast and lingering hand. . . .

You need but lift a pearl-pale hand. . . .

White woman that passion has worn. . . .

With her cloud-pale eyelids falling on dream-dimmed eyes. . . .

Pallor, dimness, and whiteness, one lifted hand, an abundance of hair, and an indistinct bosom give her the generalized look of a Burne-Jones figure. The reiteration of the word *dream* assists in making her seem some immemorial archetype.

Yet while Yeats's early verse resembles the tapestry of the Pre-Raphaelites, its insistent symbolism differentiates it from their work. The forms in his tapestry, as he said of *The Shadowy Waters*, only half reveal themselves. In spite of their simple and repetitious vocabulary, the poems are not simple. While Rossetti and Morris are occasionally symbolical in their paintings and verse, they do not rival Yeats's steady and highly organized symbolic design. A quatrain which he wrote suggests the prominence of symbols in his esthetic :

> God loves dim ways of glint and gleam ;
> To please him well my verse must be
> A dyed and figured mystery ;
> Thought hid in thought, dream hid in dream.

It is this mystery which we must now try to anatomize.

III. THE SYMBOLIC INFLECTION

Symbolism was for Yeats an effort to restore the unity of mind and nature which had existed until the seventeenth century. Shakespeare's mind had not been troubled by the difference between Locke's primary and secondary qualities, or by any sort of abstraction, whether scientific, religious, or philosophical, that could keep it from wholeness. But during the seventeenth century there came into being the modern fragmentary man, who sets up in the mind gigantic philosophical or religious abstractions, and sets up outside the mind a nature which is a scientific abstraction. T. S. Eliot's term for this change is 'dissociation of sensibility', Yeats's is 'bursting into fragments'. What Yeats hoped to do was to bring man and nature into harmony again, and to reconcile the demands of intellect with those of the imagination. Symbolism would pull the external world back into the mind by establishing the correspondence of nature and mental states. It would make the connections among the personal, national, and natural worlds.

Yeats began very early to unearth particular correspondences. At the age of twenty he proposed to the Hermetic Society, a group of young Dubliners with literary and occult leanings, that they assemble the affirmations of the great poets in 'their finest moments' and make a new religion out of them. The word 'religion' is misleading ; this was to be no outworn creed or collection of ethical apophthegms, but a poetic mythology taken seriously. The poets had testified, for example, that man was not surrounded by dead material objects, but by 'spirits of water and wind'. These were not mere fancies but, as he gradually came to see, aspects of a symbolical construct or 'fabric'.

He did not neglect to define symbolism. In his edition of Blake's poetry which appeared early in 1893, Yeats distinguished between the symbol and the metaphor. Borrowing another image from the art of tapestry, he said that metaphors were relatively sporadic and accidental images, and that they became symbols only when they were part of a close and continuous weave :

Whoever has understood the correspondence asserted by Blake between (say) sight, hearing, taste and smell, and certain mental qualities, feels at once that much in his own intellect is plainer to him, and when Shakespeare compares the mind of the mad Lear to the 'vexed sea', we are told at once something more laden with meaning than many pages of psychology. A 'correspondence', for the very reason that it is implicit rather than explicit, says far more than a syllogism or a scientific observation. The chief difference between the metaphors of poetry and the symbols of mysticism is that the latter are woven together into a complete system. The 'vexed sea' would not be merely a detached comparison, but, with the fish it contains, would be related to the land and air, the winds and shadowing clouds, and all in their totality compared to the mind in its totality.

He still assumes, although later he would give up the notion, that symbolism is the mystic's special aptitude, and implies that the poet must therefore be a mystic. Actually, mysticism is already playing the ambiguous role of a supplier of symbolic materials. By its interconnecting correspondences, symbolism holds the cosmos together, and the poem too ; a whirl of warring atoms becomes an intricate harmony. Everything is related to everything else.

In a later essay on symbolism Yeats asserted that it often appeared in poetry without the poet's being consciously aware he was using it. For illustration he took a passage from Burns :

The white moon is setting behind the white wave,
And Time is setting with me, O !

'These lines', Yeats declared, 'are perfectly symbolical.'

Take from them the whiteness of the moon and of the wave, whose relation to the setting of Time is too subtle for the intellect, and you take from them their beauty. But, when all are together, moon and wave and whiteness and setting Time and the last melancholy cry, they evoke an emotion which cannot be evoked by any other arrangement of colours and sounds and forms.

His remarks are important because they make clear that the correspondences must not be merely mechanical, and that they must command an emotion which is untranslatable. Yeats is needlessly unkind to the subtlety of the intellect, however, to which the relations of moon and sea, and moon and time, and time and sea, and whiteness and old age (in turn associated with setting time and the waning moon) are not inscrutable. At this stage in his career he was hard on the intellect, feeling that it was the chief culprit in depriving the imagination of control over the world. But he is closer to the point in showing that the evocative power of the juxtapositions does not depend solely upon rational explanation.

    In articulating the pattern of his own symbolism, Yeats relied heavily upon what he learned in the Theosophical Society from 1887 to 1890, in the Golden Dawn from 1890 to 1901, and in the process of editing a three-volume edition of Blake's poetry from 1889 to 1892. The Theosophists, who drew their theories from every quarter, were much concerned with correspondences between the natural and spiritual worlds, which they conceived of as parallel and interlocked. One of their theories which engaged Yeats's attention for a time was that human nature was divisible into seven principles, and with habitual thoroughness he attempted to divide all natural scenery into seven correlative types to correspond with them. A more developed project was setting up the associations of the seasons, and the journal which he kept while a member of the Esoteric Section of the Theosophical Society displays the results :

Spring	Summer	Autumn	Winter
Morning	Noon	Evening	Night
Youth	Adolescence	Manhood	Decay
Fire	Air	Water	Earth
East	South	West	North

Some of these combinations may be arrived at without benefit of Theosophy; they have, like spring and youth, the sanction of tradition and observation. Others, like summer and air, were based upon intuition, for if the need for symmetry alone had dictated their selection, they would have been valueless. The force of these correspondences, for occultist and poet alike, derives from the assumption that they have deep roots in the mind, so that only one member of a group needs to be tapped to awaken the whole group into life. Mentioning fire, for example, evokes youth, the time of greatest energy, and thus spring, morning, and sunrise in the east. Parallels in external nature, and a wide area of unconscious associations, are evoked together. To know the genuine correspondences is to be master of the switches that control life and poetry.

The Golden Dawn, an occult society in London, had less doctrine than the Theosophists, and was even more active in research into symbols. Certain symbols evoked certain kinds of dreams or 'visions'. Yeats made many experiments with his friends to see if similar dreams would result in many people from the same symbolic stimulus, for example, the Tantric symbol of fire, and was gratified by his success. The linking of qualities to the four elements in particular became habitual with him. Long afterwards he still felt under the influence of a Kabbalistic ceremony in which he participated as a young man, where there were 'two pillars, one symbolic of water and one of fire. . . . The water is sensation, peace, night, silence, indolence; the fire is passion, tension, day, music, energy.' But the example of Blake was perhaps most important in keeping the poetic usefulness of this collection of correspondences always before his mind.

Although Yeats had heard Blake's lyrics from his father when he was fifteen years old, his serious interest in him began in 1889. At that time he learned that his father's friend, Edwin Ellis, had a way of explaining the song at the beginning of the second book of *Jerusalem*. Ellis conjectured that the English place names in the passage might be related to the four points of the compass and to the four elements. When Yeats informed him that these are

the familiar hinges by which the occultist boxes and controls the
universe, they resolved to do a complete exegesis, and they
published their results in three large volumes in 1893.

The three years' study of Blake's symbolism helped Yeats to
develop his own. As he wrote to Katharine Tynan, 'It has done
my own mind a great deal of good in liberating me from formulas
and theories of several kinds. You will find it a difficult book,
this Blake interpretation, but one that will open up for you as it
has for me new kinds of poetic feeling and thought.' Blake's
symbolism was astonishingly comprehensive. The four elements,
and the four symbolic personages or 'Zoas' whom he connects
with them, radiate through the universe in a remarkable way.
He saw the world in terms of a quaternion to which he gave the
strange names of Urizen, Luvah, Tharmas, and Urthona ; they
are four aspects of the human mind, to begin with — Yeats
identified them roughly as Reason, Emotion, Sensation, and
Energy ; but they are also the four elements in nature, the four
points of the compass, four parts of the human body, and, as Ellis
suspected, four parts of London. There is no necessity to cavil
at the quadripartite division ; it has to be accepted as a useful
and ancient metaphor. What is essential is the conception of a
unity which is everywhere visible if only we have eyes to see.

Blake conceived of the Zoas as originally and ultimately in
harmony, and called this harmonious state 'Jerusalem'. They
may be upset and distorted, however, so that they battle one
another. In this state of confusion, the Zoas lose their identities
and split off various sections of themselves. One of these sections
is known as the *emanation* or the Zoa's affective life, and another
is the *spectre* or the Zoa's abstract reasoning power. These
segments retain their independent life until harmony is regained.
Although the terms are not familiar, they seem a more adequate
description of mental conflict than the traditional simplistic
terminology of higher self and lower self, and are no more
unwieldy than Id, Ego, and Super-Ego.

The resemblance of Yeats's scheme to Blake's becomes
clearer in Yeats's later work, *A Vision*. In *A Vision* four 'facul-

ties' fulfil some of the same functions as the four Zoas. The harmony of the Zoas, Blake's 'Jerusalem', finds an approximate parallel in Yeats's Unity of Being and sphere. The emanation and spectre bear some resemblance to Yeats's 'daimon' and 'anti-self'. The closest parallels in Yeats's early work, however, are in his notes for an Irish mystical order, dating from about 1898 and 1899. In the first draft of his *Autobiographies* he recounts his efforts to work out symbolic correspondences for the 'four talismans', often with the help of other ardent Celts :

At any moment of leisure, we obtained in vision long lists of symbolic forms that corresponded to the cardinal points, and the old gods and heroes took their places gradually in a symbolic fabric that had for its centre the four talismans of the Tuatha De Danaan [legendary inhabitants of Ireland], the Sword, the Stone, the Spear, and the Cauldron, which related themselves in my mind with the suits of the Tarot.

Although Yeats did not publish these correspondences, his notes about them have survived. The talismans of sword, stone, spear, and cauldron are related to the elements of earth, air, water, and fire ; each of these represents an aspect of the mind (a Zoa) that must be controlled. The spear is associated with passion, the sword with intellect, the cauldron with moving images (presumably imagined), and the stone with fixed ones (presumably seen). The man who has mastered each of these can hope to attain to the fifth element or final harmony ('Jerusalem'), where he is at one with universal forces, and where passion and intellect, desired image and actual fact, are united into one whole.

The parallels indicate Blake's influence, and also Yeats's insubordination. Perhaps the main effect of Blake on Yeats is not in specific symbols, striking though the resemblances of these are, but in the fact that from 1890 on there is a gradually increasing pressure in his poetry from powerful congeries of symbolic images.

IV. MARSHALLING THE ELEMENTS

Because classification, which only compiles, is not symbolism, which reveals, Yeats never allowed his methods to become rigid.

But with his tentative congregations of symbols and symbolic ramifications in mind, we can penetrate some distance into his manner of composition and into the structure of his poetic imagery. The four elements appear steadily. They can be recognized easily under various guises : water is often 'dew', 'wave', or 'flood'; air is 'wind'; fire is 'stars' or 'flame'; earth is 'clay' or 'woods'. These readily extend themselves : the darkness of earth suggests a connection with night and sleep such as Yeats made in his Esoteric Section journal, and, because of the connotations of blackness, is often regarded as malevolent. Since Satan, supreme power of darkness, has his seat in the north (originally, perhaps, because of climatic considerations), that cardinal point may come to be associated, by successive stages, with earth. Water suggests tears and sorrow, therefore loss and therefore death ; since death is traditionally 'stepping westward', water comes to be related to the west. Fire, being crimson and suggesting the fires of passion — a metaphor which indicates how irresistible this way of thinking has always been, may become a symbol of love and, being hot, call up the south. The remaining cardinal point is east, and the element remaining is air ; by identifying these for the sake of congruence we obtain a connection between air and the rising sun and dawn, and thus hope.

These associations are not quite the same as those we have already examined for the four elements. And we come here to an important symbolic principle. Any given situation can be put in elemental terms, but in no two situations will the elements be in exactly the same configuration. Their relationship is not fixed, although the amount of variation is limited by the number of possible associations for each element. Yeats immersed his mind in all likely correspondences and drew upon those he needed. This particular set of associations provided material out of which he wove his poem, 'Michael Robartes Bids His Beloved Be at Peace', in 1895. He invested the elements there with mysterious, frightening power, by making them interact with apocalyptic horses whose role was the more threatening because unexplained :

I hear the Shadowy Horses, their long manes a-shake,
Their hoofs heavy with tumult, their eyes glimmering white,
The North unfolds above them clinging, creeping Night,
The East her hidden joy before the morning break,
The West weeps in pale dew and sighs passing away,
The South is pouring down roses of crimson fire :
O vanity of Sleep, Hope, Dream, endless Desire,
The Horses of Disaster plunge in the heavy clay.[1] . . .

The function of the cardinal points is kept deliberately diffuse, and the diffuseness exploited.

As occasion demanded, then, Yeats varied the use and significance of the elements, always, however, keeping them within traditional contexts. Sometimes he contrasts them, as aspects of the material world, with the heroic spirits who rise above them:

> *Him who trembles before the flame and the flood*
> *And the winds that blow through the starry ways,*
> *Let the starry winds and the flame and the flood*
> *Cover over and hide, for he has no part*
> *With the lonely, majestical multitude.*

In a variation on this theme, he employs fire as the immortal element with which he can connect Kathleen-Ny-Hoolihan, a personification of Ireland, and makes the other elements the mortal ones which contrast with it. Each stanza of 'Red Hanrahan's Song about Ireland' in its original version begins with one of these inferior elements, and the poem culminates in Kathleen and fire :

Veering, fleeting, fickle, the winds of Knocknarea . . .

Weak and worn and weary the waves of Cummen Strand . . .

Dark and dull and earthy the stream of Drumahair
When the rain is pelting out of the wintry air ;

---

[1] Yeats had a note on these associations in *The Wind Among the Reeds* : 'I follow much Irish and other mythology, and the magical tradition, in associating the North with night and sleep, and the East, the place of sunrise, with hope, and the South, the place of the sun when at its height, with passion and desire, and the West, the place of sunset, with fading and dreaming things'. The correspondences, as we have noticed, are even thicker than his statement admits.

> Dark and dull and earthy our souls and bodies be :
> But pure as a tall candle before the Trinity
> Our Kathleen-Ny-Hoolihan.

The elements need not, however, be antipathetic to the spirit. In several of the poems they reflect a different mood and provide a consolatory choir for the poet's beloved :

> Great Powers of falling wave and wind and windy fire,
> With your harmonious choir
> Encircle her I love and sing her into peace
> That my old care may cease. . . .

> When you are sad,
>   The mother of the stars weeps too,
> And all her starlight is with sorrow mad,
>   And tears of fire fall gently in the dew.

> When you are sad,
>   The mother of the wind mourns too . . .

> When you are sad,
>   The mother of the wave sighs too. . . .

Their presence is not always so readily ascertainable. In 'The Two Trees', for example, they are almost out of sight in the last five lines of this passage :

> Beloved, gaze in thine own heart,
> The holy tree is growing there ;
> From joy the holy branches start,
> And all the trembling flowers they bear.
> The changing colours of its fruit
> Have dowered the stars with merry light ;
> The surety of its hidden root
> Has planted quiet in the night ;
> The shaking of its leafy head
> Has given the waves their melody. . . .

Yet the lady's unity with the elements is important in the conceptual scheme of the poem.

Nature in Yeats never appears for its own sake ; it reinforces either the poet's anxieties or his aspirations. In 'The Pity of Love', the elements of earth, fire, water, and air appear sequentially under some disguise to symbolize his anxieties :

> A pity beyond all telling
> Is hid in the heart of love ;
> The folk who are buying and selling,
> The stars of God where they move,
> The mouse-grey waters on flowing,
> The clouds on their journey above,
> And the cold wet winds ever blowing,
> All threaten the head that I love.

Their appearance is not very impressive ; the images, conventional except for 'mouse-grey waters', secure their interest only because the last line asserts their rather surprising disconnection from the lady. In 'Who Goes with Fergus ?' and more subtly, in 'The Lake Isle of Innisfree', the elements are intrinsically more interesting ; here they symbolize his aspirations at the same time that they order the scenic details :

> For Fergus rules the brazen cars,
> And rules the shadows of the wood,
> And the white breast of the dim sea
> And all dishevelled wandering stars.

And I shall have some peace there, for peace comes dropping slow,
  Dropping from the veils of the morning to where the cricket sings ;
There midnight's all a glimmer, and noon a purple glow,
  And evening full of the linnet's wings.

Yeats is particularly fond of manipulating the opposition of fire and water. The effect is to encompass strongly contrasted associations, even though their symbolic meaning is usually kept imprecise :

> And when you sigh from kiss to kiss,
> I hear white Beauty sighing, too,
> For hours when all must fade like *dew*,
> But flame on flame, deep under deep . . .
> Brood her high lonely mysteries.

White woman that passion has worn
As the tide wears the dove-grey sands,
And with heart more old than the horn
That is brimmed from the pale fire of time. . . .

We who still labour by the cromlech on the shore,
The grey cairn on the hill, when day sinks drowned in dew,
Being weary of the world's empires, bow down to you,
Master of the still stars and of the flaming door.

And therefore my heart will bow, when dew
Is dropping sleep, until God burn time. . . .

And candle-like foam on the dim sand,
And stars climbing the dew-dropping sky,
Live but to light your passing feet.

While time and the world are ebbing away
In twilights of dew and of fire.

There is no injustice to Yeats in hunting down the elements
in this way. He himself declared, with more accuracy than a
casual reader might recognize, that 'the elemental creatures go /
About my table to and fro'. These lines, addressed 'To Ireland
in the Coming Times', were a frank statement of his method of
writing. He went still further with his correspondences when he
modelled a set of symbolic personages according to the preponderance in them of one element or another. Some of these
appear in his prose, and some in his verse. An early letter to
O'Leary reveals that Yeats was fearful that his characters in
John Sherman might suffer from over-stylizing as a result : 'It
is all about a curate and a young man from the country. The
difficulty is to keep the characters from turning into Eastern
symbolic monsters of some sort which would be a curious thing
to happen to a curate and a young man from the country.' In
his verse he created the characters Hanrahan, Robartes, and
Aedh, each of whom represented a particular collocation of the
elements, and attributed certain poems to each. Eventually,
however, he decided to remove this scaffolding, and took their

THE SEARCH FOR LIMITS

names out of the titles of his poems. Yet the poems retain their elemental emphasis.

Yeats remained loyal to this technique of composition. It provided him with an excellent means of introducing nature, a nature stylized and dilute, scarcely at all dependent upon observation. Waves, woods, winds, and stars were subject to his imagination because he saw them through a formal pattern of special meaning and correspondence. With them he was able to enlarge his context steadily so as to give poems about love and frustration a traditional weight. By couching his feelings in the framework of the elements, he anchored them in universal forces and lent them added dignity and sanction. The protagonist of the poems is more than a frustrated lover ; he is all frustrated lovers, and nothing that is frustrating in the universe is alien to him.

So the elements continue to appear in Yeats's later work. Such splendid poems of his maturity as 'Sailing to Byzantium' and 'Byzantium' depend on fire and water as much as do 'Michael Robartes Remembers Forgotten Beauty' and 'The Valley of the Black Pig'. They depend, in fact, even more, for the later poems contain more action, and the elements participate more vigorously in it. The water, instead of being 'the white breast of the dim sea' that Fergus knew, swirls violently about the Byzantine shores, and the fire, no longer Red Hanrahan's 'tall candle before the Holy Rood', purges all that it touches. Yeats said of himself that he was of those subjective men who must, like the spider, weave their web out of their own bowels, and as he grew older, while he increased the number of components in his verse, he kept the restrictive intricacy of the early pattern.

The elements can be found again in the four lunar quarters of *A Vision*, which underlie most of the verse written in the last twenty years of his life. A good example of their later use comes in a letter from Yeats to Mrs. Shakespear of July 24, 1934 :

Notice this symbolism [he writes]

Water under the earth⎫
The Earth   ⎭   The bowels, etc.   *Instinct*

The Water	= The blood & the sex organs	*Passion*
The Air	= The lungs, logical thought	*Thought*
The Fire	*Soul*	

They are my four quarters : The Earth before [lunar phase] 8, the Water before 15, the Air before 22, the Fire before 1 (see *A Vision*, page 86). Notice that on page 85 of *A Vision* the conflict on which we now enter is 'against the Soul', as in the quarter we have just left it was 'against the intellect'. The conflict is to restore the body.[1]

Another letter, written two weeks later, elaborates and explains the first :

> Yesterday I put into rime what I wrote in my last letter.

THE FOUR AGES

He with Body waged a fight ;
Body won and walks upright.

Then he struggled with the Heart ;
Innocence and peace depart.

Then he struggled with the mind,
His proud Heart he left behind.

Now his wars with God begin ;
At stroke of midnight God shall win.

> They are the four ages of individual man, but they are also the four ages of civilization. You will find them in that book you have been reading. First age, *earth*, vegetative functions. Second age, *Water*, blood, sex. Third age, Air, breath intellect. Fourth age Fire, Soul etc. In the first two the moon comes to the full — resurrection of Christ & Dionysus. Man becomes rational, no longer driven from below or above.

Yeats's symbolism here, while basically elemental, is less patently so, and the symbols *are* the meaning instead of verging on embellishments of it, as they often do in the early poems. They are

---

[1] Yeats gives the wrong page number here. In a letter dated the following day he corrects 85 to 35 and says, 'In the last quarter of a civilization (the quarter we have just entered,) the fight is against body and body should win.'

also extended to include aspects of history as well as of psychology, the human soul recapitulating the development of a civilization.   Finally, they are represented with increasing turbulence.

In arriving at these changes, Yeats subtly shifted his view of his art.   In 1893 he wrote a statement of his early artistic aims which was forthright, if not felicitous, and fell incidentally into a weaving image :

> I pray that I ever be weaving
>   An intellectual tune,
> But weaving it out of threads
>   From the distaff of the moon.
>
> Wisdom and dreams are one,
>   For dreams are the flowers ablow
> And Wisdom the fruit of the garden :
>   God planted him long ago.

Bringing together wisdom and dreams does not entail major difficulties at this period.   But in a poem which he wrote, but did not finish, thirty-six years later, this pacific image is put aside and a more violent metaphor chosen :

> Imagination's bride
> Having thrown aside
> The skin of the wild beast
> And laid her wilful breast
> There by the bride groom
> Beauty becomes.
>
> Reason named his bride
> That so long had hid,
> That so long had fled,
> And the slut's in bed
> Truth is her name.
>
> The first, a kind of flame
> That last a bird of night
> They in mutual spite
> Suspicion, rage and scorn
> Live though sisters born.

Now truth (reason's bride) and beauty (imagination's bride), which correspond roughly to wisdom and dreams, are bitter and hostile to each other, in spite of their mutual dependence. The concepts are alive instead of mechanical. Powerful images of sexuality and family hatred suit the mature poet better than flowers and fruits.

This alteration occurred gradually. By 1902, in a poem called 'Adam's Curse', Yeats could still refer to his craft as 'stitching and unstitching', but by 1910 he announced in 'A Coat' that he had put aside his early conception of poetry as embroidery and henceforth would walk 'naked'. He did not mean that he would give up his early symbols, but that the elements, for example, would from now on be part of his skin instead of part of his outer garments.

Of the three major developments in his early verse, its Irish setting, its tapestry-like effects, and its symbolic inflection, Yeats put only the second aside. If any single art can be said to have replaced tapestry, it is that of the goldsmith. And, while this is a much more violent art than the weaver's, it has the same strict elaboration.

CHAPTER III

ASSERTION WITHOUT DOCTRINE

I. BELIEF

YEATS'S poetry abounds in challenging statements about the world. How sympathetically these are to be taken by the reader, and how firmly they are asserted by the writer, are problems that have vexed his critics. They also vexed Yeats himself. He did not describe his assertions as statements of belief, and his not doing so is the more surprising because he freely and unequivocally criticized disbelief.

The inconsistency is only superficial. To hold certain ideas as 'beliefs' would give them a sort of autonomy; the mind, whose independence Yeats demanded, would become subservient to them, instead of their being necessary expressions of it. Man would be surrounded by a group of mammoth pyramidal conceptions outside his control. But the object of Yeats's verse was, we have seen, to eliminate just such cold-blooded relationships; an external set of ideas held as beliefs was as dangerous as an external nature. He therefore argued that the word 'belief' did not belong to our age.

Yet if his statements are not beliefs, what are they? To give them a name he sometimes spoke of them as ideas which he had held for so long that he could now call them his convictions; here the test was not their philosophical validity, but the length of time the mind could encompass and cherish them. In the same vein, he referred to them as ideas which he could not help drawing on whenever he wrote. The fact that they were useful in his art was also relevant, because art would not endure them if they were nonsensical. Yeats's approach to the problem is epitomized in his remarks about immortality, an idea frequently set forth in his verse. When he defends immortality, he argues pragmatically that confidence in it is necessary to human survival; without it no course of conduct except brute pleasure-seeking would hold any attraction. He is close to Nietzsche's contention that some ideas are life-furthering and some not, and that we must hold to those that are. Yeats's second argument is also pragmatic : to those who denied immortality he was likely to point out that scepticism destroyed the integrity of the mind. These arguments are alike in that they emphasize not immortality, but man, and insist upon the mixture of ideas with other human experiences.

Yeats was encouraged to take this position, which has so contemporary a sound, by his agnostic father. John Butler Yeats held that the poet must feel disengaged from doctrine, able to use it if it suited a poetic purpose, and to abjure or modify it if it did not. He said that the poet must not attach himself so strongly to his ideas that his verse becomes bothersomely credal and to that extent unpoetic. The poem may use beliefs, but must never seem to have been written merely to express them. They must be fused, along with emotional and formal patterns, into a unit with its own autonomy, where their function as beliefs is lost or unimportant. Most critics today maintain that we do not have to share the beliefs of Dante or Milton in order to appreciate their poetry ; but J. B. Yeats's contention goes further, in suggesting that neither Dante nor Milton necessarily believed what he wrote, and that if either did, he embodied his belief in his poetry for artistic and not religious reasons. I. A. Richards has proposed that the statements in poetry can be regarded as pseudo-statements which organize the reader's responses ; this theory arises from the same roots as Yeats's poetry.

But Yeats differed from his father, and from Mr. Richards, in being fascinated by belief, or rather, by the believer's stance, as fascinated as Shelley was by atheism. He had a great interest in any thought which had aroused the passions of masses of men or of some small group of gifted individuals. Yet he was unable to hold it with the same enduring fervour that they had. His use of Irish fairy tales is a good example. He was much impressed by the survival in the Irish countryside of a belief in fairies. In *The Celtic Twilight* (1893) he described this and other beliefs with sympathy, but took care to explain that his own beliefs were not necessarily identical with theirs. In another of the weaving images to which he customarily resorted, he attempted to describe belief as a gradual conscious formulation of experience, a personal formulation which drew its strength not from its truth but from the energy and sufficiency of the experience :

I have . . . been at no pains to separate my own beliefs from those of the peasantry, but have rather let my men and women, dhouls and faeries, go their way unoffended or defended by any argument of mine. The things a man has heard and seen are threads of life, and if he pull them carefully from the confused distaff of memory, any who will can weave them into whatever garments of belief please them best. I too have woven my garment like another, but I shall try to keep warm in it, and shall be well content if it do not unbecome me.

The word belief is already an embarrassment to him. In later life he identified it with 'the sense of spiritual reality', and, characteristically for his later manner, said that it was not the result of a slow weaving process, but 'comes whether to the individual or to crowds from some violent shock'. But both metaphors emphasize the intimacy and immediacy of the poet's relation to an idea.

Before he was thirty Yeats framed his principle of including statements in his verse without implying that they had any validity outside the particular poem where they appeared. He put his position roundly in a review of Buchanan's *Wandering Jew* for the *Bookman* in 1893 : 'The belief of the typical literary man of the time, that you can separate poetry from philosophy and from belief, is but the phantasy of an empty day'. Beliefs had to be included in some form, but, as he wrote George Russell in 1900, poetic expression should never be compromised if it got in the way of a poet's philosophy. He argued that there could be no fundamental conflict :

I do not understand what you mean when you distinguish between the word that gives your idea & the more beautiful word. Unless of course you merely mean that beauty of detail must be subordinate to beauty of general effect, it seems to me just as if one should say 'I don't mind if my sonata is musical or not so long as it conveys my idea !' Beauty is the end & law of poetry. It exists to find the beauty in all things, philosophy, nature, passion, — in what you will, & in so far as it rejects beauty, it destroys its own right to exist. If you want to give ideas for their own sake write prose. In verse they are subordinate to beauty which is their soul if they are true. Isn't this obvious ?

Ideas, like nature and the passions, furnish the poet with material, and his task is to weld them into poems. Ideas which are true are those which lend themselves to this treatment. Ideas which are false or insincere remain isolated abstractions and spoil the poem ; they divert to themselves attention which should focus on the poem of which they are only a part.

Because he wished to use ideas without being submerged by them, Yeats kept throughout his life to the dramatic lyric and the drama, where the test of an idea is not its significance outside poem or play, but its relevance to the speaker's dramatic situation. The author forgets himself in the role that he assumes in the poem ; this role is not pretence, but is often a simplification and intensification of something in his mind whose presence there he may hardly have recognized. A later letter to Sean O'Casey expresses Yeats's lifelong position. It was written to explain the Abbey Theatre's rejection of O'Casey's play, *The Silver Tassie*, on the grounds that it was too full of O'Casey's own views :

Among the things that dramatic action must burn up are the author's opinions ; while he is writing he has no business to know anything that is not a portion of the action. Do you suppose for one moment that Shakespeare educated Hamlet and King Lear by telling them what he thought and believed ? As I see it Hamlet and Lear educated Shakespeare, and I have no doubt that in the process of that education he found out that he was an altogether different man to what he thought himself, and had altogether different beliefs. A dramatist can help his characters to educate him by thinking and studying everything that gives them the language they are groping for through his hands and eyes but the control must be theirs, and that is why the ancient philosophers thought a poet or dramatist Daimon-possessed.

To be successful the poet must be humble before his own *personae*.

In Yeats's verse, we shall find, a series of ideas recur, but they recur as expressions of his characters. These ideas attract his characters not as conceptions external to themselves to which they owe allegiance ; they are better described as necessary counters to express pride of life, defiance of vulgarity, anxiety about the future, or refusal to accept despair. The only way in which poetry can be philosophical, Yeats brilliantly declared, is by portraying 'the emotions of a soul dwelling in the presence of certain ideas'. Without ideas at all the poet is shallow, timid, and sentimental ; with ideas gripped tightly as beliefs the poet is gullible, opinionative, and biased ; but with ideas as perches, or habitual surroundings, or, like the elements, symbolic counters, he is made free.

II. IDEAS OVERPOWERED

Among the recurrent ideas in his verse, the most imaginatively seductive was reincarnation. The notion that the soul passes through round after round of lives was steeped in folklore and ancient religions. It had the advantage, to a man who prided himself on iconoclasm, of being un-Christian, unscientific, and unconventional. Darwinism, on the other hand, was a creed to be disbelieved or believed like religion ; and even if considered as a myth rather than a solemn scientific faith, its concern with sub-human development was of little use to Yeats, whose interest was in the highest human faculty — the imagination. 'Romantic poetry', Ezra Pound has shrewdly suggested, 'almost requires the concept of reincarnation as part of its mechanism. No apter metaphor having been found for certain emotional colours.'

Yeats adopted reincarnation in his verse not really because he needed it, or because he believed it, but because he liked it.

His interest in reincarnation was aroused very early. Perhaps through his friend Russell, who was precociously versed in all the Indian literature that had been translated, he took to reading Indian poetry such as Kalidasa's, and then Theosophical books like A. P. Sinnett's *Esoteric Buddhism*. He was aided in his studies by the visit to Dublin in 1885 of a Bengali Brahmin named Mohini Chatterjee, who came as a representative of the Theosophical Society. Yeats asked if he should pray, and the Brahmin replied : No, one should say before sleeping : 'I have lived many lives, I have been a slave and a prince. Many a beloved has sat upon my knees and I have sat upon the knees of many a beloved. Everything that has been shall be again.'

In making a poem out of this pronouncement, Yeats at once appreciated the danger of its seeming merely didactic. He put it into a dramatic setting by calling it 'Kanva on Himself', Kanva being a fictitious Indian to whom several of the early poems were originally attributed, and had Kanva speak it as a series of rhetorical questions. Even these precautions did not save it :

> Now wherefore hast thou tears innumerous ?
>   Hast thou not known all sorrow and delight
> Wandering of yore in forests rumorous,
>   Beneath the flaming eyeballs of the night,
>
> And as a slave been wakeful in the halls
>   Of Rajas and Mahrajas beyond number ?
> Hast thou not ruled among the gilded walls ?
>   Hast thou not known a Raja's dreamless slumber ?
>
> Hast thou not sat of yore upon the knees
>   Of myriads of beloveds, and on thine
> Have not a myriad swayed below strange trees
>   In other lives ? Hast thou not quaffed old wine
>
> By tables that were fallen into dust
>   Ere yonder palm commenced his thousand years ?
> Is not thy body but the garnered rust
>   Of ancient passions and of ancient fears ?

Then wherefore fear the usury of Time,
    Or Death that cometh with the next life-key ?
Nay, rise and flatter her with golden rhyme,
    For as things were so shall things ever be.

Although the image of the body as the 'garnered rust' of passions
has some interest, it does not compensate for the clumsy 'in-
numerous' and 'rumorous' and for the stilted and exhausted
diction.   The poem's failure comes largely from the lack of
resistance offered in it.   It is too single-minded, as if Kanva were
an advocate for reincarnation as a doctrine.   When, many years
later, Yeats rewrote it, he demonstrated the way to make reincarnation serve the poem :

MOHINI CHATTERJEE

I asked if I should pray,
But the Brahmin said,
'Pray for nothing, say
Every night in bed,
"I have been a king,
I have been a slave,
Nor is there anything,
Fool, rascal, knave,
That I have not been,
And yet upon my breast
A myriad heads have lain."'

That he might set at rest
A boy's turbulent days
Mohini Chatterjee
Spoke these, or words like these.
I add in commentary,
'Old lovers yet may have
All that time denied —
Grave is heaped on grave
That they be satisfied —
Over the blackened earth
The old troops parade,
Birth is heaped on birth

That such cannonade
May thunder time away,
Birth-hour and death-hour meet,
Or, as great sages say,
Men dance on deathless feet.'

In its revised form the poem could please no orthodox Hindu. The significance of reincarnation as doctrine has abated, and the poem is much more than a statement of belief. Mohini's remarks become an assertion of the paradox that women have loved even fools, rascals, slaves, and knaves, as well as kings, that the soul will encounter during its cycle every possible state and yet always experience love. The whole poem is now argued in terms of love ; the cannonade of rebirth is the desperate struggle with time to enable frustrated lovers to be satisfied. The propositions are arrived at by necessity and after struggle. Mohini, too, is no longer a wise man speaking, like Kanva, oracularly ; instead his advice is motivated in part by a desire to calm his young pupil, and the pupil later is able to speak for himself with western energy. A dramatic relation is established between them.

Not only has Yeats enlivened the later poem by a sense of importunacy absent from the quietism of the earlier version, but he makes no claim upon the reader's belief, or even, to use Coleridge's term, his suspension of disbelief. In his assumed role of commentator, he explicates a text by exploding passion in the philosophical lesson. The subjunctive 'that' clauses ('That they be satisfied', 'That such cannonade . . .') can be clauses of either result or purpose ; the certainty of the result is not the poet's concern so much as the harried ceaselessness of the struggle towards the result. He is deeply disturbed, too, although he says so only indirectly, by the frenzied handling of human lives. Both of these reactions are overwhelmed in the splendid final lines, which envisage the end of the rebirth cycle in an ecstasy of contemplative desire beside which belief would seem a trivial attitude. Reincarnation is important because of the human implications that can be attached to it. The poem envelops and transcends reincarnation as a belief by making it the only possible outlet for the speaker's thoughts and feelings.

By the early 'nineties Yeats had learned how to employ ideas in this larger context. He was delighted to discover hints of the rebirth cycle in ancient Irish legends, for it thus became part of the tradition of his own country and the west as well as of the east. In his poem 'Mongan Thinks of His Past Greatness When a Part of the Constellations of Heaven', he combined some rather confused Irish legends of Mongan with the clearer Welsh legend of Taliesin, and made his hero avow his past incarnations; but he shifted the emphasis from the remarkable cycle of new lives to the fact that so many incarnations have led at last only to the sorrow of Mongan's present life as a frustrated lover. Fergus in the poem 'Fergus and the Druid', from the *Countess Kathleen* volume (1892), discovers through the druid's aid all the lives he has lived in the past :

> I see my life go dripping like a stream
> From change to change ; I have been many things —
> A green drop in the surge, a gleam of light
> Upon a sword, a fir-tree on a hill,
> An old slave grinding at a heavy quern,
> A king sitting upon a chair of gold,
> And all these things were wonderful and great ;
> But now I have grown nothing, being all,
> And the whole world weighs down upon my heart. . . .

The theme, however, is not his discovery of past lives, but the pain which he experiences on surrendering his power as a king and man of action in return for even such spectacular knowledge. So doctrine is overshadowed here as well.

While it is conceivable that Yeats might have had outside his poems beliefs of a more obtrusive kind than those he put in his poems, he apparently did not. We have unusual evidence for his state of mind about reincarnation. The unpublished first draft of his *Autobiographies* recounts a conversation he had with Maud Gonne and George Russell in the middle 'nineties :

He [Russell] had seen many visions, and some of them had contained information about matters of fact that were afterwards verified ;

but though his own personal revelations were often original and very remarkable, he accepted in the main the conclusions of Theosophy. He spoke of reincarnation and Maud Gonne asked him 'how soon a child was reborn, and where'. He said, 'It may be reborn in the same family'. I could see that Maud Gonne was deeply impressed and I quieted my more sceptical intelligence, as I had so often done in her presence. I remember a pang of conscience. Ought I not to say 'The whole doctrine of the reincarnation of the soul is hypothetic; it is the most plausible of the explanations of the world, but can we say more than that?' or some such sentence?

This scruple is characteristic; although Yeats came to present the theme of reincarnation with a vehemence that increased with age and with the general strengthening of his mature verse, it was never more for him than the 'most plausible of the explanations of the world'. As such it stood him in good stead as a poet.

Reincarnation is closely related to a second concept in Yeats's verse. There, as in Eastern thought, the wheel of endless becoming can be escaped and the soul transported to some kind of supreme existence which is changeless and immortal. This ideal state is neither exactly the Christian heaven nor the Buddhist Nirvana. Yeats invigorated and personalized it by giving it the irreligious names of 'the happy townland', 'the glittering town', and later on, 'the predestined dancing-place'. A good deal of mystery surrounds this state: do we achieve it in this life, or must we bide our time until the afterlife? He took no permanent stand on this question, for to do so would have made him, like his friend Russell, a mystic given to unqualified assertion rather than a poet given to passionate longing. Russell's heaven was an abstraction, he thought, and he wrote his father in 1909: Russell 'has set his ideal in so vague and remote a heaven that he takes the thoughts of his followers off the technique of life, or leaves only their poorer thoughts for it'. He accepted instead J. B. Yeats's statement in a letter of 1914, 'Poetry concerns itself with the creation of Paradises. I use the word in the plural for there are as many paradises as there are individual men — nay — as many as there are separate feelings.' Heaven, then, is a name we apply to an ideal condition ; whether it exists or not is of less importance than the fact that we demand its existence. What form we give it depends upon our feelings at a particular time.

Yeats's heaven is therefore startlingly variable. A comparison of the uncorrected and the corrected proof sheets of the 'Apologia Addressed to Ireland in the Coming Days' (1892) reveals his determination to keep it so. The first version represents the perfect state as a union with truth which is attained only post-humously :

> From our birthday until we die,
> Is but the winking of an eye.
> And we, our singing and our love,
> The mariners of night above,
> And all the wizard things that go
> About my table to and fro,
> *Are passing on to where there is*
> *In truth's consuming silences*
> No place for love and dream at all ;
> For God goes by with white footfall.

The italicized lines contained two implications that Yeats felt obliged to alter. One was the dogmatic certainty of the state described, the other was the unpalatableness of even truth's transcending love and dream. He did not remove the lines, but he entered a significant qualification :

> Are passing on to where *may be*
> In truth's consuming ecstasy. . . .

Now his emphasis is not on the ideal state itself but on the possible peril to love and dream within it, and certainty or uncertainty are equally irrelevant.

The revision brings the poem closer to his statements in *The Shadowy Waters*, a play which elaborates his conceptions more lengthily than any other work in the 'nineties. Here the ideal state is the perfect union of hearts, not truth. Will the hero and heroine attain union in life or in death ? Yeats admits the question without deciding it, preferring to celebrate the consummateness of their love,

> Whether among the cold winds of the dead,
> Or among winds that move in the meadows and woods.

On the other hand, the wise man Dathi in 'The Blessed' does not associate heaven only with love; he contends, too, that the state of blessedness can be reached in life in all sorts of ways, including drunkenness :

> O blessedness comes in the night and the day
> And whither the wise heart knows,
> And one has seen in the redness of wine
> The Incorruptible Rose. . . .

Yeats was not required in his verse to side with a heaven attained through love, or a heaven attained through drunkenness, or to decide heaven's exact composition. He could admit as many paradises as separate ideals and longings. Yet the various heavens he describes have certain negative qualities in common : they are never thin, spiritualized, or fleshless. For a heaven that was purely spiritual seemed to him alien to poetry, which, he considered, must satisfy body as well as soul with its ideals. When in 1926 he came to write 'Among School Children', he described his mature paradise consistently :

> Labour is blossoming or dancing where
> The body is not bruised to pleasure soul.

The location of 'where' is left in doubt, but not the body's right to be the soul's peer in whatever heaven there may be.

A third theme, the approaching end of the world or its transmutation, is developed with the same constancy of attention and diversity of treatment. Several early poems picture a beast who will uproot the world in a consummation which sometimes appears to be the ultimate one, and at other times to be the upheaval heralding, in Theosophical doctrine, every new cycle. The beast, who invites comparison with the sphinx-like creature in 'The Second Coming', which Yeats wrote in 1919, and with the donkey in *The Herne's Egg* (1938), is variously represented in the early poems as a grunting boar without bristles, a black pig, and a death-pale deer. While the first two, if not the third, are based on Irish folklore, the zoological variety is symptomatic of a variation in attitude. Sometimes Yeats diffidently heralds the approaching event ; at other times he longs for it but sees no immediate prospect of its coming about ; and elsewhere he half-regrets its coming. The eschatology is straightened or loosened to serve the particular poem and (to anticipate a little) the particular state of mind.

The introduction of religious imagery, especially of God or the gods, is a fourth problem of ideology in both Yeats's prose and verse. So much of this imagery is Christian that we might at first suppose that he attached religious significance to it. Mrs. Yeats has remarked that her husband prayed all his life ; but if so it was not to any orthodox Christ. His attitude toward Christianity is complicated ; like Blake he sometimes accepts Christ as divine because a symbol of imagination. So he wrote his friend William Horton in 1896, urging him to join the Golden Dawn on the grounds that this view of Christ was held by that society :

Nor is our order anti-Christian. That very pentagram which I suggested your using is itself as you would presently have learned, a symbol of Christ. I am convinced however that for you progress lies not in dependence upon a Christ outside yourself but upon the Christ in your own breast, in the power of your divine will and divine imagination and not in some external will or imagination however divine. We certainly do teach this dependence only on the inner divinity but this is Christianity. The uttermost danger lies for you in emotional religion, which will sap your will and wreck your self-control. I do not mean that you cannot progress outside the G[olden] D[awn] but that you should read or study in some unemotional and difficult school.

Of course, as a poem on Father Rosicross confirms, Yeats would have accepted other symbols of the imagination just as readily as Christ.

Well before 1900, Yeats displays an increasing reluctance to employ Christ even as a symbol, for his birth and life seemed to him to be excessively spiritual. The hero of the unpublished novel, *The Speckled Bird*, proposes to improve Christianity by reconciling it with natural emotions and particularly with sexual love:

He was going to the East now to Arabia and Persia, where he would find among the common people so soon as he had learnt their language some lost doctrine of reconciliation ; the philosophic poets had made sexual love their principal symbol of a divine love and he had seen somewhere in a list of untranslated Egyptian MSS. that certain of them dealt with love as a polthugic [*sic*] power. In Ireland he [found] wonderful doctrines among the poor, doctrines which would have been the foundation of the old Irish poets, and surely he would find somewhere in the East a doctrine that would reconcile religion with the natural emotions, and at the same time explain these emotions. All the arts sprang from sexual love and there they could only come again, the garb of the religion when that reconciliation had taken place.

In an article of 1897, Yeats argued that Irish Christianity was at its best when it had retained an infusion of paganism :

Nothing shows more how blind educated Ireland — I am not certain that I should call so unimaginative a thing education — is about peasant Ireland, than that it does not understand how the old religion which made of the coming and going of the greenness of the woods and of the fruitfulness of the fields a part of its worship, lives side by side with the new religion which would trample nature as a serpent under its feet ; nor is that old religion faded to a meaningless repetition of old customs, for the ecstatic who has seen the red light and white light of God smite themselves into the bread and wine at the Mass, has seen the exultant hidden multitudes among the winds of May, and if he were philosophical would cry with the painter, Calvert : — 'I go inward to God, outward to the gods'.

This point of view accorded with his other preoccupations, for he laboured to reunite nature and man by imaginative perception, and to evolve a poetry, with the force but without the constriction of religion, to educate humanity to an ampler life. His friend Russell suggested to him about this time that they build a chapel for fairy worship so that the Catholic worshippers might 'become worshippers of the Sidhe without knowing it', a prospect which seemed to him as salutary as it was mischievous.

He, like Yeats, wanted to break down the barriers in the interest of a higher unity.

When God appears in Yeats's verse, it is as an ultimate counter with which the imagination can round out its world. A good example is the morphology of a line in 'He Remembers Forgotten Beauty'. Yeats originally wrote :

> Where such grey clouds of incense rose
> That only God's eyes did not close ;

then he altered the second line for a later edition, so that it read :

> That only the gods' eyes did not close ;

and finally, for another edition, he restored the first version. The only motivation for this monotheism seems to be rhythm.

Elsewhere God is referred to as the 'Eternal Darkness', 'the Supreme Enchanter' (which makes his connection with the imagination especially close), the 'Ineffable Name', 'the Light of Lights', the 'Master of the still stars and of the flaming door'. In old age Yeats evolved more unusual terms still, like 'the old man in the skies' and 'the Thirteenth Cone'. He had cause for his ingenuity. No abstraction, as Blake had taught him, was more dangerous than a god abstracted from humanity, and frequent reference to divinity under conventional names seemed to him likely to erect just such an abstraction. Triteness could separate the poet from his object, and spiritual exaltation, even if not trite, could be poetically inapposite. Yeats wrote a shrewd letter in 1898 to Russell about the use of God. A tireless reviser of his friends' work as well as his own, he objected to a line in Russell's 'Carrowmore' which read :

> Yet his sleep is filled with gold light by the King of all the world,

and explained, 'I have changed "King of all the world" which sounds a little commonplace to "the masters of the world", and "gold light" which the verse puts out of the usual accentuation to "music" which gives a full sound'.[1] Russell meekly accepted

---

[1] Yeats followed his own advice in a poem, '*The Players Ask for a Blessing on the Psalteries and on Themselves*', where they address their prayer, or request, to the 'masters of the glittering town'.

the shift. Divinity might have a place in poetry, but not a prerogative. The poem, in short, came first.

Yeats's fixed policy was to shun the vast religious generalizations which were popular at the end of the nineteenth century. A year and a half before his death he had a talk with a Hindu professor, to whom he asserted that he was no mystic. While he always took the westerner's part when talking to anyone from the East, just as in writing for a western audience he habitually introduced eastern conceptions, he was not speaking merely *ad hoc*. 'In my own poetry', he said, 'I have always aimed at perfect clearness of conception and a perfectly logical expression. Tagore, who is of course a great personal friend of mine, writes a great deal about God. My mind resents the vagueness of all references to God. I keep to what is clear and rational. . . . In my poetry there is always a clear conception expressed in language as perfect as I can command.' It is, in fact, true that God in Yeats's writings is either a poetic property like destiny, filling out the picture of the cosmos by providing it with leadership, or a symbol of some imaginative power, or imagined state of being, closely associated with man, and that in neither capacity is He likely to be described with vagueness. A very early poem, 'The Indian upon God', is an excellent illustration. The Indian hears a moorfowl assert that God is 'an undying moorfowl', a lotus protest that 'He hangeth on a stalk', a roebuck that 'He is a gentle roebuck', and a peacock that 'He is a monstrous peacock'. The poem would be equally congenial to Hume and Madame Blavatsky. Hume would say that it meant that all religions were founded on personal prejudice and therefore were false, and Madame Blavatsky would interpret it to mean that all religions, whatever their particular forms, sprang from a common and valid instinct. Yeats would say that he had not written the poem to express either of these dogmas, and that neither inference was an adequate restatement. Primarily the poem meant to him that these creatures were right in imagining their God as like themselves, concrete and personal, while man was wrong when he tried to create his God out of some other substance than humanity.

The essential standard for the poet is one of 'dwelling in the presence of certain ideas' rather than of positing them as truths demanding adherence; he relies on the complexity of poetic structure to prevent his verse from being doctrinal. The references to God in most of the early poems are alike in exhibiting no affection for Him and not much attention to His present power in the world. Rather Yeats summons Him from the sky to destroy or transmute the world in the near future, and so concentrates on the attitudes of fear and hope rather than of piety. This treatment is not atheism, but it should not be mistaken for orthodoxy or devotion either. Far from being a God-intoxicated man, Yeats has only to think of God to become sober and extremely wary.

Instead of worshipping an abstraction, Yeats advocates, in one of his short stories, the 'unfolding' of the individual's heart. This personal ethic, which he opposes to conventional ethics, is the fifth recurrent idea in his verse. Critics have sometimes identified him with a doctrine of art for art's sake, and so misinterpreted him. Like his father, Yeats was disinclined to discuss ethical questions theoretically; he had had enough of the emphasis on conduct in nineteenth-century letters. At the age of twenty, in some notes about George Eliot, he irritably announced : 'There is too much talk of the moral law, surely the tongue of the poet is for other teaching. Is there not a pulpited million of disconsolate voices shouting the moral law for so much a day?' Sometimes he impatiently opposed morals altogether, sometimes he simply indicated his satiety with them, and sometimes he reconstituted them.

His fundamental position was that good and bad in their usual senses were, as Blake had said, nets of convention. The writer, and any man of personality, must steer clear of them. As he put it in *The Celtic Twilight* (1893), fantasy and caprice would lose their necessary freedom if united either with evil or good. The hero of 'The Tables of the Law' is incapable of sin, because he 'had discovered the law of my being, and could only express or fail to express my being'. If one must have sins, they should be one's own and no one else's; in a lecture in 1909, Yeats spoke of 'the old writers as busy with their own sins and of the new writers as busy with other people's', ranking Shakespeare on one side and Milton on the other. He had said in his edition of Blake that truth is the dramatic expression of the most complete man, and the same definition would have served for his notion of good.

In youth as in old age, he was struggling to be rid of stereotyped ethical judgments. His notes for the first edition of *A Vision* contain a curious passage on the problem :

We have never solved the central problem of the system, that of good and evil. I think we must consider that there are gyres within the being of the man. That the coming of one of these gyres to its subjective state must cause the creation of some knot. Genius, for instance, has I think been described as the harmonising or disorganising of such knots.

The word 'knot' is an attempt to get away from valuative language. When *A Vision* was published early in 1926, it contained a prediction that for men of the coming age, as distinguished from men of the present, the good would be that 'which a man can contemplate himself as doing always and no other doing at all'.

These statements are at bottom related, and they imply an ethical attitude. The self has the task of expressing itself, but it can be judged by its own completeness, and by the completeness of its expression. It has to be able to respect itself, and to do so tries to live up to some image of desirable life. The hero at Mount Meru, or Troy, or the Dublin Post Office, the poet at his desk framing the most complex experiences, and the young girl in the indolence of her youth have other things to be concerned with than the tables of abstract law. Their self-imposed ideals of conduct, through which they aspire to completeness, possess their thoughts.

III. SYMBOLIST THEORY

The centre of a Yeats poem is not its ideological content. It is rather, Yeats said as a young man, a mood, or as he later put it, a state of mind. He meant both terms to be large enough to include both emotions and ideas. Moods and states of mind are conspicuously, but not exclusively, emotional or temperamental ; they differ from emotions in having form and, often, intellectual structure. Less fleeting than a mere wish, and less crystallized than a belief, a mood is suspended between fluidity and solidity. It can be tested only by the likelihood of its being experienced at all, and being so, by many people. Ideas which occur in moods are 'lived' and lose their abstractness ; beliefs are dramatized and lose their affiliations with dogmas to take on affiliations with the dramatic speaker of the poem.

Moods are not aroused by the rational faculty or by 'undisciplined squads of emotion', but by the imagination, which has both at its disposal. If, for example, the reason tells us that the reality we see is the only reality, the imagination may contradict it, affirming that the corporeal eye is only an instrument and not a very important one. More important than that eye is our dreaming or visionary faculty, which is second-sighted and conceives a reality more fundamental than Zola's. Of dreams, visions, folklore, and works of art, Yeats writes in the *National Observer*, 'They are an existence and not a thought, and make our world of the tea-tables seem but a shabby penumbra'.

No reader would be so brazen as to defend the reality of tea-tables, yet one might object that the poet exploits this scorn to justify discarding the world of appearance altogether. He does not go so far, however. His fondness for words like dream, ideal, phantasy, symbol, delusion, glamour, and image permits him to 'exchange civilities with the world beyond' ; to carry it further would be to isolate one part of the mind from the rest.

By keeping up a running battle with the world of appearance, Yeats gives it covert recognition. As early as 1893, he writes in *The Celtic Twilight*, 'I too had by this time fallen into a kind of trance, in which what we call the unreal had begun to take upon itself a masterful reality . . .'. Everything exists, everything is true, and the earth is only a little dust under our feet.' Sometimes he transvaluates the word 'dream' so that the world of appearance is the dream, and the *au-delà* is the reality, as when Niamh invites mortals to 'Empty your heart of its mortal dream'. But 'dream' may also have its more conventional meaning, as in 'The Song of the Last Arcadian', where the poet urges, 'Dream, dream, for this is also sooth'. These statements do not offer philosophical distinctions between appearance and reality, but tensions between them ; while either term is likely to shift its meaning, Yeats regularly exalts all that is imagined and denigrates all that is seen if it falls short of what is imagined. He well knew Blake's declaration that to him the sun was not a round disc of fire somewhat like a guinea but an innumerable company of the heavenly host crying, 'Holy, holy, holy is the Lord God Almighty'. But Yeats did not wish to deprive the moods of their ties with common perception, only to free them from absolute dependence on those ties.

In the same way, he freed them from dependence on rational foundations. 'It is better doubtless', he wrote winningly, 'to believe much unreason and a little truth than to deny for denial's sake truth and unreason alike. . . . When all is said and done, how do we not know but that our own unreason may be better than another's truth ?' The tortured syntax may well put a hard-headed reader on Yeats's side, and lead him to ignore the fact that all denial is not for denial's sake. Yeats was not necessarily so elliptical. Speaking to the Irish Literary Society in London, he asserted that there were truths of passion which were intellectual falsehoods ; in many of his writings he insisted that the peasant knew and revealed more in his folklore than the metropolitan in his technical books. 'Folk-lore', he announced, 'is at once the Bible, the Thirty-Nine Articles, and the Book of Common Prayer, and well-nigh all the great poets have lived by its light. Homer, Aeschylus, Sophocles, Shakespeare, and even Dante, Goethe, and Keats, were little more than folk-lorists with musical tongues.' The respect for folklore, as for passion, was to rob the intellect of ascendancy.

Since the moods are informed by the imagination, they are the most real things or beings we know. 'The great Moods are alone immortal, and the creators of mortal things', Yeats reverently declares in *The Secret Rose*. How they appear to us, or better, befall us, he describes in 'Rosa Alchemica' :

For just as the magician or the artist could call them when he would, so they could call out of the mind of the magician or the artist, or if they were demons, out of the mind of the mad or the ignoble, what shape they would, and through its voice and its gestures pour themselves out upon the world. In this way all great events were accomplished ; a mood, a divinity or a demon, first descending like a faint sigh into men's minds and then changing their thoughts and their actions until hair that was yellow had grown black, or hair that was black had grown yellow, and empires moved their border, as though they were but drifts of leaves.

They offer a sanction for the 'monumental moments' of dramatic lyrics, for at bottom, Yeats explained in an important essay in 1895, art has no content but moods :

Literature differs from explanatory and scientific writing in being wrought about a mood, or a community of moods, as the body is wrought about an invisible soul ; and if it uses argument, theory, erudition, observation, and seems to grow hot in assertion or denial, it does so merely to make us partakers at the banquet of the moods. It seems to me that . . . argument, theory, erudition, observation, are merely what Blake called 'little devils who fight for themselves ', illusions of our visible passing life, who must be made serve the moods, or we have no part in eternity. Everything that can be seen, touched, measured, explained, understood, argued over, is to the imaginative artist nothing more than a means. . . .

Beyond the moods there is no more ultimate reality, unless it is their union. In his edition of Blake, Yeats, having pointed out the divergencies of different mystical systems, justified them as expressions of moods :

Sometimes the mystical student, bewildered by the different systems, forgets for a moment that the history of moods is the history of the universe, and asks where is the final statement — the complete doctrine. The universe is itself that doctrine and statement. All others are partial, for it alone is the symbol of the infinite thought which is in turn symbolic of the universal mood we name God.

It is characteristic of his point of view that the final 'doctrine and statement' turns out to have no formulation except that of the universe which is itself a symbol. It is the symbol of God, Himself a symbol of 'the universal mood', the *prima materia*. Mood is piled on mood to such an extent that everything is symbolically related, and we can define any given mood only by establishing precisely its correspondence with others. So considered, heaven, hell, purgatory, and fairyland may be simply names attributed to certain moods; thus hell is 'the place of those who deny' its existence.

Whether the human imagination creates moods, or only evokes them, was a question that Yeats asked himself. Sometimes he took the solipsist position. So in some notes for his unpublished novel, *The Speckled Bird*, he went as far as he could : 'The Rosicrucian magic means the assertion of the greatness of man in its extreme form. His [the hero's] letter should give some eloquent expression to this. He may even claim with the Druids that man created the world.' A quarter of a century later Yeats made this claim in 'The Tower' :

> Death and life were not
> Till man made up the whole,
> Made lock, stock and barrel
> Out of his bitter soul,
> Aye, sun and moon and star, all,
> And further add to that
> That, being dead, we rise,
> Dream and so create
> Translunar Paradise.

Yet if such a claim had complete pre-eminence over all others, it would have contradicted his conception of poetry as an assemblage of moods. He justifiably did not base all his poems on the solipsist theory.

The value of the moods to his poetry was threefold. First, they exempted it from the powerful conscriptive pressure of conventional beliefs and fashionable doubts ; they made imagination, whether the breeding-house or the nursery of moods, more important than reason and more permanent than emotion. 'Whatever we build in the imagination', he wrote Florence Farr in 1899, 'will accomplish itself in the circumstance of our lives.' Second, they unified the world into one imaginative substance; they replaced the *matter* of the scientists with the *mood* of the poets. Third, they made forceful asseveration possible to a man whose point of view was flexible. They admitted the poet to a world which the scientist, the banker, the clergyman, and the philosopher, clutching like dolls their substitute-realities, were forbidden to enter.

CHAPTER IV

ICONOGRAPHY

I have no speech but symbol, the pagan speech I made
Amid the dreams of youth.

YEATS, 'Upon a Dying Lady'

I. THE STRUCTURE

THE word 'phantasmagoria' was one which Yeats, following Rimbaud, Baudelaire, and Poe, grew fond of during
the 'nineties. It designated for him that structure of
related images through which he could express himself, and
through which, as he later said, 'the dream and the reality' might
'face one another in visible array'. What was personal and
transitory might be welded with what was impersonal and permanent through a group of images which had attracted men for
hundreds of years. These images were phantasmagoric not in
that they were illusory, but in that they represented, more than
they participated in, the secret essences of things.

Because of his view of reality as consisting ultimately of
moods, and of moods as having an eternal or archetypal character,
it is not easy to say precisely for what the phantasmagoric image
stands. A. G. Lehmann has ingeniously defined the Yeatsian
symbol entirely in terms of its effect as 'any representation serving
as a sign of a general attitude which either tradition or supernatural decree has invested with powerful emotional resources'.
The definition needs amending in two ways: the word *attitude*
detracts from the symbol's self-sufficiency, and must yield to
mood; that is, the symbol serves as an aspect of the total mood
of the poem. Moreover, the powerful resources of the symbol
must be intellectual as well as emotional, for Yeats would not
have countenanced purely emotional symbols.

On this point he was perfectly definite. He distinguished between two kinds of symbols, those 'that evoke emotions alone', and those 'that evoke ideas alone, or ideas mingled with emotions'. His clear preference was for the second sort. As he explained in his essay on 'The Symbolism of Poetry' (1900), 'If I say "white" or "purple" in an ordinary line of poetry, they evoke emotions so exclusively that I cannot see why they move me ; but if I bring them into the same sentence with such obvious intellectual symbols as a cross or a crown of thorns, I think of purity and sovereignty'. Through intellectual symbols the poem could impart 'an indefinable wisdom' :

It is the intellect that decides where the reader shall ponder over the procession of the symbols, and if the symbols are merely emotional, he gazes from amid the accidents and destinies of the world ; but if the symbols are intellectual too, he becomes himself a part of pure intellect, and he is himself mingled with the procession.

Intellectual symbols never grew stale ; the more they were used, the richer they became.

Among the intellectual symbols we can distinguish two sorts, or better, two functions : cooperative and emphatic. While any symbol could serve either function, the four elements of earth, air, fire, and water frequently are good examples of cooperative symbols. They set up eddies of association which are auxiliary to the main symbol of the poem. That main or emphatic symbol is a centre of attraction around which the mood gathers, and many of Yeats's poems, from 'The Rose of the World' to 'The Black Tower', are built around such centres.

Two phantasmagorias or symbolic structures can be found in his work, the first built up from boyhood and retained until after 1900, the other accumulating mainly from 1915 to 1929. The period from about 1903 to about 1914 lacks a clearly articulated structure though it has occasional elements of the early and late ones ; and towards the close of Yeats's life, from about 1935 to his death in 1939, the power of the second symbolic structure is noticeably abated. The early structure was largely made up of familiar symbols treated in an unfamiliar way, while the later structure contained much less common symbols which Yeats made to seem familiar. His attitude differed towards the two : he advertised the second in *A Vision*, but was more reticent about the first. His most explicit statements of it are in the notes to *The Wind Among the Reeds* and in a programme note on *The Shadowy Waters* among his published work, and in his rituals for his Irish mystical order among his unpublished papers ; but these do not present a unified picture. For this we can look to the elaborate gilded covers of his books of verse and short stories from 1897 to 1900, because on them Yeats had Althea Gyles draw intricate designs of his symbolism.

The cover of *The Secret Rose* (1897) was intended to make the book resemble a *grimoire*. At its centre is a four-petalled rose joined to a cross, occupying a place just below the middle of a tree. The boughs of the tree resemble a serpent's folds ; among them, just above the rose, are the kissing faces of a man and a woman.

These emblems pervade much of Yeats's early verse. Forms so archetypal as the cross and the circle, which the petals of the rose form, have of course a great many implications, some of which we can fix. The four petals are then, chiefly, the four elements. The conjunction of rose and cross which suggests the fifth element or quintessence is the central myth of Rosicrucianism, and Yeats was an active member of the Rosicrucian order of the Golden Dawn throughout the 'nineties. In the order, the conjunction is often referred to as a 'mystic marriage', as the transfiguring ecstasy which occurs when the adept, after the long pain and self-sacrifice of the quest in this world, a world in which opposites are for ever quarrelling, finds his cross — the symbol of that struggle and opposition — suddenly blossom with the rose of love, harmony, and beauty. Such a meaning is indicated in *The Shadowy Waters* :

> I can see nothing plain ; all's mystery.
> Yet, sometimes there's a torch inside my head
> That makes all clear, but when the light is gone
> I have but images, analogies,

YEATS'S EARLY SYMBOLISM

The cover design of *The Secret Rose*, designed for Yeats by Althea Gyles (and here copied by Mary Gelb), showing the conjunction of Rose and Cross, and of man and woman, in the midst of the serpentine folds of the Tree of Life. The three roses at the top represent the three principal states of being (Sephiroth) of the Kabbalistic Tree, and the skeleton at the bottom represents the lowest state of being or nature.

> The mystic bread, the sacramental wine,
> The red rose where the two shafts of the cross,
> Body and soul, waking and sleep, death, life,
> Whatever meaning ancient allegorists
> Have settled on, are mixed into one joy.
> For what's the rose but that ? miraculous cries,
> Old stories about mystic marriages,
> Impossible truths ? But when the torch is lit
> All that is impossible is certain,
> I plunge in the abyss.

Obviously Yeats intended to keep the symbols as manifold as possible in their suggestibility. Elsewhere he offers further meanings. In a manuscript book he noted down in 1901 a recent dream :

I woke up saying that father Rosy Cross was the first who [proclaimed] that beauty was holiness and all that is ugly unholiness. I thought between waking and sleeping, 'He set the rose upon the cross and thereby united religion and beauty, the spirit and nature, and the universe of spirit and of nature in magic'.

The conjunction can also be regarded as sexual symbolism, in which Yeats, as comparative mythologist and occultist, was already well versed ; the masculine principle, the cross, merges with the feminine principle, the rose. The cross has the apparent connotation of Christ and Christianity, while the rose, although a Christian symbol too, sometimes implies, as in his dream, a kind of pagan beauty.

These associations help to clarify one of the more cryptic of Yeats's early poems. He published it in the *Bookman* in 1895, without explanation, as 'A Song of the Rosy Cross':

> He who measures gain and loss,
>   When he gave to thee the Rose,
> Gave to me alone the Cross ;
>   Where the blood-red blossom blows
> In a wood of dew and moss,
>   There thy wandering pathway goes,
> Mine where waters brood and toss ;

> Yet one joy have I, hid close,
> He who measures gain and loss,
> When he gave to thee the Rose,
> Gave to me alone the Cross.

The magical-mystical-religious symbolism is appropriated here for special amorous and poetic purposes. The poet says that, since his beloved is endowed with perfect beauty, and since he has the obligation of suffering for her in a way which seems divinely appointed if only because uniquely unpleasant, he can find consolation for his pain in the conviction that perfect beauty and perfect suffering reflect the archetype of perfect union, and thus reflect the basic principles of world order. The rose and cross are emphatic symbols, while earth and water are cooperative. Yeats evidently decided that the poem was too arcane in its references, or too lavish in its apportionment of attributes to lover and beloved, so he did not reprint it.

A later poem, 'The Travail of Passion', has the air of using traditional symbols more familiarly than 'A Song of the Rosy Cross', but on close examination turns out instead to be more subtle and skilful in its diversion of tradition to the poet's ends. The religious context of the women weeping for Christ is secularized so as to be connected, like many of the poems in *The Wind Among the Reeds*, with the transcendent passion of love :

> When the flaming lute-thronged angelic door is wide ;
> When an immortal passion breathes in mortal clay ;
> Our hearts endure the scourge, the plaited thorns, the way
> Crowded with bitter faces, the wounds in palm and side,
> The vinegar-heavy sponge, the flowers by Kedron stream ;
> We will bend down and loosen our hair over you,
> That it may drop faint perfume and be heavy with dew,
> Lilies of death-pale hope, roses of passionate dream.

In its careful contrivance, this poem holds back the person to whom it is addressed until the close, so that the sentence seems to struggle in the middle describing the travail, and to reach its difficult end simultaneously with the revelation of the object of such suffering. The syntax suits the sense with comparable neatness in a later poem about a quest, 'The Magi'. There the Christian symbols are enlarged by making the Magi into symbols of all men who struggle to accommodate their experience to miracle ; here, in the second line, Yeats implies that an immortal passion incarnates itself in every true lover as in Christ. If the 'lilies of death-pale hope, roses of passionate dream' seem at first a peculiar description of Christ as every lover, it should be recognized that on one level they simply describe the pink and whiteness of the face. On another level they describe two of his attributes, hope and dream, and implicitly in the lily and rose, purity and passion. The poem is nevertheless unsatisfying ; it does not have enough force to warrant its powerful religious images and their special use, which Donne might have carried off. The last two lines, like the second, lose weight and dwindle into epithets which seem adequate only until we take the trouble to grasp the sense beneath their nebulous charm.

The rose blossoms so thickly over the poems and stories that its ontogeny needs to be traced. As a decorative device it attracted Yeats almost from the time that he began to write. He started *Mosada*, his early play, when he was nineteen or twenty, with the words :

> Three times the roses have grown less and less,
> As slowly Autumn climbed the golden throne
> Where sat old Summer fading into song. . . .

No precise moment can of course be found when the rose gives up its place in the garden to become a symbol. By the time of *The Wanderings of Oisin* (1889), it is a frequent feature of the landscape, and by the second edition of that poem, in 1895, Yeats inserts it more frequently still. While the Golden Dawn encouraged him in this, he was also affected by the practice of his contemporaries, among whom the rose then had the currency which the bone attained in English poetic symbolism during the nineteen-twenties. Yeats's friends Lionel Johnson and Ernest Dowson, for example, took to the rose symbol with ardour, probably because of the current vogue of Catholicism among

English men of letters, and made it a constant feature of their
expression. But while Johnson employed the symbol in the
Dantean way, relating it to the Virgin and to heaven, Dowson
followed another tradition in using it as an un-Christian symbol
of sensual delight, as in his famous phrase, 'Flung roses, roses
violently with the throng'. We do not have to suppose that
Yeats, who drew upon both traditions of the rose, was following
them ; the evidence in fact indicates that he experimented with it
before he knew them or their work well. But he found support
in sharing an iconography with them, just as in later life he was
gratified to discover that Dorothy Wellesley and Edith Sitwell
were writing with symbols like his own. As usual, however, he
went further than they did.

The relation of rose and meteor offers an example of his
construction of symbolic relations and overtones. In *Oisin*, the
rose is compared to a meteor, but only by way of simile :

> We danced to where within the gloom
> Hung, like meteors of red light,
> Damask roses in the night. . . .

In 'The White Birds', a poem he wrote three years later, he made
the same comparison, but this time introduced much more
symbolic activity:

I would that we were, my beloved, white birds on the foam of the sea !
We tire of the flame of the meteor, before it can fade and flee ;
And the flame of the blue star of twilight, hung low on the rim of
   the sky,
Has awaked in our hearts, my beloved, a sadness that may not die.

A weariness comes from those dreamers, dew-dabbled, the lily and rose;
Ah, dream not of them, my beloved, the flame of the meteor that goes,
Or the flame of the blue star that lingers hung low in the fall of the dew;
For I would we were changed to white birds on the wandering foam :
   I and you !

I am haunted by numberless islands, and many a Danaan shore,
Where Time would surely forget us, and Sorrow come near us no
   more ;

Soon far from the rose and the lily and fret of the flames would we be,
Were we only white birds, my beloved, buoyed out on the foam of
the sea !

The rose, lily, meteor, and evening star are so insistently and
oddly linked as to make the reader ask what their relation is.
The Shadowy Waters, a play which Yeats worked on from about
1885 to 1899, almost the span of his early verse, is helpful. Its
hero appears with a lily embroidered on his breast, its heroine
with a rose ; Yeats explained in a note on the play that these
were masculine and feminine symbols, for he conceived of man
as for ever seeking death, and of woman as for ever seeking life.
This explanation helps to make precise what the poem makes
only misty, that the speaker is anxious to escape from the world
where such distinctions of desire, and such opposite states as life
and death, trouble the inhabitants. More standard associations
are also at work. The lily, as in 'The Travail of Passion', has
its traditional aura of purity, hope, and frustration, and the rose
its implications of beauty, love, and fulfilment. And the meteor
suggests both the glow of passion and the transitoriness of time,
while Venus, the flaming star of evening, suggests love and
death ; they are contrasted with the maternal ocean, to which
their tensions drive the poet to flee with his beloved in the form
of a bird.

But birds are not free of all these pressures. We are dealing
here, however, with special birds, close to the discarnate species
in 'Sailing to Byzantium'. The poet intimates as much in the
third stanza by allying them with 'many a Danaan [fairy] shore'.
Yet, while the poem dwells upon the bird-like shape for which
the poet longs, it draws more of its interest from the implied
misery which causes so extreme a wish than from the wish
itself.

'The White Birds' is obviously not one of Yeats's best poems.
Put next to its mature counterpart, 'Sailing to Byzantium', it
looks loose and wasteful in method. The poems share the emphatic symbol of the birds, and the cooperative symbols of fire and
water, but the later poem leaves the overworked rose, lily, meteor,

and evening star alone. Instead of relying on pictorial beauty to justify imprecise symbols, it makes clear the reason why the poet wishes to change his state to that of a bird ; and, instead of conveying a rather eccentric aspiration for an unidentified state beyond life and death, it identifies the state tightly with the perfection of art. It locates the bird in space (Byzantium) and roughly in a historical period, and substitutes a *jusqu'auboutiste* vitality and self-possession for helpless wistfulness and longing. The earlier symbols seem by comparison to be obfuscating rather than illuminating ; at this stage Yeats was often excessively attracted by the enigmatic character of his symbols, as if their power depended upon their forms being, as he said, 'only half-revealed in the shadowy folds'. The occult maxim '*Tout secret divulgué est perdu*' may sometimes have underlain his poetic practice. To the complaint of obscurity Yeats replied that he expected his symbols 'to explain themselves as the years go by and one poem lights up another', but this expectation was not always fulfilled.

II. THE GAMUT OF ROSES

His most ambitious and original effort during his early period is, however, a group of poems centred about the rose that he began late in 1891 and concluded near the end of the century. The symbol was so prominent that he applied the collective title of 'The Rose' to all the lyrics in the *Countess Kathleen* volume, explaining in a note dated 1895 that 'in them he has found, he believes, the only pathway whereon he can hope to see with his own eyes the Eternal Rose of Beauty and of Peace'. Three years later he humorously admitted to 'a passion for the symbolism of the mystical rose, which has saddened my friends'. It was a passion to which he yielded with remarkable adroitness.

In an unpublished draft of his *Autobiographies*, Yeats ruefully attributed the temper of his rose poems to his association with the Theosophists. He spent a great deal of time with them in Dublin during the 'nineties :

   Probably I had made matters worse for myself by the choice of a
lodging. Some half dozen theosophists who lived together in Ely
Place invited me to join them and as I never earned more than a
pound a week and knew that some of them had no more I accepted
and was grateful. Beside the resident members others would call
during the day and the reading room was a place of much discussion
about philosophy and the arts for we never spoke of politics. If we
spoke of love poetry we preferred the love poetry when one sang at
the same moment not the sweetheart but some spiritual principle —
'all must be vita nuova'. We were full of Platonism, not of Plato
but of current conversation, and it was perhaps now that I began
to write love poems which my fellow countrymen, discerning the
presence of some abstraction plainly not 'the finest peasantry above
earth', found very obscure.

The love poems which he wrote are, in fact, love poems with a
difference. The beloved hovers in them somewhere between an
actual woman and a symbol. While she manifests herself in the
form of a rose, the rose is often described with horticultural
indifference as footed and skirted. As if combining the roses of
Johnson and Dowson, she is sometimes physical, sometimes
spiritual. Her significance and aspect change from poem to
poem, somewhat as Blake's symbolic personages shift facets
continually in what Yeats called 'the circulation of the Zoas' as
they create or yield to pressures.

   The pattern of circulation is ascertainable. For example, in
'To the Rose upon the Rood of Time', a title which employs the
rose-cross conjunction of 'A Song of the Rosy Cross' and of
'The Travail of Passion', the rose is identified (and originally
capitalized) as 'Eternal Beauty', so excellent that the poet begs
her not to dazzle him for fear that he will lose sight of the less
ecstatic but still desirable features of ordinary, simple life. Yet
she is not altogether transcendental, this 'Red Rose, proud Rose,
sad Rose of all my days', since she is apparently within human
call, and is sad because of her voluntary participation in human
sorrows. For, Yeats said, 'The quality symbolized as The Rose
differs from the Intellectual Beauty of Shelley and of Spenser in
that I have imagined it as suffering with man and not as something

pursued and seen from afar'. His use of the word 'quality' recognizes and even exaggerates the odd impersonality of his love poems. The rose in the poem originally entitled 'They Went Forth to the Battle, But They Always Fell' is less transcendent than in 'To the Rose upon the Rood of Time'; she is closer to incarnation, and her sadness is explained as due not to her growing sad with human sorrows, but to having 'grown sad with Eternity'. She may even long for anthropomorphosis. Sorrow comes from being human, and from not being human.

An opposite pattern takes hold in 'The Rose of the World' and 'The Peace of the Rose'. Yeats starts with a genuine woman in these poems, red lips and all, and then proceeds to apotheosize her.

THE ROSE OF THE WORLD

Who dreamed that beauty passes like a dream ?
  For these red lips with all their mournful pride,
  Mournful that no new wonder may betide,
Troy passed away in one high funeral gleam,
  And Usna's children died.

We and the labouring world are passing by :—
  Amid men's souls that day by day give place,
  More fleeting than the sea's foam fickle face.
Under the passing stars, foam of the sky,
  Lives on this lonely face.

Bow down archangels in your dim abode :
  Before ye were or any hearts to beat,
  Weary and kind one stood before His seat,
He made the world, to be a grassy road
  Before her wandering feet.

The present woman quickly becomes Helen of Troy (an insertion of Greek mythology which is unusual for Yeats in the 'nineties), then Deirdre, for whom the sons of Usna died, then beauty herself before God's throne, a conception familiar to Shelley and Spenser, and indebted to the Kabbalistic and neo-Platonic theory that the *Shekhinah* or eternal womanhood is coeval with God.

Yeats either begins, then, with a symbolic abstraction and humanizes it, or begins with a woman and renders her symbolically impersonal. When she appears initially as a woman, she will, as like as not, begin shortly to unfold as a multifoliate rose, to be sought unavailingly among mortal women. On the other hand, when she is a rose at the beginning of a poem, she generally ends up with characteristics that have nothing to do with the flower. Some interpenetration of the opposites qualifies the method a little ; the rose of the world is still 'weary and kind' in her exalted station next to God. But the basic pattern holds fairly firm.

No doubt all poetry moves in these arcs, but, characteristically, Yeats is more deliberate about them than most poets. That he had a conscious principle of creation behind his method is intimated by his letter to Russell of May 14, 1903, where he writes of two movements in poetry : 'Long ago I used to define to myself these two influences as the Transfiguration on the mountain and the Incarnation . . .'. Both transfigurative and incarnative imagery — terms which aptly describe the upward and downward movements of the rose — tend to hold the lady apart from excessively intimate contact with poet or reader. They also equip her to reside comfortably in the region which Yeats depicted in 1893 as 'that great Celtic twilight, in which heaven and earth so mingle that each seems to have taken upon itself some shadow of the other's beauty'. They helped Yeats to idealize woman in a way which was, like that of the pre-Raphaelites, anachronistic. So he wrote in the first draft of his *Autobiographies* :

I had much trouble with my senses, for I was not naturally chaste and I was young. All young men that I knew lived the life Edwin Ellis told me of, but I had gathered from the romantic poets an ideal of perfect love. Perhaps I should never marry in church but I would love one woman all my life. . . . I was a romantic, my head full of the mystical women of Rossetti, and those hesitating faces, in the art of Burne-Jones, which seemed always waiting for some Alcestis at the end of a long journey.

Most of his characters move, like Hanrahan and Dermot in *The*

Secret Rose, towards spirituality or away from it to humanity, and find no contentment in either.

The personality of the rose is clarified by the cover of *The Secret Rose*. The rose grows there upon a tree which is the tree of life. A note to *The Wind Among the Reeds* justifies its position :

Because the Rose, the flower sacred to the Virgin Mary, and the flower that Apuleius' adventurer ate, when he was changed out of the ass's shape and received into the fellowship of Isis, is the western Flower of Life, I have imagined it growing upon the Tree of Life.

The note has Yeats's characteristic fusion of Christian and pre-Christian traditions, based on the assumption that they are equivalent fulfilments of the same mental needs. Yeats does not mention, however, what may well have been his primary source, an open secret of Kabbalism according to which the tree of life is made up of ten *Sephiroth* or states ; the sixth of them, known as the heart, is customarily identified with beauty. This *Sephirah* (*Tiphareth*) is regarded as the connecting link between the upper and lower selves and the upper and lower worlds. That Yeats did not mention *Tiphareth* when he related the rose to it may have been due to his early habit of making public only the more communicable and respectable of the traditional associations of his symbols. It must be said for him that he would never have drawn on Kabbalistic doctrine had he not known of its analogues in other, non-occult literature.

Symbols run their course in Yeats's work, and he grew to dislike the rose. Contemporary taste also finds the poems rather tiresome in their frustrated rosolatry. They are, however, subtly worked, and Yeats's agility and originality in controlling the slide from physical to spiritual is remarkable. It can be seen at its best by comparing the efforts of Rossetti to do the same thing, efforts which frequently verge on the ludicrous :

> But soon, remembering her how brief the whole
> Of joy, which its own hours annihilate,
> Her set gaze gathered, thirstier than of late,
> And as she kissed, her mouth became her soul.

Apart from the ineptness of the third line, the conversion of body into spirit is unconvincing. It is so because the world of the spirit seems to enter only as a euphemistic extravagance, and because the physical imagery is too literal to permit of such rapid transformation. Yeats has a more considered view than Rossetti of the two worlds, and arranges their meetings less obtrusively, with more warranty and majesty. The distance between the lover and his love is already so great, even in physical terms, that it can be enlarged without incongruity. Casting his beloved into the rose symbol helps to enforce the exaltation of his love, and the poet's frustration promotes his credibility.

III. THE TREE AND THE SERPENT

Our next symbol, the tree of life, is of course a standard Biblical one, but Yeats was for a time almost as familiar with the Kabbalah as with the Bible. The Kabbalah is helpful in interpreting his poem 'The Two Trees', because the Sephirotic tree has two aspects, one benign, the reverse side malign. On one side are the *Sephiroth*, on the other the dread *Qlippoth*. Since the Kabbalists consider man to be a microcosm, the double-natured tree is a picture both of the universe and of the human mind, whose faculties, even the lowest, can work for good or ill. Yeats can therefore write,

> Beloved, gaze in thine own heart,
> The holy tree is growing there . . .

and at the same time warn her not to look in 'the bitter glass', where the tree appears in its reverse aspect :

> For there a fatal image grows,
> With broken boughs and blackened leaves,
> And roots half-hidden under snows
> Driven by a storm that ever grieves.

Although the poem is comprehensible without the esoteric source, the source helps to explain how it came to be written.

The symbol of the tree of life appears conspicuously in three other early poems. It is curiously bedizened in 'He Thinks of His Past Greatness when a Part of the Constellations of Heaven', where the speaker says,

> I have been a hazel-tree, and they hung
> The Pilot Star and the Crooked Plough
> Among my leaves in times out of mind. . . .

The hazel-tree, Yeats explained in a note, is the 'common Irish form' of the tree of life, an attribution which was less certain than he and George Russell assumed. We may still wonder why the Pilot Star and the Crooked Plough are hung from it. Yeats's note says only that they are Gaelic names for the North Star and the constellation of the Bear. The answer, which he does not divulge, is that the Pilot Star, like the rose, suggests direction, guidance, and a goal, while the Crooked Plough, like the cross, suggests difficulty and hardship. The union of the two on the tree of life is thus a fresh way of presenting the rose-cross conjunction.

Although he does not mention the tree of life in 'Aedh Pleads with the Elemental Powers', he has it in mind in this elaborate passage :

> The Powers whose name and shape no living creature knows
> Have pulled the Immortal Rose ;
> And though the Seven Lights bowed in their dance and wept,
> The Polar Dragon slept,
> His heavy rings uncoiled from glimmering deep to deep ;
> When will he wake from sleep ?

A note on the imagery comments :

> I have made the Seven Lights, the constellation of the Bear, lament for the theft of the Rose, and I have made the Dragon, the constellation Draco, the guardian of the Rose, because these constellations move about the pole of the heavens, the ancient Tree of Life in many countries, and are often associated with the Tree of Life in mythology.

What then is the Polar Dragon, with his uncoiling heavy rings ?

Looking again at the cover of *The Secret Rose*, we find the serpent's folds encircling the trunk of the Tree of Life as if it were indeed the 'guardian of the Rose'. In Kabbalism this serpent is the serpent of nature in its benign aspect, and the occultist is said to follow the serpent's winding path upwards through many initiations, corresponding to each of the *Sephiroth*, until he reaches the top of the tree. Since in the poem the polar dragon sleeps, like earth in the 'Introduction' to Blake's *Songs of Experience*, the meaning seems to be that the natural world has become uncoiled or detached from beauty.

The third appearance of the tree of life, in 'Aedh Hears the Cry of the Sedge', is esthetically an improvement. The tree, Yeats explains, is here represented as the 'axle' or 'axle-tree' of the heavens :

> I wander by the edge
> Of this desolate lake
> Where wind cries in the sedge :
> *Until the axle break*
> *That keeps the stars in their round*
> *And hands hurl in the deep*
> *The banners of East and West*
> *And the girdle of light is unbound,*
> *Your breast will not lie by the breast*
> *Of your beloved in sleep.*

The superiority of this poem over the three others that we have considered is due to many causes : the diction of some lines is powerful and unusually free of expressions that Yeats standardized in the 'nineties ; the suspended sentence is well maintained to bring out its climax ; and the metrics are very skilful. Another reason, and perhaps the most important, is that the symbol is not gloated over for its own sake, as in 'Aedh Pleads with the Elemental Powers', but subordinated to its role in the poem. The danger with Yeats's emphatic symbols in much of his early work lay in their taking on what he hoped to avoid, a value of their own apart from their poetic contexts. They interfered with vigorous expression by distracting the reader, and 'Aedh Hears the Cry of the Sedge' is an exception which anticipates Yeats's later development.

Whatever their limitations, the great symbols of four-petalled rose, cross, tree of life, and serpent enabled Yeats to put order upon his imagination, as, he wrote Lady Gregory, all his symbolic labours were intended to do. Other symbols supplement the main ones and give the emblematic skeleton further articulation. For example, Yeats uses the dance to represent both the state of fairyland and the state of blessedness, realms not identical but akin. Dancing has one or the other of these senses in such early poems as *Oisin*, 'The Man Who Dreamed of Fairyland', the story 'Rosa Alchemica' (where for the first time the dance is ritualized), and 'The Withering of the Boughs'. It becomes even more prominent in his later poetry, as in 'The Double Vision of Michael Robartes' and 'Among School Children'. Another emblem for the state of blessedness is the meeting of sun and moon or of gold and silver. So in 'The Happy Townland' the boughs of heaven are golden and silver, and in 'The Song of Wandering Aengus' the hero seeks

> The silver apples of the moon,
> The golden apples of the sun.

The same rather easy symbolism, familiar to Yeats from alchemical writers as well as more accessible sources, shows up afterwards in the golden king and silver lady of 'Under the Round Tower', in the sun's 'golden cup' and moon's 'silver bag' of 'Those Dancing Days Are Gone'. Its most successful appearance is in 'The Tower', where Yeats writes, daringly,

> O, may the moon and sunlight seem
> One inextricable beam,
> For if I triumph I must make men mad.

Madness — the blotting out of common perception — will enable men to understand the perfection which the miraculous blending of solar and lunar light will symbolize. Much of the individuality of the poetry of Yeats comes from such repetitions, with fresh variations, of the same or equivalent symbols.

IV. A SYMBOLIC DRAMA

Towards the end of the 'nineties Yeats's symbolic clusters thickened to the point of crowding. They reach their greatest abundance in *The Shadowy Waters*. This play is full of what Valéry describes as the poet's '*secrets d'état*'. Its subject, Yeats told Russell, was 'the relations of man and woman in symbol'. He placed its action in 'the heroic age' in accordance with a theory that this was the best setting for a symbolical poem. As he remarked in a review in the *Bookman*, the new movement in the arts 'has made painters and poets and musicians go to old legends for their subjects, for legends are the magical beryls in which we see life, not as it is, but as the heroic part of us, the part which desires always dreams and emotions greater than any in the world, and loves beauty and does not hate sorrow, hopes in secret that it may become'.

From the start, readers of *The Shadowy Waters* were perplexed by it. The editor of the *North American Review*, on agreeing to publish the play, asked Yeats for an exegesis. Yeats replied, 'The more one explains, the more one narrows the symbols', and offered only the most general hints. But a few years later, when the play was produced and there was danger of boring, by baffling, the audience, Yeats decided to become more communicative. His summary of the plot in 1906 gives some help :

Once upon a time, when herons built their nests in old men's beards, Forgael, a Sea-King of ancient Ireland, was promised by certain human-headed birds love of a supernatural intensity. These birds were the souls of the dead, and he followed them over seas towards the sunset, where their final rest is. By means of a magic harp, he could call them about him when he would and listen to their speech. His friend Aibric, and the sailors of his ship, thought him mad, or that this mysterious happiness could come after death only, and that he and they were being lured to destruction. Presently they captured a ship, and found a beautiful woman upon it, and Forgael subdued her and his own rebellious sailors by the sound of his harp. The sailors fled upon the other ship, and Forgael and the woman drifted on alone following the birds, awaiting death and what comes after, or some mysterious transformation of the flesh, an embodiment of every lover's dream.

The alternative possible expectations at the end are characteristic of Yeats's unwillingness to commit his poetry to locating the perfect state definitely in death or in life. His résumé can be supplemented by an unsigned programme note, obviously by his hand, written for the performance of the play on July 9, 1905, at the Abbey Theatre :

The main story expresses the desire for a perfect and eternal union that comes to all lovers, the desire of Love to 'drown in its own shadow'. But it has also other meanings. Forgael seeks death ; Dectora has always sought life ; and in some way the uniting of her vivid force with his abyss-seeking desire for the waters of Death makes a perfect humanity. Of course, in another sense, these two are simply man and woman, the reason and the will, as Swedenborg puts it.

The second flaming up of the harp may mean the coming of a more supernatural passion, when Dectora accepts the death-desiring destiny. Yet in one sense, and precisely because she accepts it, this destiny is not death ; for she, the living will, accompanies Forgael, the mind, through the gates of the unknown world. Perhaps it is a mystical interpretation of the resurrection of the body.

These hints will bring us closer to the intent of the symbolism. Even the stage setting is symbolic. It shows the deck of a galley, with a sail which has 'a conventional pattern' of three rows of hounds, 'the first dark, the second red, and the third white with red ears'. In the programme note, Yeats offers the suggestion that these may 'correspond to the *Tamas*, *Rajas*, and *Sattva* qualities of the Vedanta philosophy, or to the three colours of the Alchemists'. With the aid of Max Müller, who was probably the main source of Yeats's early knowledge of Vedanta, the passage may be glossed as meaning that the hounds symbolize thesis, antithesis, and reconciliation. As Müller puts it, 'Tension between these qualities produces activity and struggle : equilibrium leads to temporary or final rest'. In later life Yeats identified *Tamas* as darkness and exhaustion, *Rajas* as activity and passion, *Sattva* as brightness and wisdom. The three hounds signify, in terms of the play, Forgael's death-wish, Dectora's life-wish, and their fusion in 'some mysterious transformation of the flesh'. Yeats chooses hounds for his symbols to suggest pursuit, and their colours reflect their qualities — the dark being related to death, the red to life and passion, and the white with red ears to some kind of transmutative fusion of the two.

The rest of the play contributes heavily to the paradigm of symbols. We have already noticed that the hero and heroine wear a lily and a rose on their breasts to signify their respective aspirations towards death and life, towards pure transcendence and passionate embodiment. But Yeats heaps symbol upon symbol. He took over from *Oisin* the hound which follows a hornless deer and added a red hound which runs from a silver arrow. The first, he now explained, was a symbol of 'the desire of the man "which is for the woman" and the desire of the "woman that is for the desire of the man"'. He was not to embody this 'ninetyish conception of the relations of the sexes until long afterwards. As for the red hound running from the silver arrow, this is the passionate Dectora fleeing the silver (and therefore lunar, idealizing) love of Forgael.

Forgael's harp is also of special significance. He has received it from a fool in a wood, and we learn from Yeats's note that this is not *a* fool but *the* fool, 'the fool of the Rath, the fairy fool of modern Irish folklore, from whose touch no man recovers — the divine fool'. Yeats and Russell had some correspondence about this fool, in the course of which Yeats conjectured that the fool was associated with Aengus, god of lovers, presumably as some lower manifestation of him. Hence the appearance of the fool along with the symbol of perfect love in the union of Aengus and Edain. The harp is primarily, of course, the poetic imagination, vauntingly described in the play as 'mightier than the sun and moon, / Or than the shivering casting net of the stars'. Twenty-six years later, in 'The Tower', Yeats said that the imagination 'Made sun and moon and star', choosing a similar figure for his hyperbole.

On his harp Forgael plays two songs, a repertoire that will not seem strange when we recall that Yeats, throughout his poetry, celebrates two faculties of his art, the one praising life, the other praising a superhuman state beyond life. The contrast can be found in the two shapes near the beginning of the second book of *Oisin*, who gaze, one at the sea of life, the other at the stars, just as it can be seen in the difference between the 'cocks of Hades' and the golden birds of 'Byzantium'. Appropriately, therefore, Forgael's first song rouses in his hearers dreams of love, while his second rouses dreams of a love beyond mortal love.

The Shadowy Waters carries its symbolic involutions still further. Since hero and heroine have opposite longings, they respond oppositely to one another. As Dectora falls in love with Forgael, her heart is said to grow young, his to grow old. As their warring hearts and opposite desires are joined, symbols of reconciliation appear on the scene. The arrow at last succeeds in piercing the red hound's heart, and Dectora imagines that she sees apple blossoms over a stream. Such blossoms, Yeats makes plain in an occult diary kept while he was writing his poetic play, 'are symbols of dawn and of air and of the earth and of resurrection in my system and in the poem'. A wood of precious stones has also a symbolical meaning, according to Yeats's note ; the stones 'are perhaps emotions made eternal by their own perfection' ; and the first draft of his *Autobiographies* gives corroborative evidence : 'I thought we [Maud Gonne and himself] became one in a world of emotion eternalized by its own intensity and purity, and this would have for its symbol precious stones'. The wood appears in the play to signalize the lovers' union.

So many symbols may well lead us to the conclusion that the play is overpopulated by them. One cannot turn a corner in it without finding them perched enigmatically in one's way. Yeats said he had written the play 'for a few people who love symbol', a limitation of audience which, even allowing for his frequent overstatements of his dramatic intentions, verges on the doctrine of symbol for symbol's sake. Thoroughly charged with special significance as it is, the drama plays tag with boredom none the less. Its defects cannot be attributed to the strange birthplace of many of the symbols ; Yeats knew he was a poet and not a magician, and displayed his talismans for their artistic, not their occult, utility. Yet, in his delight with his symbols, he often preens them too much ; *The Shadowy Waters* is too much their showcase, not enough a dramatic contest.

On two counts, however, the nobility of its ideal and the virtuosity of its experimentation, the play must be defended. It embodies the central theme of all Yeats's early work, which is, to modify his language, the hunger to build everything anew. By casting all things into symbols he gave them a meaning and presence which they otherwise usually lacked. It represents, too, the farthest range of symbolism in dramatic poetry in English until the twentieth century. Like *The Player Queen*, a work which occupies the same prominence in his writing from 1907 to 1917 that *The Shadowy Waters* has from 1885 to 1899, it attempts to enlarge the possibilities of the theatre. The later play is more successful ; its symbols are more disciplined and essential ; but its achievement was made possible by *The Shadowy Waters*.

By the end of the century, then, Yeats's symbolical framework was fully formed. He remained loyal in later life to many of his early symbols, such as the four elements and the dance, but his principal symbols, the rose and cross, made way for unusual substitutes, and even the familiar symbols gradually took on a different aspect. It is well to remember, however, as Yeats's world begins to move faster and faster, that it pivots on the same axis.

CHAPTER V

THE PURSUIT OF SPONTANEITY

John Synge, I and Augusta Gregory thought
All that we did, all that we said or sang
Must come from contact with the soil, from that
Contact everything Antaeus-like grew strong.
We three alone in modern times had brought
Everything down to that sole test again,
Dream of the noble and the beggar-man.

YEATS, 'The Municipal Gallery Revisited'

I. THATCH AND GUTTER

BY naming his next book *In the Seven Woods* (1903), Yeats implied a symbolic change of locale and of element from *The Wind Among the Reeds* (1899) and *The Shadowy Waters* (1900). The culmination of his elaborate manner at the end of the century may have been wilfully extreme, the result of a desire to force, by reaction, a new departure upon himself. It is clear, for instance, that his remarks about the necessity of simplicity in art became especially frequent at the very moment that he was driving his art to its farthest pitch of symbolic complexity. At that time, too, he began to devote whole summers to collecting folklore with Lady Gregory in the west of Ireland. Until about 1900 these expeditions had little effect on his writing ; but after that time they provided him with literary reserves on which to draw.

Having become surfeited with the glossy, attenuated style of his youth, Yeats was eager to expose his art to what Synge called 'the shock of new material'. He set forth this purpose explicitly in an account which he wrote of his first meeting with James Joyce in 1902. He originally intended to use it as a preface to *Ideas of Good and Evil* (1903), but changed his mind. The interview occurred when both men were at important points in their

85

careers : Joyce, only twenty years old but already formidable, was almost ready to burst out of Dublin and make his name on the continent. He was paradoxically bent both on conquering Yeats in argument and on winning his respect. Yeats, seventeen years older, had left the period of certainty and was in that stage where the choice among many alternatives perplexes the artist. And he was particularly sensitive about his work at the moment because he was busy changing it. With Lady Gregory's help he was embarked on a series of short plays about peasant life, but he did not intend to write peasant plays exclusively, and was less certain of the value of his attempts in this *genre* than he allowed others to know. Joyce's outspoken and powerful attack was therefore a little nettling to him, and he retained from it a permanent impression of a brilliant but cruel mind. He was not, of course, overwhelmed, and his remarkably honest story of the interview is humorous and detached :

I had been looking over the proof sheets of this book one day in Dublin lately and thinking whether I should send it to the Dublin papers for review or not. I thought that I would not, for they would find nothing in it but a wicked theology, which I had probably never intended, and, it may be, found all the review on a single sentence. I was wondering how long I should be thought a preacher of reckless opinions and a disturber who carries in his hand the irresponsible torch of vain youth. I went out into the street and there a young man came up to me and introduced himself. He told me he had written a book of prose essays or poems, and spoke to me of a common friend.

Yes, I recollected his name, for he had been to my friend who leads an even more reckless rebellion than I do, and had kept him up to the grey hours of the morning discussing philosophy. I asked him to come with me to the smoking room of a restaurant in O'Connell Street, and read me a beautiful though immature and eccentric harmony of little prose descriptions and meditations. He had thrown over metrical form, he said, that he might get a form so fluent that it would respond to the motions of the spirit. I praised his work but he said, 'I really don't care whether you like what I am doing or not. It won't make the least difference to me. Indeed I don't know why I am reading to you.'

Then, putting down his book, he began to explain all his objections to everything I had ever done. Why had I concerned myself with politics, with folklore, with the historical setting of events and so on? Above all why had I written about ideas, why had I condescended to make generalizations? These things were all the sign of the cooling of the iron, of the fading out of inspiration. I had been puzzled, but now I was confident again. He is from the Royal University, I thought, and he thinks that everything has been settled by Thomas Aquinas, so we need not trouble about it. I have met so many like him. He would probably review my book in the newspapers if I sent it there. But the next moment he spoke of a friend of mine [Oscar Wilde] who after a wild life had turned Catholic on his deathbed. He said that he hoped his conversion was not sincere. He did not like to think that he had been untrue to himself at the end. No, I had not understood him yet.

I had been doing some little plays for our Irish theatre, and had founded them all on emotions or stories that I had got out of folklore. He objected to these particularly and told me that I was deteriorating. I had told him that I had written these plays quite easily and he said that made it quite certain; his own little book owed nothing to anything but his own mind which was much nearer to God than folklore.

I took up the book and pointing to a thought said, 'You got that from somebody else who got it from the folk'. I felt exasperated and puzzled and walked up and down explaining the dependence of all good art on popular tradition. I said, 'The artist, when he has lived for a long time in his own mind with the example of other artists as deliberate as himself, gets into a world of ideas pure and simple. He becomes very highly individualized and at last by sheer pursuit of perfection becomes sterile. Folk imagination on the other hand creates endless images of which there are no ideas. Its stories ignore the moral law and every other law, they are successions of pictures like those seen by children in the fire. You find a type of these two kinds of invention, the invention of artists and the invention of the folk, in the civilization that comes from town and in the forms of life that one finds in the country. In the towns, especially in big towns like London, you don't find what old writers used to call the people; you find instead a few highly cultivated, highly perfected individual lives, and great multitudes who imitate them and cheapen them. You find, too, great capacity for doing all kinds of things, but an impulse towards creation which grows gradually weaker and weaker. In the country, on the other hand, I mean in Ireland and in places where the towns have not been able to call the tune, you find people who are hardly individualized to any great extent. They live through the same round of duty and they think about life and death as their fathers have told them, but in speech, in the telling of tales, in all that has to do with the play of imagery, they have an endless abundance. I have collected hundreds of stories and have had hundreds of stories collected for me, and if one leaves out certain set forms of tale not one story is like another. Everything seems possible to them, and because they can never be surprised, they imagine the most surprising things. The folk life, the country life, is nature with her abundance, but the art life, the town life, is the spirit which is sterile when it is not married to nature. The whole ugliness of the modern world has come from the spread of the towns and their ways of thought, and to bring back beauty we must marry the spirit and nature again. When the idea which comes from individual life marries the image that is born from the people, one gets great art, the art of Homer, and of Shakespeare, and of Chartres Cathedral.'

I looked at my young man. I thought, 'I have conquered him now', but I was quite wrong. He merely said, 'Generalizations aren't made by poets ; they are made by men of letters. They are no use.'

Presently he got up to go, and, as he was going out, he said, 'I am twenty. How old are you ?' I told him, but I am afraid I said I was a year younger than I am. He said with a sigh, 'I thought as much. I have met you too late. You are too old.'

And now I am still undecided as to whether I shall send this book to the Irish papers for review. The younger generation is knocking at my door as well as theirs.

Joyce's position in this peculiar interview is less immediately comprehensible than Yeats's. Although he said little, he evidently took Yeats's interest in folklore as a narrow ideology, and therefore a denial of the personal immediacy and concreteness, and of the haughty autocracy, of great art. Yeats, on the other hand, hoped to capture from the peasantry first, an insouciant spontaneity, and second, a multitude of images sanctioned by tradition. His pastoral impulse was not naïve ; he did not think of folk art

as the talented creation of an untalented group of country bump-
kins, but regarded it as mainly the work of individual artists who
had escaped the infection of current intellectual and literary movements and of an excessive self-consciousness like his own. Not
that the images were to be adopted without thought : his goal
was to bring his schematic insights into experience — his themes,
correspondences, and oppositions — which he called *ideas* in
talking with Joyce, together with fresh images of the folk. The
artist's individualized consciousness must be married to ancient,
anonymous, popular, unconsidered images. Joyce saw nothing
beneath the ingratiating metaphor of marriage except abstraction
and theory, not knowing that his own work would one day
follow a similar pattern.

As for Yeats, who with some reason thought himself a pioneer
both in the symbolist movement and in a new Irish dramatic
movement, to be treated as an elderly decadent by this brilliant
young man was discomfiting. Besides, Joyce had pricked an old
wound, for men like Johnson and Dowson in the Rhymers' Club
had been equally contemptuous of Yeats's theorizing. In his
Autobiographies he admitted,

A young Irish poet [Joyce], who wrote excellently but had the
worst manners, was to say a few years later, 'You do not talk like a
poet, you talk like a man of letters', and if all the Rhymers had not
been polite, if most of them had not been to Oxford or Cambridge,
the greater number would have said the same thing. I was full of
thought, often very abstract thought, longing all the while to be full
of images. . . .

The special character of Yeats's verse made the danger of generalization particularly alarming. Wishing to create moods, and
unable to work without an impressive organization of themes and
symbolic ramifications, he ran the risk of creating schematizations
instead.

Increasingly now, he wished his art to constitute a marriage,
balance, or reconcilement. He wrote in the preface to *The
Unicorn from the Stars* (1908) that what he aspired to do was to
bring 'together the rough life of the road and the frenzy that the

poets have found in their ancient cellar — a prophecy, as it were, of the time when it will be once again possible for a Dickens and a Shelley to be born in the one body'. He amused and shocked the refined Lady Gregory by telling her that their art would have to 'accept the baptism of the gutter'. Because art had its roots in the earth he symbolized it as a centaur, and told Florence Farr that the imagination should rest 'as upon the green ground'.

In his critical writings he made clear this preoccupation with popular art. The essays which he wrote for *Ideas of Good and Evil* (1903) and *The Cutting of an Agate* (1915) are mainly attempts to estimate literature according to its admixture of images and ideas. Poetry might be judged by its proximity to the earth and qualities associated with earth. So William Morris pleased him by his abundance and ease, while Spenser, who possessed these qualities too, had marred them by accepting allegory with its excessive deliberateness, its submergence of image by idea to suit the overdeveloped moral sense of Puritanism. Yeats lamented the quarrel between man and nature which began in the late sixteenth century, when poets became urban, and the old qualities of irresponsibility, caprice, energy, and wildness were sacrificed. Even Shakespeare, whom Yeats reread about 1903, had not altogether escaped, for while he had the popular love of personality for its own sake, regardless of moral direction, he adopted too complex and deliberate a diction, and English literature lost the unity and simplicity which might have made it like Greek literature. Of all the poets, perhaps Chaucer was closest to what Yeats desired because closest to the folk tradition.

Gradually, as Yeats speculated on what art should be, he became aware that his own work was undergoing a permutation. This was accelerated by his having to write plays for a popular audience at the newly founded Abbey Theatre. In the preface to his 1906 volume of *Poems*, he remarked :

To me drama . . . has been the search for more of manful energy, more of cheerful acceptance of whatever arises out of the logic of events, and for clean outline, instead of those outlines of lyric poetry that are blurred with desire and vague regret.

Drama, which was the creation of a central mood out of the moods of all the characters, ensured his freedom from abstract thought. In all his work he discovered that his interest in symbols *qua* symbols had begun to flag. A letter to Florence Farr of about 1907 explains what has happened :

I at last find that I can move people by power, not merely — as the phrase is — by 'charm' or 'speaking beautifully' — a thing I always resented. I feel this change in all my work and that it has brought a change into the personal relations of life — even things seemingly beyond control answer strangely to what is within. I once cared only for images about whose necks I could cast various 'chains of office' as it were. They were so many aldermen of the ideal, whom I wished to master the city of the soul. Now I do not want images at all, or chains of office, being contented with the unruly soul.

This statement differs from his pronouncements in the 'nineties in making clear that even the symbols in a poem must be subordinated to the whole, and in emphasizing the unruliness of the soul whose moods would be represented, rather than its potential perfection.

II. THE SCHEMATIZATION EXPANDED

After 1900 Yeats reconsidered his old psychological and cosmological thoughts and enlarged upon them. His results may best be displayed by comparing them with those of Friedrich Nietzsche, for reading Nietzsche in the early years of the century proved to be almost as enthralling for Yeats as unravelling Blake had been from 1889 to 1892. The eloquence, psychological acuteness, arrogance, and messianic fervour of the German philosopher delighted him and gave European authority for many ideas which he had come upon either by himself or in strange places.

He began reading Nietzsche in the summer of 1902 at the suggestion of his friend and patron, the New York lawyer John

Quinn. For a time he could do nothing else. He felt compelled to apologize to Lady Gregory in a letter of August 1902 for neglecting her :

DEAR FRIEND,

I have written to you little and badly of late I am afraid, for the truth is you have a rival in Nietzsche, that strong enchanter. I have read him so much that I have made my eyes bad again. They were getting well it had seemed. Nietzsche completes Blake and has the same roots — I have not read anything with so much excitement since I got to love Morris's stories which have the same curious astringent joy.

Yeats rightly perceived that there were few irreconcilable differences between the English poet and the German. Both denounced conventional morality, Blake with his 'marriage of heaven and hell', Nietzsche by moving 'beyond good and evil'. They were equally hard on conventional Christianity, although their conclusions were not the same. For Nietzsche Christ was a weak, impotent, and illusory god, whom the Orient created as a revenge upon Roman power. For Blake Christ was divine, but had been distorted from his true character of a strong, brave, and violent hero-god. Yeats for the most part accepted the Nietzschean position.

Nietzsche was especially helpful on cyclical theory. For while cycles appear in Blake's 'Mental Traveller' and other poems, they are described gnomically, and Blake's theory about them is hard to paraphrase. Nietzsche puts the matter more plainly, having his Zarathustra speak of taking his way through a hundred souls and through a hundred cradles, birth-throes, and farewells. 'Thou teachest that there is a great year of Becoming, a prodigy of a great year ; it must, like a sand-glass, ever turn up anew, that it may anew run down and run out.' In this passage Yeats may have found the title of the play, *The Hour-Glass*, which he wrote in 1902. It can be said with more certainty that he discovered in Nietzsche an attitude towards the cycles which was akin to his own. Instead of an eastern resignation towards 'eternal recurrence', Zarathustra is full of western exultation. 'He who climbeth on the highest mountains', says the sage, 'laugheth at all tragic plays and tragic realities.' When, towards the end of his life, Yeats wrote his two fine poems 'The Gyres' and 'Lapis Lazuli', he framed the Nietzschean lines, 'All things fall, and are built again, / And those that build them again, are gay', and 'We that look on but laugh in tragic joy', and perhaps also recalled Nietzsche in the picture of the three Chinese on top of the mountain, staring on 'the tragic scene' of life with eyes full of gaiety.

Yeats's views of man and of human psychology were not identical with those of Blake and Nietzsche, but may instructively be juxtaposed. Blake calls for a regeneration of man, and symbolizes it by the new Jerusalem; Nietzsche, influenced by meliorist doctrines somewhat at variance with his cyclical theory, envisages a magnification of the individual, symbolized by the superman. The first says, 'Restore man', the second, 'Surpass him'. Here Yeats is closer to Blake, while less violent. In analysing the individual self, where Blake sees an interplay between self, its emanation, and its spectre, Nietzsche envisages a simpler relation between the self and its 'mask', and Yeats, whom the term 'mask' had already attracted, followed Nietzsche on this point. Nietzsche had not much systematized his reflections about the mask, but his writings were full of suggestions. The advantage of the mask of Nietzsche over the 'pose' of Oscar Wilde was that the former was virile and unconnected with estheticism. Yeats, who had been concerned since childhood over the discrepancy between what he was and what he wanted to be, between what he was and what others thought him to be, now made 'mask' a favourite term.

According to Nietzsche, the superman wears a mask he has designed for himself, while 'the objective man', whom he (and Yeats after him) describes as 'a mirror', creeps into 'a God's mask'. In the one case personality is asserted, in the other rejected. With Nietzsche, as with Yeats, the mask has several functions. Not the least is its severance of the hero from the mob, for whom his open-faced candour would be too dangerous. Then too, for the hero to reveal himself would be *lèse-majesté*.

since isolation and disguise are heroic properties. The mob is protected from too much reality, the hero from debasement.

Both Nietzsche and Yeats go deeper still. Other Nietzschean passages represent the mask as a weapon in an internal war, with heroic minds imposing the masks and heroic hearts rejecting it. Of this form of self-discipline and struggle he says, in a sentence that might be from Yeats's *Vision*, 'There are free insolent minds which would fain conceal and deny that they are broken, proud, incurable hearts (the cynicism of Hamlet — the case of Galiani). . . .' Finally, the mask may be an image of himself which the heroic spirit sets up as his goal, and then proceeds to become. Nietzsche's remarks on this process use other terms than mask, but Yeats, more methodical in his organization, could easily see such a sentence as this in the light of it : 'What? A great man? I always see merely the play-actor of his own ideal.'

The conception of the mask shuttles between the unblemished dream image and the actual face, and assumes that the former is more real as well as more prepossessing than the latter. It is based, in Nietzsche as often in Yeats, on a further postulate, that the individual creates his own world.[1] Nietzsche's oblique presentation of this position was closer to Yeats's attitude than Blake's frontal aggression. The philosopher declared that what we know as reality is only a group of symbols, a mythology, Yeats's 'phantasmagoria'. So-called objective philosophies turn out to be merely symbolic expressions of the philosophers' wishes and needs. Plato's work, for example, was involuntary and unconscious autobiography. That his own philosophy of the will to power might be similarly autobiographical and mythological Nietzsche admitted, and even added, with an unphilosophical rashness that Yeats must have admired, 'So much the better'. Notwithstanding this admission, and his repeated statement that

---

[1] Nietzsche may have derived this conception from Schopenhauer ('*Die Welt ist meine Vorstellung*'); Yeats's sources were partly occultism, where it is a favourite notion, partly the writings of Blake and the French symbolists. For example, in Villiers de l'Isle-Adam's *Axël*, which Yeats called his 'sacred book', solipsism is tirelessly espoused: '*Si tu veux posséder la vérité, crée-la! comme tout le reste! tu n'emporteras, tu ne seras que ta création. . . . Son apparaître (celui du monde) quel qu'il puisse être, n'est en principe que fictif, mobile, illusoire, insaisissable.*'

we spend our lives in a condition of untruth, Nietzsche was also quite capable of claiming that he had succeeded in piercing the veil, or that at any rate his mythology was more firmly grounded in the life process than that of others. Yeats's *Vision* is at times equally presumptuous in its claims to be ultimate truth, with the same inconsistency.

Nietzsche, closer in time to Yeats than Blake, often presented formulations with which Yeats found himself astonishingly in sympathy. His impatience with abstraction and argument provided the poet with a favourite quotation, 'Am I a barrel of memories that I should give you my reasons?' He eschewed sentimentality and demanded hardness, a quality which Yeats admired more and more as his own disposition began to toughen. Zarathustra's exhortation to man to laugh helped to shape the rather Nietzschean hero of Yeats's play, *Where There Is Nothing* (1902), who very seriously announced that he was in search of laughter; it may also have encouraged Yeats to celebrate in his verse 'a written speech / Wrought of high laughter, loveliness and ease', and the heroes 'Who have lived in joy and laughed into the face of Death'. Although Yeats never accepted the superman, J. M. Hone has pointed out that the ending of *The King's Threshold* (1904) echoes Nietzsche in its reference to 'the great race that is to come'. A distinction which Nietzsche drew, in *The Birth of Tragedy*, between the Apollonian and Dionysian principles in Greek art, also struck Yeats's eye, and his letter to Russell of May 14, 1903, makes use of it to describe his altered art:

I am no longer in much sympathy with an essay like the Autumn of the Body, not that I think that essay untrue. But I think I mistook for a permanent phase of the world what was only a preparation. The close of the last century was full of a strange desire to get out of form, to get to some kind of disembodied beauty, and now it seems to me the contrary impulse has come. I feel about me and in me an impulse to create form, to carry the realization of beauty as far as possible. The Greeks said that the Dionysiac enthusiasm preceded the Apollonic and that the Dionysiac was sad and desirous, but that the Apollonic was joyful and self sufficient.

But the meanings given to the terms are Yeats's; it is hard to think of the ebullient Dionysus as his muse of the 'nineties. The misappropriation of Nietzsche's distinction is evidence that Yeats kept his independence. In the same way, his equivalent for Nietzsche's brotherhood of supermen was not a gang of superb Irish roughnecks but an intellectual élite like that of Duke Ercole in Castiglione's *Courtier*.

The volume of Nietzsche which Yeats read in 1902 contains annotations that suggest the limits of his debt to the German philosopher. Yeats marks such a passage as this one on the morality of the noble man :

The noble type of man regards *himself* as the determiner of worth.

This theme appears in a poem he wrote in 1913, 'To a Friend Whose Work Has Come to Nothing' :

> Now all the truth is out,
> Be secret and take defeat
> From any brazen throat,
> For how can you compete,
> Being honour bred, with one
> Who, were it proved he lies,
> Were neither shamed in his own
> Nor in his neighbours' eyes ?
> Bred to a harder thing
> Than Triumph, turn away
> And like a laughing string
> Whereon mad fingers play
> Amid a place of stone,
> Be secret and exult,
> Because of all things known
> That is most difficult.

He marked another passage in Nietzsche with less favour :

The morality of the ruling class, however, is more especially foreign and irritating to the taste of the present day, owing to the sternness of the principle that one has *only obligations* to one's equals, that one may act towards beings of a lower rank, and towards all that is foreign to one according *to discretion*, or 'as the heart desires', and in any case 'beyond Good and Evil'.

Beside this he notes : 'Yes but the necessity of giving remains. When the old heroes praise one another they say "he never refused any man". Nietzsche means that the lower cannot create obligation for the higher.' And in another note he complains : 'His system seems to lack some reason why the self must give to the selfless or weak, or itself perish or suffer diminution'. A poem of 1912, 'To a Wealthy Man Who Promised a Second Subscription to the Dublin Municipal Gallery If It Were Proved the People Wanted Pictures', emphasizes what Nietzsche had omitted :

> Look up in the sun's eye and give
> What the exultant heart calls good
> That some new day may breed the best
> Because you gave, not what they would,
> But the right twigs for an eagle's nest !

He discarded the brutal implications of the philosopher's ethics.

The annotations show that Nietzsche's contrast of slave morality with master morality helped Yeats to set the pattern of opposition between self and soul which became central in *A Vision* and much of the later verse. Under Nietzsche's stimulus he writes in the margin of one page :

Night	{ Socrates { Christ	one god —	denial of self in the soul turned towards spirit, seeking knowledge.
Day	Homer	many gods —	affirmation of self, the soul turned from spirit to be its mask and instrument when it seeks life.

He objects, however, to Nietzsche's blanket condemnation of Socratic-Christian spirituality, and comments : 'But why does Nietzsche think that the night has no stars, nothing but bats and owls and the insane moon ?' The utter rejection of spirit meant the unpardonable exclusion of an important human mood.

Compared with Nietzsche, as compared with Blake, Yeats seems less outlandish while still highly unorthodox. Attentive to the need of making literature as complete as possible an expression of mental life, he held himself back from an extremism that might subject his mind and verse.

III. A POETRY OF PARTIAL REACTION

The ferment of his intellectual searches and discoveries after 1900 made certain changes in his verse inevitable. Where the earlier verse had for foundation the reverie or dream, the middle verse has the 'wild thought' as the later verse would have a subtler mixture of gay abandon, the considered view, and the nightmare. Previously he had been occupied mainly with moods of temptation and frustration ; now he is more often concerned with the aftertaste and afterthought of experience, the *pensée de l'escalier* rather than the trepidation in the anteroom of experience. The art of tapestry is put aside in favour of a lively succession of carefully selected images of vitality. Earlier Yeats had kept his gestures slow, now he hastened them ; he had cherished statuesque poses, or horizontal images of a carpet of dreams or of his love dead under boards ; now the poses are more natural, as of people sitting together at the end of day, and less recumbent, with his beloved breathing steadily and apparently in the best of health. The verse is no longer prone.

His conception of the poet also altered. Previously he had lived up to the role of an attendant upon Lady Beauty, full of humility. By the time he composed an unpublished dialogue of about 1915, *The Poet and the Actress*, he was on his way to becoming an urbane public man :

The Actress. I saw Mr. Shaw's *Candida* last night. There was a poet there who shudders to the depths of his soul because he sees his sweetheart is cutting onions. I had always thought a poet was like that, that everything moved him. . . .

The Poet. Do you know any great poet or great writer who is easily moved ?

The Actress. Well, when I come to think of it, I have found all poets, great or small, exceedingly blasé. It has done more for my chastity even than my knowledge of their unfaithfulness. When they have paid me compliments, I have wondered if they were laughing at me.

The urbane view develops slowly, and is not present until after Yeats's solemn defence of poetry in *The King's Threshold* (1904). But his poems grow steadily more aware of what people look like and of what varying motives may make them act. The perfect world of his imagination abates in prominence without losing its integrity.

His images accordingly become more muscular and seem the products of less precious care. Apple blossoms, which in the 'nineties had been spread about his verse as symbols of extra-mundane perfection and resurrection, now describe his beloved's bosom :

> Tall and noble, but with face and bosom
> Delicate in colour as apple-blossom.

The arrow, which a few years before would have denoted for him the mystic's direct access to divinity, or, in another mood, the shaft of Kama, the Indian correlative of Cupid, appears in more active senses in the first two poems of *In the Seven Woods*, his first volume of twentieth-century verse. Setting the key for the book, the arrow may be matched against the winding hair of *The Wind Among the Reeds* ; it implies a more direct confrontation of his subject-matter.

We can follow his metamorphosis by tracing the history of one of his images, that of quiet. It first appears in a poem published in 1887, 'She Who Dwelt Among the Sycamores : A Fancy' :

> A little boy outside the sycamore wood
>> Saw on the wood's edge gleam an ash-grey feather ;
>> A kid, held by one soft white ear for tether,
> Trotted beside him in a playful mood.
> A little boy inside the sycamore wood
>> Followed a ringdove's ash-grey gleam of feather.
>> Noon wrapt the trees in veils of violet weather,
> And on tiptoe the winds a-whispering stood.

Deep in the woodland paused they, the six feet
Lapped in the lemon daffodils ; a bee
In the long grass — four eyes droop low — a seat
Of moss, a maiden weaving.   Singeth she :
'I am lone Lady Quietness, my sweet,
And on this loom I weave thy destiny'.

This amusingly callow poem shows Yeats struggling with the
task of personification, and accomplishing it by setting off the
last two personifying lines from the rest of the poem with quotation marks, by separating them from the detail of the previous
lines, and by conceiving the image of the lady as static in contrast
to the gradually slowing movement of the little boy.   Compare
with this a poem first printed in *The Secret Rose* (1897), to which
Yeats later gave the title of 'Maid Quiet' :

I never have seen Maid Quiet,
    Nodding her russet hood,
For the winds that awakened the stars
    Are blowing through my blood.
I never have seen Maid Quiet,
    Nodding alone and apart,
For the words that called up the lightning
    Are calling through my heart.

The poet is now cut off from Quiet and opposed to her ; but, in
spite of her russet hood, she is little more than a personified
counterweight for the poet's distress.   In 1902, however, Yeats
invoked her in less decorous fashion :

IN THE SEVEN WOODS

I have heard the pigeons of the Seven Woods
Make their faint thunder, and the garden bees
Hum in the lime-tree flowers ; and put away
The unavailing outcries and the old bitterness
That empty the heart.   I have forgot awhile
Tara uprooted, and new commonness
Upon the throne and crying about the streets
And hanging its paper flowers from post to post,
Because it is alone of all things happy.

I am contented, for I know that Quiet
Wanders laughing and eating her wild heart
Among pigeons and bees, while that Great Archer,
Who but awaits His hour to shoot, still hangs
A cloudy quiver over Pairc-na-lee.

What is in contrast to Quiet is even more thoroughly established. As for the maid herself, she is not called a maid now, and her abandoned autophagy is close to misconduct. The image has been rendered raw and barbaric instead of prettified and civilized ; it conveys a more original meaning ; and the suggestion of a pagan ritual heralds a new emphasis in his art.

Not only do the images become more forceful ; they are also more specific. An early poem had asked, 'Where are now the warring kings ?' and answered, 'An idle word is now their glory'. He could lump all kings together in this way by having in mind only legendary ones. But the reference to kings in 'In the Seven Woods' is of a different stamp. It is true that his concern for Tara, the seat of ancient Irish kings, is a little precious even when translated into a lament for lost Irish independence, but the reference to the newly crowned Edward VII as 'new commonness upon the throne', and the specific actions attributed to this commonness, show Yeats welding past and present more drastically than he had been accustomed to do before. By comparing the new king with an ancient, almost legendary line, he both derides the present and gives the past a reality it might otherwise lack. The method is not yet altogether successful, but in later life it enabled him to obtain some astonishing effects, as in 'Crazy Jane on the Mountain', or in this poem which he wrote in 1929 for the Crazy Jane series but did not publish :

CRACKED MARY'S VISION

Yesternight I saw in a vision
Long-bodied Tuatha de Danaan
Iron men in a golden barge,
Those great eyes that never wink
Mirrored on a winking wave
That a righteous king must have —

When I think of him I think
May the devil take King George.

Saw the sages wait the king
Seven fingers cautioning ;
Saw the common people surge
Round a wave-wet landing stair
Banging drums and tambourines ;
Saw that lucky eye-ball shine
On the lewd and learned there —
May the devil take King George.

On the moment he has gone
Nothing there could hold him down,
Nor hammered iron of the forge
Upon his body and his head
Nor that great troop I saw in a vision
Long-bodied Tuatha de Danaan —
But long or short when all is said
May the devil take King George.[1]

The later poem is of course open to the objection that attacking
the English king is *vieux jeu*, but its directness and pungency
illustrate Yeats's effortless force in old age.

In general, Yeats shifted his direction in the book *In the Seven
Woods* and subsequent volumes towards 'incarnation' and away
from 'transfiguration', to return to his own terms. The beloved
who, in the earlier volumes, is too fragile and intangible for
detailed description, now at least has hair that can be particularized as turning grey. Communication between her and the poet
had previously been by way of the latter's apostrophes, usually
delivered on his knees or, at any rate, with upturned brow. Now,
in poems like 'Adam's Curse', she sits beside him. Instead of
apostrophe there is dialogue, although it is her friend who speaks.
(She herself never utters a word until 'The People', written in
1915, but in the intervening period she has obviously grown

[1] Yeats suppressed the poem on the advice of that paragon of prudence, Ezra Pound,
who said to Mrs. Yeats, 'Do you really think he ought to publish it ? After all, the poor
old king is ill. . . .'

capable of articulate speech.) The dialogue is for the first time urbane and even witty :

> 'To be born woman is to know —
> Although they do not talk of it at school —
> That we must labour to be beautiful.'

Even God participates in the disruption : He is no longer represented, as in *The Countess Cathleen*, as 'the Light of Lights', but almost playfully as the 'Great Archer' in the poem 'In the Seven Woods'. The last lines of this poem refer to the familiar Yeatsian theme of the turning of the cosmic tables ; if we set next to them the concluding two lines of a poem from *The Wind Among the Reeds*, 'The Secret Rose',

> Surely thine hour has come, thy great wind blows
> Far-off, most secret, and inviolate Rose ?

we find that Yeats has so tempered the lines of 'In the Seven Woods' that they can be taken as forecasting merely a change in the weather ; the Archer himself may be only Jupiter Pluvius about to send a thunder shower. While the image is still high-flown in the later poem as in the earlier, it has more freshness ; and the possibility of reading it in either apocalyptic or climatic terms, and the impossibility of so reading the earlier, indicate Yeats's increasing mindfulness of his predominantly secular audience.

The secularization affects other images as well. In 'Adam's Curse', for instance, seasons and times of day are chosen as premeditatedly as ever ; the end of love is depicted at the end of summer and at the end of day ; but the concatenation occurs without mystery or special emphasis. The poet emerges from his candle-lit room into the open air, and seems almost ready to stretch and rub his eyes in the light.

IV. RECONSTRUCTING THE PHANTASMAGORIA

'I will maintain', said André Gide in his *Journal*, 'that an artist needs this: a special world of which he alone has the key. It is not enough that he should bring *one* new thing, although that is already an achievement; but rather that everything in him should be or seem new, seen through a powerfully colouring idiosyncrasy.'

Yeats's verse had already its own colouring, and the alteration in it now was not a universal upheaval. He in no sense gave up the special world of his earlier writing, but he set himself the task of remaking it. He dropped the rose and cross and shifted other symbols about, so that his symbolic patterns took on a new appearance. The work was difficult ; he wrote only a handful of short poems between 1902 and 1908, when he emerged in full control of his lyrical medium again.

During those years he developed symbolic patterns in a series of plays. The contrasts which he had evolved in *The Shadowy Waters* remained the basis of his dramaturgy ; he represented them, however, with greater subtlety and matter-of-fact ease. In modified form he retained the distinction between Forgael and Dectora, as in the analysis, at the beginning of *The King's Threshold* (1904), of 'the two kinds of music' :

> . . . the one kind
> Being like a woman, the other like a man.
> Both you that understand stringed instruments,
> And how to mingle words and notes together
> So artfully, that all the Art's but Speech
> Delighted with its own music ; and you that carry
> The long twisted horn, and understand
> The heady notes that, being without words,
> Can hurry beyond Time and Fate and Change.

Other plays keep the opposition without making it depend upon the sex of the character. In *Deirdre* (1907) and *On Baile's Strand* (1903), the personae are either dreamers or realists, either other-worldly or worldly in their desires and actions. Yeats tells us in a note on the latter play that the fool, who hears voices and sees visions, and the blind man, who is extraordinarily alive to everything around him and entirely practical, represent in some sense the 'combatants who turn the wheel of life'. Neither is complete in himself; they despise and yet need one another.

Yeats was eager to explain his dramatic method. He main-

tained that it was not mechanical to set up s
fool and blind man or King Conchubar and C
Shakespeare and every great dramatist had done the sam
contest pervades all life, he said in his dialogue of 1915, *The*
and the Actress, which unfortunately he left incomplete :

Now the art I long for is also a battle, but it takes place in the
depths of the soul and one of the antagonists does not wear a shape
known to the world or speak a mortal tongue. It is the struggle of
the dream with the world — it is only possible when we transcend
circumstances and ourselves, and the greater the contest, the greater
the art. . . .

In every great play — in Shakespeare for instance — you will
find a group of characters — Hamlet, Lear, let us say, who express
the dream, and another group who express its antagonist and to the
antagonist Shakespeare gives a speech close to that of daily life. But
it is not only the mere speech that must be heightened, there must
be whole phantasmagoria through which the lifelong contest finds
expression. There must be fable, mythology, that the dream and the
reality may face one another in visible array. Even when real life
moves us deeply, so profound is the scorn the heart feels for all created
things, so unutterably proud it is, we cease to be realists. The lover
forgets the living woman who has set fire to his haystack, to think of
Helen, and the mother forgets her own child, so full of idiosyncrasy,
to dream of the child at Bethlehem. Only the intellect is humble
despite that false fable of the fallen angels, is content with what the
eye sees and the intellect only wishes to understand. That is why we
poets pass on age after age an artificial language inherited from the
first poets and always full of reminiscent symbols, which grow richer
in association every time they are used for new emotion.

. . . Those who try to create beautiful things without this battle
in the soul, are merely imitators, because we can only become conscious of a thing by comparing it with its opposite. The two real
things we have are our natures and the circumstances that surround us.
We have in both a violent antithesis, nor do I believe art has anything
to do with happiness. . . . The end of art is ecstasy and that cannot
exist without pain. It is a sudden sense of power and of peace that
comes when we have before our mind's eye a group of images which
obeys us, which leaves us free, and which satisfies the needs of our

ind if we left out a single painful fact,
in those images.

read as some easy romantic rejection
ys the word 'dream' now to mean the
imaginative exercise. He holds that an
...ist for us only when we have freed it from
chaos of circumstances. The imagination
possible by linking present actions with actions
o.   ast; Yeats's examples of this process, the lover'
who se...   ...oved as Helen or the mother who sees her infant
as the Chris.. ..hild, appear impressively in the same context in
'Among School Children' ten years later. The experience is in
no sense rejected or lightly transcended; the imagination has to
struggle with visible counters, and learns to master them by
relating them to all that has been dreamt of in the life of humanity
as well as the individual life.

By ecstasy Yeats means no romantic agony; it is the libera-
tion which comes from the perception of a pattern in intense
human experiences. It frees the reader, like the writer, from
isolating external circumstances. He escapes from confusion to
radiant knowledge.

In applying his theory to Shakespeare Yeats over-simplified
the plays by dividing their characters into two groups, one
expressing the dream, the other expressing the reality. The
theory might better be applied to the battle that takes place
within the minds of heroes like Lear and Hamlet, between the
data and the desires of their lives. Yeats's division is much
more applicable to his own plays, where, for example, Deirdre
and Naisi, Cuchulain, and Seanchan represent the reckless ideal,
and the kings with whom they war represent the inglorious reality.

He is intensely schematic. He borrows, from Shakespeare
and from older tradition, the fool as a stock character, but binds
him more narrowly than Shakespeare to his functions. Usually
Yeats's fool is a detached spokesman for the dream, who because
of his ancient lineage can say what he likes and be, in the par-
liamentary sense, privileged. He was an expression of Yeats's

pastoral affinities — a peasant who had successfully avoided cities and science and education, and because he was supposed to know nothing, in fact knew everything. His wisdom could not be reduced to reason, nor his instinct to emotion. Yeats used him in four of the early plays (*The Countess Cathleen, The Shadowy Waters, The Hour-Glass,* and *On Baile's Strand*) and from time to time afterwards. He appears also in the poems, along with the madman and the untutored spiritualist medium ; Yeats was so pleased with the device of the knowing fool or madman that in 'Beggar to Beggar Cried', where the beggar speaks quite rationally but very frankly, the poet shields him by representing him as 'frenzy-struck', and therefore not responsible for what he says. He is the mind at its most daring or exuberant, in short, the mind at its best.

A parallel aspect of Yeats's schematizing of these years is the appearance of something like a bestiary in his verse and drama. He had had an interest in the beast fabulist's way of looking at things before, but he now extended it. His hero, in *Where There Is Nothing*, classifies people by cutting his hedges into the shapes of what he takes to be their armorial images. Bothersome relations are cackling chickens ; a well-meaning but weak-kneed priest is a pigeon ; he imagines himself more impressively as some creature having a great iron beak and claws, perhaps a mammoth eagle or vulture. Among the creatures let loose in the poems are the lion, Pegasus, the dog, the eagle, birds, fish, the crab, the barnacle-goose, the seamew, the dragon, the peacock, the squirrel, the magpie, and a man with a cat-head. Each embodies some special sort of personality or mood. Yeats confounded his friends by carrying the technique of the bestiary into his private conversation, as when he told Gilbert Murray in the early years of the century that he mistrusted a friend because he had seen him followed by a 'small green elephant'.[1]

---

[1] One beast, the unicorn, is darkly associated in *The Player Queen* with the millennium like the apparently virginal boar without bristles of the early verse. It is not merely coincidence that in Yeats's later poetry the millennium is accomplished by the mating of a swan, a unicorn, or a herne, with a woman, while in the early verse no sexual intercourse is required.

His explanation of his fabulous creatures is contained in a poem called 'The Realists', written about 1912 :

> Hope that you may understand !
> What can books of men that wive
> In a dragon-guarded land,
> Paintings of the dolphin-drawn
> Sea-nymphs in their pearly wagons
> Do, but awake a hope to live
> That had gone
> With the dragons ?

The purpose of reviving dolphins and dragons or sea-nymphs, or of turning people into images, was the same as for reviving mythology in general : it was to restore to the mind its almost lost faculties of unity and vitality, which created mythologies in the past. One of Yeats's symbols of the imagination is, appropriately, Noah's ark, the storehouse of images that could withstand the floods.

The image was important to everyone. In *The Player Queen*, a play on which he worked from 1907 until it was published in 1919, Yeats showed how it directly affected life. As a character in the play says, 'Man is nothing till he is united to an image'. That is, man must have a dream of what he might be in order to become it.[1] The next remark is less clear : 'Now the Unicorn is both an image and beast ; that is why he alone can be the new Adam'. The unicorn is both symbol and body ; when the self attains this unity it is reborn. Yeats sees all human beings engaged in a great struggle to become united to their images of themselves. At the moment of unification the temporal and the permanent are one. As the heroine of *The Player Queen* remarks in a 1915 draft of the play, 'Septimus told me once that no one finds their genius [until] they have found some role, some image, that gives them a pose towards life, that liberates some-

---

[1] Gide arrived at a similar conception, but only in relation to the artist, and described it as 'a kind of reverse sincerity'. He writes : 'Rather than recounting his life as he has lived it, he must live his life as he will recount it. In other words, the portrait of him formed by his life must identify itself with the ideal portrait he desires. And, in still simpler terms, he must be as he wishes to be.'

thing within them, that had else been deaf and numb. Only by images, he said, do we make the eternal life become a part of our ephemeral life.' In a letter written about 1910 to his father, Yeats said the theme of his play was 'that the world being illusive one must be deluded in some way if one is to triumph in it'. He cited part of the dialogue, never published, in elucidation :

> Queens that have laughed to set the world at ease
> Kings that have cried 'I am great Alexander
> Or Caesar come again' but stir our wonder
> That they may stir their own and grow at length
> Almost alike to that unlikely strength,
> But those that will not make deliberate choice
> Are nothing or become some passion's voice
> Doing its will, believing what it choose.

The sense of the verse is beyond Yeats's prose statement : it is that self-development is only possible through the imagination's creating an image. Without such an image, we are but loose dough.

From now on Yeats's work is full of this conception of the image. In his *Deirdre*, the two lovers spend their last and most heroic hours playing chess because they have heard of two legendary lovers, Lughaid Redstripe and his seamew wife, who died in that way. And the climax of *The Player Queen* occurs when the actress who likes to play queens' roles is actually crowned and becomes a real queen because she is the only woman capable of playing the part. It is the signal for a new cycle.

To provide himself and his characters with images of desirable life Yeats went as before to mythology, which gave him a scheme of moods related by narrative to supplement the subtler associations of his non-narrative symbolism. After 1900 his most notable mythological variation was that, while he continued to treat Irish myths in his plays, he almost abandoned them in his verse. To most of his readers, after all, these myths were still exotic and unknown ; in the plays they could be unfolded in sufficient detail to make them understandable, and in the early poems their mysteriousness, and the difficulty of pronouncing

names in them, had the virtue of contributing to the dimness of
the atmosphere. But the verse which he was now writing was
intended to stir the reader more urgently and actively.

Fortunately, at this juncture he took up the Greek mythology.
Although a few years before, in the flush of his enthusiasm for
Irish texts, he had announced that Greek mythology was dead,
he now began to use it as if it was remarkably alive. Like many
comparative mythologists, such as John Rhys, he had laboured to
construct an Irish Pantheon on the Greek model; but in the
'nineties this work had aimed only at reinforcing the Irish gods
and at showing that Homeric analogues persisted in the Irish
countryside. Allusions to Greek mythology became, at the beginning of the new century, more insistent. The hero of *Where
There Is Nothing* (1902) declared, 'I am the beggarman of all the
ages — I have a notion Homer wrote something about me'. By
1908 such references were no longer scattered. In that year
Yeats represented his beloved not as a virginal, transcendental
rose, but as the experienced Helen of Troy. The whole texture
of his attitude towards her had changed, and his mythology
with it.

Of course, he wanted to invoke only a small part of the story
of Helen. Like Marlowe and Goethe, he ignored Paris completely, or else referred to him lightly as 'her boy'. And he
edged farther away from her by making her so deeply legendary,
and his own failure with her so completely manifest, as to pre-
clude any supposition that he was himself to be identified with
her Trojan lover or Grecian husband. The first poem in which
she appears is 'No Second Troy', a triumph of mythopoeic
technique :

> Why should I blame her that she filled my days
> With misery, or that she would of late
> Have taught to ignorant men most violent ways,
> Or hurled the little streets upon the great,
> Had they but courage equal to desire ?
> What could have made her peaceful with a mind
> That nobleness made simple as a fire,

With beauty like a tightened bow, a kind
That is not natural in an age like this,
Being high and solitary and most stern ?
Why, what could she have done, being what she is ?
Was there another Troy for her to burn ?

The success of the poem comes partly from the poet's withholding the identification of his beloved with Helen until the
last line, when it fairly explodes. Yeats manages this by basing
the identification not merely on beauty, but also on destructive
power, and thus shunning sentimentality. At first the poet's
theme seems to be the extreme pressure that he feels to put blame
upon her for what she has done both to him and to Ireland. But
the fact that the wrong can be stated in national and mythological
as well as personal terms lends it a kind of grandeur.

Nevertheless, the first of the four rhetorical questions puts
the case against her so strongly as to appear to require an answer.
She has filled his days with misery — and this seems the greater
because he says no more about it — and urged on a vulgar
revolution. But the poet's way of describing her revolutionary
activity is the bridge to the second question. He disapproves of
her revolutionary efforts, yet he emphasizes not his disapproval
but his contempt for both her partisans and her opponents. Her
battle is made to seem futile by a reference to her supporters'
ignorance, trivial by setting it up as a contest between little streets
and great streets (the adjective *great* being conspicuously restricted in its meaning to size, as the word *desire* is limited to *want*),
and contemptible because her supporters lack even courage. The
second question takes up the challenge of the first : the reader
expects more complaints about her conduct, but instead her
justification begins. Her nobility, simplicity, and beauty were
too great for our age, and therefore she could not be peaceful.
The word *natural* carries the pejorative implication of conventional or prosaic, as if nature itself had decayed since the Homeric
time. The third question emphasizes the impossibility of her
doing anything but what she has done, yet leaves the matter of
her guilt unresolved. Only in the fourth and final question is

she completely vindicated, for all the guilt of her actions is showered upon her age. The poet attacks the Troy-less present for not being heroically inflammable. And the act of burning Troy is glorified as embodying passionate, heroic action, and as expressing with adequacy her towering personality.

Such a position might be objectionable were it not for the pity which pervades the poem, a pity for the beloved that makes the speaker forget to pity himself and find his misery irrelevant, her actions inevitable. To speak of Yeats's work as he spoke of Lady Gregory's, the past draws itself together, comes to birth as present personality. The myth is reanimated by a subtle but sure-footed identification of the actual and the legendary woman, of reality and the dream, and by making the counterpoint between them the dramatic situation with which the contemporary woman is faced. The difficulties of being mythical are so central and pressing that the fact that she is a mythical person can be taken for granted and by-passed.

This reanimation of myth through parallel and contrast is soon displayed in other poems. Yeats is careful to make the myth full-bodied, as in his choice of words in 'Peace', where he laments his beloved's growing old :

> Ah, that Time could touch a form
> That could show what Homer's age
> Bred to be a hero's wage.

The word 'wage' calls attention to a feature of Homeric culture which a poet like Tennyson would have euphemized. Yeats never loses sight of the physical reality of Greek life :

> She might, so noble from head
> To great shapely knees
> The long flowing line,
> Have walked to the altar
> Through the holy images
> At Pallas Athene's side,
> Or been fit spoil for a centaur
> Drunk with the unmixed wine.

His Homeric reference in 'When Helen Lived' recognizes that
to the Trojans Helen was another unfaithful wife, but he finds a
half-excuse for them in the fact that he and his friends would have
thought the same :

> Yet we, had we walked within
> Those topless towers
> Where Helen walked with her boy,
> Had given but as the rest
> Of the men and women of Troy,
> A word and a jest.

The great architectural feat of these poems is to introduce the
myth naturally and effortlessly. In 'A Woman Homer Sung',
the Homeric reference of the title is slipped with surreptitious
relevance into a peculiarly isolated phrase in the middle of a long
sentence :

> For she had fiery blood
> When I was young,
> And trod so sweetly proud
> As 'twere upon a cloud,
> A woman Homer sung,
> That life and letters seem
> But an heroic dream.

The power of the living woman, as she fuses with the mythical
one, is to transform reality into a dream ; she becomes an image,
and makes all life into one.

The Greek strain endured in Yeats's writing ; ancient Athens
was an image that he thought modern Dublin might emulate,
and he wished to recognize in Homer his own archetype : 'Homer
is my example and his unchristened heart'. This mythology was
common and acquired its freshness by Yeats's remarkable rework-
ing ; after 1910 he added a less common mythology, or quasi-
mythology, to his phantasmagoria, a mythology made up of
ghosts of the dead. Ghosts were part of the historical past, but
death had brought them close to legend. Through death their
lives had been conveniently sifted and stylized into a pattern
comparable to that of orthodox mythological heroes. Without

turning into elemental personages, like Robartes and Aedh in the early poems, ghosts were manipulatable as living men were not. Close to life, they yet kept a distance from it which dignified them.

So one of Yeats's favourite methods in the volume *Responsibilities* (1914–16) in particular, and in later verse, is to pose the experiences of the present against these shadowy judges and their high, non-mortal standards. In the prefatory poem of the book he calls upon the ghosts of his ancestors, whom death has cast into a noble group, to pardon his childlessness. He invokes his friends of the Rhymers' Club in 'The Grey Rock', men like Dowson and Beardsley who were dissolute and confused when alive, but whom he conceives as having been purged in death of all except their finest quality, their steadfast belief in their art. They are a proper audience for a poem which balances the life of art against the life of action. 'To a Shade' addresses Parnell as 'thin shade', not only because a ghost has no body but because Parnell's desires for the future have been so starved since his death ; as in his unpublished poem on Robert Gregory, '"Reprisals"',[1] Yeats employs the ingenious manœuvre of calling up Parnell's ghost to listen, and then sending him away because there is nothing good for him to hear.

The ghostly dead, and the people of legend, are all the 'companions / Beyond the fling of the dull ass's hoof', whom Yeats refers to in the concluding poem of the volume. By seeing his experiences through their eyes — although it must be remembered that by coincidence they also see with his — he imparts majesty and authority to his comments on his time and his own affairs. The living man sits in judgment, but with a jury of ghosts and legended heroes, like Parnell, Duke Ercole, or Homer, who can be relied upon to render a fitting verdict. The reader's attention is diverted from the reality of the jury to the more interesting question of their attitudes towards the contemporary world.

The poet would lack the prerogative of ranking his selected

[1] See below, pp. 231-2.

dead men and heroes on his own side if his standards were anything but exalted.   Throughout the poetry of this period Yeats
sets up rigorous criteria of behaviour, never on the basis of right
and wrong, but of greatness and meanness of soul.   Often with
considerable bitterness, he scorns the apes of his early style, the
mob which hissed Synge's *Playboy of the Western World*, Ireland's
lapse from its romantic past.   He isolates and insists on the isolation of the persons and conduct he admires ; instead of ranking
himself, as he did in his youth, with his fellow-countrymen
Mangan, Davis, and Ferguson, he claims kinship with the
remoter poets Landor and Donne.   Coldness as well as passion
are the requisites of poetry which he demands in 'The Fisherman', and they are also the requisites of conduct.   Paradoxically,
Yeats seems never farther from the community than now when
he is the most fervent advocate of standards for it.

In the second decade of the century his *ex officio* role slowly
gives way to the assumption of the joys and woes of the community as a participating member.   The gradual increase in his
sympathy at this time is especially exhilarating to a generation
extraordinarily conscious of the range of inhumanity.   While
many illustrations could be chosen, one that he himself might
have approved is his treatment of sexual love.   In contrast to the
idealized celibacy of his early verse, the lyrics of the middle
period made allusions to sensuality which were usually baldly
physical ; not until about 1918, in such poems as the series
about Solomon, did he bring together warm affection with
sexuality.   When he did his noble isolation was over.

CHAPTER VI

STYLE AND RHETORIC

Style, biche derrière les balustrades.
HENRI MICHAUX

I. EARLY PRACTICE

TO most of the writers of the 'nineties style was a matter of craftsmanship, which could be discussed in purely artistic terms. Yeats's conception of style, while not without precedent, was quite different. He considered it to be the element which in literature corresponded to the moral element in life ; that is, by its emphases it determined delicate gradations of value and was a direct indication of the writer's personality. This definition followed from his concern over belief, tradition, emotion, reason, sincerity, and unity. For style was a question of the vigour with which positions were taken and of the honesty with which qualifications were made ; it had to do with the degree of emotion to be expressed, and with the degree of contemporaneity in the expression. How a man decided when he faced the alternatives of being affirmative, negative, sceptical, or mealy-mouthed, modern or archaistic, cautious or brazen, affected his choice of words, his clarity or obscurity in setting forth his themes, his sentence structure. Would he try *donner un sens plus pur aux mots de la tribu*, like Mallarmé and Eliot, or abide with the flaccidity of words as they had been handed down to him ? Would he make his art independent of his own weaknesses, so far as he knew them, and so far as he could, or a confession of those weaknesses ? To consider style apart from these questions, Yeats believed, was to consider it superficially ; if form and content met at all, they met at such points of encroachment as these.

The quest for style was therefore a primary interest of Yeats because it was also a quest for his own character, freed from the accidents of every day. Only through style could he establish communication with the self which often seemed so different from his floundering quotidian personality that he began to label it his 'anti-self', or, as we have seen, his 'image'. In terms of this quest his passion for revision of his poems turns out to be central and not eccentric in his career; it was part of the process of what he himself described as 'self-conquest'.

He began to discipline his style in the lee of Victorian verse. A poet of the nineteen-twenties or 'thirties would have campaigned against the major poets of the late nineteenth century because of their lax and sentimental language; for Yeats these defects were not separable, but went with other unfortunate traits of characters which caused the choice of wrong subjects as well as wrong words. He attacked their 'irrelevant descriptions of nature, the scientific and moral discursiveness of *In Memoriam* . . . the political eloquence of Swinburne, the psychological curiosity of Browning, and the poetical diction of everybody'. He made no sudden break with them, however, as Hardy and Hopkins did. Nor did he attempt to follow the radical experiments of Walt Whitman, whose verse he knew because his father, Rossetti, and Dowden had been among the signers of a tribute to Whitman from across the sea. In his early poetry, written up to his twenty-fourth year, he was content to write verse which looked more like William Morris's than it was.

Morris thought, in fact, that he had found a disciple in Yeats, and told him, after having read *The Wanderings of Oisin*, 'You write my sort of poetry', meaning the poetry of his late period rather than of his early psychological narratives. The late verse of Morris reflected his admiration for simplicity of structure and outline, delicacy of ornament without vagueness, bright and clear colour, organic structure, and stately loveliness and quietude. There are passages in *Oisin* which have these qualities, although they have others as well :

Many a shell
That in immortal silence sleeps

> And dreams of her own melting hues,
> Her golds, her azures, and her blues,
> Pierced with soft light the shallowing deeps,
> When round us suddenly there came
> A far vague sound of feathery choirs.
> It seemed to fall from the very flame
> Of the great round sun, from his central fires.
> The steed towards the music raced,
> Neighing along the lifeless waste ;
> And, as the sun sank ever lower,
> Like sooty fingers many a tree
> Rose ever from the sea's warm floor,
> And they were trembling ceaselessly,
> As though they all were beating time
> Upon the centre of the sun
> To the music of the golden rhyme
> Sung of the birds.   Our toil was done ;
> We cantered to the shore, and knew
> The reason of the trembling trees,
> For round each branch the song-birds flew,
> Or clung as close as swarms of bees,
> While round the shore a million stood
> Like drops of frozen rainbow light,
> And pondered in a soft vain mood
> On their own selves in the waters white,
> And murmured snatches of delight. . . .

The difference between Yeats and Morris is that the shell and birds, which in Morris would have been mere scenery, are in Yeats symbols, like the great sun itself, of a world of perfect self-sufficiency.

Apart from its symbolism and from an occasionally aggressive tone, *Oisin* is not particularly heterodox in style for the year 1889. Its fluid line tastes of Tennyson as well as Morris. Yeats describes nature elaborately if emblematically, describes ornate clothing elaborately and with no further motive. The verse forms are loose enough to permit much dawdling. He is fond of adjectives, unduly so of compound adjectives such as 'pearl-pale', 'foam-oozy', 'gold-shod', 'tumultuous-footed'. There is much clumsiness : he writes, 'Dawn passioned', and speaks of 'the golden rhyme / Sung of the birds'. But with his symbols, and with exotic imagery from Irish legend and Indian poetry, he thought his verse had a new slant. His letter to John O'Leary about an uncomplimentary review of *Oisin* is ingratiatingly presumptuous :

That Freeman review will do no harm. It is the kind of criticism every new poetic style has received for the last hundred years. If my style is new it will get plenty more such for many a long day. Even Tennyson was charged with obscurity, and as to charges of word torturing, etc., the first thing one notices in a new country is its outlandishness, after a time its dress and customs seem as natural as any other.

The new country was still much like the old ones, however. As he later admitted, he had not yet discovered his own rhythm, and his poetic position was still unstabilized.

II. STYLISTIC CHANGES, 1889-99

Yeats's stylistic development proceeds in waves. The earliest manner is followed by a period of simplification and then by a period of intensification through sheering away from his images whatever united 'them to one man rather than to another'. His mature style is not developed until after 1900, although there are many hints of it before that time ; and in his last years it too undergoes modification. The first thoroughgoing change takes place after the appearance of *Oisin* in 1889. Yeats then determined to make 'ordinary modern speech' the basis of his verse. Within a few months he started to revise *Oisin*, and his copy of the book shows him, about 1890, altering the line, 'Footing in the feeble glow', to read 'Dancing by the window glow', and 'Hangs o'er all the wooded earth' to 'Overhangs the wooded earth'. A year and a half before he had had no compunction about filling his verse with words like 'yore', 'o'er', 'ere', ''tween', 'azure', ''tis', and 'outlivest', but in *The Countess Kathleen*

and Various Legends and Lyrics (1892) there are only a few of these
left. In this attack upon archaism Yeats was considerably ahead
of his time, as a comparison with Ernest Dowson or Arthur
Symons confirms.

Most of his stylistic changes of this period were intended to
divest his verse of Victorian habits of composition. Simplicity
became his watchword ; his verse would gain a distinctive
character by excluding every expression that his contemporaries
had made conventional. Such exclusion was not easy. In verse
drama, for example, which was one of his principal concerns, the
influence of Shakespeare's iambic pentameter line, softened by
Shelley, Swinburne, and Tennyson in their plays, was almost
impossible to avoid. Long before T. S. Eliot announced that
blank verse was dead, Yeats recognized how hard it was to make
it live. In desperation at the obstacles that confronted him, and
sure that his difficulty must come from some personal weakness,
the young poet considered improving his blank verse by sleeping
on a board. More to the point, he began a new play, *The Countess
Cathleen*, almost at once after the publication of *Oisin*, and wrote
it out completely in prose so as to guard himself from conventional rhetoric when he cast it in verse. In its first published
version, the play shows him wrestling with his medium. Even
the limitations and lapses are interesting :

> You are late home.   You have been lounging
> And chattering with some one, idling somehow.
> You know dreams trouble me, and how I pray,
> Yet all day long you lie sweating on the hill side,
> Or stand else in the gutter with all passers,
> Gilding your tongue with the calamitous times.

Whatever the shortcomings of the first five rather lack-lustre
lines, they are an honest attempt to represent speech ; they use
the word order of prose ; and they do not sound, like the last
line, as if they had come out of Tennyson's *Becket*. Rhetoric
was a less present temptation, for the moment, than bathos :

> When I have keened I will go be with her.

The style went unsteadily up and down :

> The years like great black oxen tread the world,
> And God, the herdsman, goads them on behind,
> When one has lain long under their hard hoofs,
> One falls forgetting.

The effect of the brilliant first two lines is sadly diminished by the last two, which repeat 'one' awkwardly, add the superfluous 'long', and make the sufferer, who is already lying down, fall. Such *gaucheries* were still likely to occur.

Scattered passages in his prose disclose some of the principles on which he was then working. He was always finding something to be rid of, he says. His long-standing hatred of generalization encouraged him, as we have noticed, to write dramas and dramatic lyrics, confrontations of personality rather than of doctrine. His suspicion of intellect was so great that, although he acknowledged its place in poetry, he gave it little play in his early verse. The result was that while he was protected from loose thinking, he was not protected from loose feeling.

Along with generalizations Yeats rejected the detailed descriptions of nature which, with some symbolic justification, had pleased him in *Oisin*. He was weary, he said, of *Oisin*'s 'yellow and its dull green', of 'all that overcharged colour inherited from the romantic movement', and felt that it was pointless to copy the painter's business. He agreed with Keats that 'Scenery is fine — but human nature is finer'. Instead of a landscape whose emblematic character was less evident than its decorative character, he began to use natural scenery exclusively to portray aspects or moods of the soul :

THE SORROW OF LOVE

> The quarrel of the sparrows in the eaves,
>   The full round moon and the star-laden sky,
> And the loud song of the ever-singing leaves
>   Had hid away earth's old and weary cry.

And then you came with those red mournful lips,
　　And with you came the whole of the world's tears,
　　And all the sorrows of her labouring ships,
　　　And all [the] burden of her myriad years.

　　And now the sparrows warring in the eaves,
　　　The crumbling moon, the white stars in the sky,
　　And the loud chanting of the unquiet leaves,
　　　Are shaken with earth's old and weary cry.

At the beginning of the poem nature seems for a moment to have
an independent power, but at the end it is entirely a symbolic
reflection of man.

The style of this poem, which Yeats wrote in October 1891,
was still inadequate. For the second stanza read as sentimental
hyperbole, and the contrast between the first and third stanzas
was ineptly arranged. Except for 'crumbling', the adjectives
were undistinguished and even, in the choice of 'star-laden', trite.
Louis MacNeice has castigated Yeats for not leaving well enough
alone, and for revising the poem in 1922 in such a way that it
lost its character. But while neither version of the poem is
wholly satisfying, the second may still be defended :

　　The brawling of a sparrow in the eaves,
　　The brilliant moon and all the milky sky,
　　And all that famous harmony of leaves,
　　Had blotted out man's image and his cry.

　　A girl arose that had red mournful lips
　　And seemed the greatness of the world in tears,
　　Doomed like Odysseus and the labouring ships
　　And proud as Priam murdered with his peers ;

　　Arose, and on the instant clamorous eaves,
　　A climbing moon upon an empty sky,
　　And all that lamentation of the leaves,
　　Could but compose man's image and his cry.

'Brawling' is too strong a word to be contrasted with 'clamorous',
but 'an empty sky' is a much more convincing picture of desola-

tion than 'the white stars in the sky'. In the second stanza the word 'seemed' now limits the hyperbole. 'Could but compose' in the third stanza is weak, but 'man's image and his cry' is more interesting than 'earth's old and weary cry'. 'That famous harmony of leaves' is a good rhetorical summing-up which replaces dull and conventional words. Even the first version had avoided direct statement of the lover's sorrow by couching it completely in terms of nature ; the second version increases the indirectness by changing 'you' to 'a girl', and makes the powerfully emotional lines that follow more convincing because more restrained. By introducing the word 'greatness', Yeats helps to justify the highflown comparisons which in the earlier version had seemed excessive. And, as MacNeice has admitted, the repetition of 'arose' in the third stanza serves to intensify by its abruptness the intended contrast. Somewhat defective as it is, the second version does not demand so much indulgence from the reader as does the first.

After the *Countess Kathleen* volume (1892), in which this lyric appeared, Yeats could afford to shift his efforts from simplifying his speech to purifying his emotions so as to render them more intense. His next book of verse, *The Wind Among the Reeds* (1899), reflects this intention, which he expounds in an essay on symbolism. His present view, he says, is that 'the beryl-stone' of poetry 'was enchanted by our fathers that it might unfold the pictures in its heart, and not to mirror our own excited faces, or the boughs waving outside the window'. In other words, only at those moments when we lose ourselves and become archetypal can poetry be made. Certainly there is only idealization, and no indication of 'our own excited faces' in the book. Although the poems use 'I' and 'we' freely, they are curiously anonymous and devoid of intimacy. The speaker of the poems, Yeats later admitted, seemed to him to be 'something unmoving and silent living in the middle of my own mind and body'. This was the distilled self, archetypal and not personal, poetry's beryl-stone. As for the beloved, to prevent detailed description from marring her perfection, a few brush-strokes sufficed to characterize her, too, in the most impersonal way. In one poem she is addressed simply by her three features, 'Pale brows, still hands and dim hair'. In his attempt to guard against reproducing what was merely intimate and transitory, Yeats fell into a more remote art than he intended, to which he later applied the label of 'still life'.

In his *Autobiographies* Yeats makes clear that he meant at this time to create verse that would include only emotions, but emotions that he conceived of as being 'cold'. To chill his emotions he found it convenient to make them somewhat mysterious, to set them in formal patterns, to couch them in a 'symbolic language' with many links to tradition, transforming an individual mood into one which generations of men had experienced, and to embody them in slow rhythms disengaged from the excitement of immediate experience. He attached great importance to this last aspect.[1] 'The Lake Isle of Innisfree', which he wrote in 1890, was his first poem, he said, with anything of his own music in it. While its metre is not new, the accented vowels vary greatly in the amount of time that they force the tongue to linger over them :

I will arise and go now, and go to Innisfree. . . .

Nine bean-rows will I have there, a hive for the honey-bee. . . .

The slow, majestic rhythms of *The Wind Among the Reeds* have their provenance here.[2]

---

[1] Although ignorant of theoretical prosody, Yeats had a fine ear and he delighted and bewildered Robert Bridges by hitting upon new effects instinctively. Bridges said that the line in Book III of *Oisin*, 'Fled foam underneath us, and round us a wandering and milky smoke', was previously unknown in English verse. For the most part Yeats did not attempt to evolve new metres, but rather reconstituted old ones.

[2] They did not come easy, as this early draft shows :

I will arise and go now and go to the island of Innisfree
And live in a dwelling of wattles, of woven wattles and wood-work made.
Nine bean-rows will I have there, a yellow hive for the honey-bee,
And this old care shall fade.

There from the dawn above me peace will come down dropping slow,
Dropping from the veils of the morning to where the household cricket sings ;
And noontide there be all a glimmer, and midnight be a purple glow,
And evening full of the linnet's wings.

His rhythmical principle is expounded more boldly in his essay, 'The Symbolism of Poetry', than elsewhere. It appears there as special pleading for the style he was developing :

> We would cast out of serious poetry those energetic rhythms, as of a man running, which are the invention of the will with its eyes always on something to be done or undone ; and we would seek out those wavering, meditative, organic rhythms, which are the embodiment of the imagination, that neither desires nor hates, because it has done with time, and only wishes to gaze upon some reality, some beauty. . . .

Yeats's vehemence comes less from a preference for one rhythm over another than from a preference for the imagination over the will. But his statement cannot be accepted. The imagination is not exclusively dispassionate or contemplative or indifferent to energy and activity. For his own reasons Yeats temporarily gave it these attributes, and had to discard most rhythms because they would have jarred with them. The absence of energetic rhythms is what one notices first in *The Wind Among the Reeds* (1899), as on entering a strange room one first remarks what is not there:

> I dreamed that I stood in a valley, and amid sighs,
> For happy lovers passed two by two where I stood ;
> And I dreamed my lost love came stealthily out of the wood
> With her cloud-pale eyelids falling on dream-dimmed eyes. . . .

Accented syllables and slurs pack the lines so closely that the reader is narcotized.

Yeats's early verse reaches its highest pitch in this volume. Since it was his first book to be made up of nothing but lyrics, with no longer narrative poem or play to occupy first place, he strove harder than ever before to make them impeccable. His writing slowed to three or four lines a day. The result was that he never had to revise this volume as he did its predecessors, and his later quarrel with it was over the kinds of mood it included rather than the way they were composed. Symbols are employed here with more determination than in *Oisin* and with more sharpness than in the rose poems of the *Countess Kathleen*. Archaisms, almost purged from the previous volume, now vanish altogether. Some of the poems in the book had previously appeared in reviews, and Yeats revised them ruthlessly before allowing them to join the volume. He was so ruthless that Lafcadio Hearn wrote from Japan to remonstrate about the omission from 'The Host of the Air' of this stanza :

> He knew now the folk of the air,
>   And his heart was blackened by dread,
> And he ran to the door of his house ;
>   Old women were keening the dead.

Yeats replied remorselessly that 'blackened' and 'dread' had become 'rhetorical' and 'threadbare', that he liked 'to close so short a poem with a single unbroken mood'. 'Surely', he insisted, 'the stanza merely tells, without rhythmical charm, what is *implied* by the other stanzas.' With the same rigour, he ensured syntactical and verbal simplicity by translating some of the poems into folk speech, and he warned George Russell in 1898 to preserve in his poems 'the natural order of the words'.

The extent of Yeats's skill can be conclusively demonstrated by comparing one of his poems with a poem influenced by it. In 'Mongan Thinks of His Past Greatness', the simplicity of the language and word order accentuates the startling images of the first seven lines ; and the equally simple but varied syntax of the last five lines throws their passionate sorrow into relief. The poem concentrates on the expression of a single emotion, and this emotion is 'cold' because it is put into the mouth of the legendary Mongan, and because he is immemorially resigned rather than immediately desperate about his failure in love. Rhythmically, the poem is astonishingly varied, the lines contracting and expanding to suit the thematic development, each shift in tempo precisely calculated, and the whole poem tightly bound together in spite of constant variation from the rhythmical norm.

> I have drunk ale from the Country of the Young
> And weep because I know all things now :

I have been a hazel-tree and they hung
The Pilot Star and the Crooked Plough
Among my leaves in times out of mind :
I became a rush that horses tread :
I became a man, a hater of the wind,
Knowing one, out of all things, alone, that his head
Would not lie on the breast or his lips on the hair
Of the woman that he loves, until he dies ;
Although the rushes and the fowl of the air
Cry of his love with their pitiful cries.

Ezra Pound, writing in 1907 or 1908, borrowed part of Yeats's theme and rhythm for his poem 'The Tree' :

THE TREE

I stood still and was a tree amid the wood,
Knowing the truth of things unseen before ;
Of Daphne and the laurel bough
And that god-feasting couple old
That grew elm-oak amid the wold.
'Twas not until the gods had been
Kindly entreated, and been brought within
Unto the hearth of their heart's home
That they might do this wonder thing ;
Nathless I have been a tree amid the wood
And many a new thing understood
That was rank folly to my head before.

Himself an excellent craftsman, Pound has imitated Yeats's loose line, but because of its diction and syntax, 'The Tree' sounds like the work of an older man writing in a bygone age. Even in the 'nineties, Yeats was more modern than his followers of a decade later.

III. SELF-PORTRAITURE

After *The Wind Among the Reeds* Yeats, we have seen, reconstructed many of his symbolic and intellectual patterns. His style and diction underwent fairly specific changes. In an interview with a San Francisco reporter in 1904, he remarked that he

could no longer produce in himself the 'mood of pure contemplation of beauty' which had pervaded his earlier work. He found
that he could picture himself 'and not some essence' when he
'was not seeking beauty at all, but merely to lighten the mind of
some burden of love or bitterness thrown upon it by the events
of life'. The name he applied to his new poetry was 'personal
utterance'.

In 1910, looking backwards at his career, he traced the term
to his friends the Rhymers, although none of them had worked
it out as fully as he. He wrote his father about a prospective
lecture :

I am describing the group of poets that met at the Rhymers' Club
more especially Ernest Dowson. The doctrine of the group or rather
of the majority of it was that lyric poetry should be personal. That a
man should express his life and do this without shame or fear. Ernest
Dowson did this and became a most extraordinary poet, one feels the
pressure of his life behind every line as if he were a character in a play
of Shakespeare's. Johnson had no theories of any sort but came to do
much the same through the example of Dowson and others and because
his life grew gradually so tragic that it filled his thoughts. His theory
was rather impersonality so far as he had any, I should say. In poetry
the antithesis to personality is not so much will as an ever growing
burden of noble attitudes and literary words. The noble attitudes are
imposed upon the poet by papers like the 'Spectator'.

The letter gives some indication of what he meant by 'personality'. Like style, it must manifest itself in every line. No popular
attitude, however noble, and no current jargon, however 'literary', must be suffered to alloy it. Personality expressed itself by
the imagination, and character expressed itself by the will, which
he did not cease to deprecate.

Yeats supplemented these statements in the lecture itself,
according to a newspaper account of it which sounds authentic :

Another comment Mr. Yeats made on Dowson's work was that
'If you express yourself sincerely I don't think your moral philosophy
matters at all. The expression of the joy or sorrow in the depth of a
spiritual nature will always be the highest art. Everything that can

be reduced to popular morality, everything put in books and taught in schools can be imitated. The noblest art will be always pure experience — the art that insists on nothing, commands nothing — an art that is persuasive because it is almost silent, and is overheard rather than heard. And when I think of that doomed generation I am not sure whether it was sin or sanctity which was found in their brief lives.'

Phrases about the expression of one's self or of the joy or sorrow in the depth of a spiritual nature, must be taken in a peculiar Yeatsian sense. The poetry he least desired remained a poetry where momentary emotions would over-bubble ; but he now felt that poetry might be personal if the self expressed by the poet was the most perfect distillation of himself that he could command. The *persona* of Yeats's verse of the 'nineties had often moved outside space and time, an eternal lover or an aspiring soul ; the new distilled being would be anchored in his own age and country, and clearly identified with Yeats.

His father complained that the resultant poetry lacked 'vision'. Yeats replied in a letter of August 1913, which summarizes his development over the past decade :

Of recent years instead of 'vision' meaning by vision the intense realization of a state of ecstatic emotions symbolized in a definite imagined pattern, I have tried for more self-portraiture, I have tried to make my work convincing with a speech so natural and dramatic that the hearer would feel the presence of a man thinking and feeling. There are always the two types of poetry — Keats the type of vision, Burns a very obvious type of the other, too obvious indeed. It is in dramatic lyrical expression that English poetry is most lacking as compared with French poetry. Villon always and Ronsard at times create a marvellous drama out of their own lives.

His poetry was then to become openly autobiographical, the creation of a man capable of living in the world as well as of contemplating perfection. To make it so, he would have to lead his life in such a way that it was capable of being converted into a symbol. Moreover, he could depict the speaker of his poems in a wider variety of situations, intellectual as well as emotional.

With his new platform Yeats altered the position of the reader as well as of the poet. In the early verse the reader was almost an intruder on the poet's contemplations ; the door was left ajar, and eavesdropping tolerated, and no further concession could be expected. After about 1900, however, he was more obviously one of the poet's concerns, and was compelled to overhear a soliloquy or an informal speech to one person, or to listen, in a few instances, to an aside delivered directly to him.

The new relationship of poet and reader required a new manner suitable for direct address. To give the impression of an active man speaking, Yeats observed that he had to use occasionally prosaic words, even dull and numb ones. 'Curd-pale moon' was an arresting phrase, but its double-adjective was unnatural, and the three strong accents in succession were too far from the rise and fall of normal cadence. He therefore turned it to 'climbing moon'. For the same reason, he began to generate more activity in his verbs, throwing out most of those which, like 'sighing', 'waning', 'brooding', 'weeping', were liable to Shaw's criticism that while he had worked to alleviate human distress, his Irish contemporaries had sung sad songs about it.

Yeats's stylistic aims are manifested in some emendations he proposed to Agnes Tobin in 1906 for her translations of Milton's Italian poems. Where she had written, 'And draws the tired moon in mid-heaven astray', Yeats suggests a series of alternatives which have for common denominator increased activity in the line :

> And draws the busy moon in heaven astray
> And draws the busy moon from heaven to stray
> And makes the moon in the mid-sky to stray
> And makes the tired moon in the sky to stray
> And draws the tired moon from mid-sky to stray

Similarly, where Miss Tobin writes, 'The dawn stands suddenly beside my bed', Yeats proposed instead, 'The Dawn runs suddenly up to my bed'.

For a few years Yeats was isolated in his stylistic purgation, but about 1908 Ford Madox Ford, T. E. Hulme, and, gradually, Ezra Pound, began in theory to emphasize qualities similar to those he desired, although none of them was as thoroughgoing in practice. Pound was a better critic than poet in this respect; no one doted more upon the virtues of the active voice than he, or had more contempt for abstractions. His influence upon Yeats, as upon T. S. Eliot, was beneficent, and the older poet permitted him to suggest revisions in his verse, and even asked him to mark all the abstractions in his prose. A few of Pound's revisions survive. In 1912 he took the final line of 'Fallen Majesty', which Yeats had written as

Once walked a thing that seemed, as it were, a burning cloud,

and excised 'as it were'. An equally typical revision may be cited here though it was made on a poem written in 1927-28. The original draft of the poem, entitled 'From the "Antigone"', read :

Overcome, O bitter sweetness,
The rich man and his affairs,
The fat flocks and the fields' fatness,
Mariners, wild harvesters;
Overcome Gods upon Parnassus;
Overcome the Empyrean; hurl
Heaven and Earth out of their places —
Inhabitant of the soft cheek of a girl
And into the same calamity,
That brother and brother, friend and friend,
Family and family,
City and city may contend
By that great glory driven wild —
Pray I will and sing I must
And yet I weep — Oedipus' child
Descends into the loveless dust.

Pound helps to clarify the poem by making the eighth line, 'Inhabitant of the soft cheek of a girl', follow the first; he removes the rather clumsy 'And into' from the ninth line, and puts instead 'That in'; he takes out the Latinate 'that' from the tenth line. These brilliant changes rendered the lament much more compact and effective.

Clarification, acceleration, and renewed disinfection of his diction were features of the introduction of what Yeats called a 'theatrical element' into his work. 'Theatrical' must be understood without pejorative implications. It seemed to him that Wordsworth, lacking this element, did not paint himself vividly enough, while Carlyle, having an excess, could neither know nor see anything. Yeats managed to steer his way between them, achieving a public manner that was not pompous and rarely affected. In this triumph the key word is oratory. He was well aware that he sometimes praised what he had once derided, and that in his youth he had equally condemned oratory, abstraction, and rhetoric. But in 1907, in some brief essays appropriately entitled *Discoveries*, he went so far as to disagree with Pater (and with the French symbolists) that music was the type of all the arts, and offered oratory in its place : 'I in my present mood am all for the man who, with an average audience before him, uses all means of persuasion — stories, laughter, tears, and but so much music as he can discover on the wings of words'. He remembered now how powerful had been the effect of the speeches of John F. Taylor, one of his Dublin adversaries during the 'nineties. These speeches, Yeats says in his *Autobiographies*, first suggested to him 'how great might be the effect of verse, spoken by a man almost rhythm-drunk, at some moment of intensity, the apex of long-mounting thought'.

Rhetoric and abstraction now revealed themselves as the two monsters who guard oratory's gate against all comers. At any cost Yeats had to foil them. By rhetoric he usually meant insincere, high-flown language, and by abstraction, passionless, narrow, opinionative, and unconcentrated language. Insincerity might come from talking about subjects not deeply felt, such as political and economic questions ; abstraction might result from an interest in ideas for their own sake rather than as projections of human personality. These had always been dangers, but were more threatening·now that he was speaking in a louder voice.

The remedy was to keep to self-portraiture, and have it always passionate. The passion could be desire or hatred, both of which he had ruled out of poetry in his essay on symbolism, or better, a combination of both. But to ensure the exalted tone of the oratory, one other element was needed. As Verlaine remarked to Yeats in 1894, the poet 'should hide nothing', but keep his 'dignity'.

To achieve this stance and style Yeats put himself through a long and arduous course of training, which led him in a way that he had not anticipated in his youth. He had reached that point where the poet, having freed himself from other people's language, can create his own. T. S. Eliot has recently suggested that modern poets, having achieved their revolt against worn-out poetical diction, might now return to writers like Milton for guidance in constructing a stylized speech. Yeats engaged in this process early in the century. 'Our common English', he said, unconsciously echoing Pater, 'needs such sifting that he who would write it vigorously must write it like a learned language.' He occasionally suggests that the basis of his verse had become the 'syntax of impulsive common life' and the rejection of archaisms and inversions in favour of 'common syntax'.

But anyone who goes to Yeats's verse of this time looking for these attributes will be disappointed. He will come upon an extraordinary syntax, for example, in the mouths of Yeats's beggars and hermits. Here is the language of the road which one Yeats beggar uses when he stumbles :

> Were it not
> I have a lucky wooden shin
> I had been hurt.

And a moment later, in the course of a dispute, he remarks in his peculiar *patois* :

> It's plain that you are no right man
> To mock at everything I love
> As if it were not worth the doing.
> I'd have a merry life enough
> If a good Easter wind were blowing,

> And though the winter wind is bad
> I should not be too down in the mouth
> For anything you did or said
> If but this wind were in the south.

Notice how casually this uninstructed old countryman falls into the subjunctive mood : 'were it not', 'as if it were', 'if a good Easter wind were blowing', 'if but this wind were in the south'. We must allow for the fact that Anglo-Irish speech is fonder of the subjunctive than English or American, but even so, it may safely be posited that only on Yeats's Connemara hills, and never in Connemara, would a beggar say 'If but', 'I should', or use the complicated clause that follows 'It's plain'. Only a Yeatsian beggar could utter three subjunctive clauses for every colloquialism like 'down in the mouth'.

This is not common syntax at all. Many years afterwards, writing to Dorothy Wellesley, Yeats declared that while '"The natural words in the natural order" is the formula', he 'would never alter a fine passage to conform to formula but one gets careless in connecting passages and then formula helps'. Even this qualification shows him to be hardly conscious of the extreme stylization of his speech. He went beyond Lady Gregory and almost as far as Synge. Lady Gregory's peasants sound more Irish than the Irish because she makes them repeat characteristic speech devices with exaggerated frequency ('It's good you'll be looking' and the like). She has been accused of unwittingly founding her Kiltartan dialect on the linguistic aberrations of a local blacksmith, but the truth is that she consciously selected and heightened the speech she heard. Synge did the same with turns of speech, and also heightened speech rhythms far beyond his friends. Yeats's specialized diction differs from theirs, however, in being based on cultivated rather than peasant talk. He daringly endowed his characters with elaborate syntactic constructions but simple words, and relied on intense, compact expression and frequent pungent expressions to force their required identities upon his personages. The particular identity is not of great consequence, for neither beggar nor hermit is allowed in Yeats's verse the independent life that Shakespearean characters often seem to have.   Yeats holds the wires taut.

Closely scrutinized, his style of this period has for a hallmark an archaistic formality. Having worked to rid himself of archaisms until he was about thirty-five, he spent the next fifteen years reviving some of them.   Writing English as a learned language, he caught up usages long out of fashion :

> 'He shadowed in a glass
> What thing her body was.'

> The daily spite of this unmannerly town
> Where who has served the most is most defamed. . . .

> . . . but now
> We'll out, for the world lives as long ago. . . .

> Maybe a twelvemonth since. . . .

> 'Would it were anything but merely voice !'

> I've stood as I were made of stone. . . .

> Enough if the work has seemed,
> So did she your strength renew,
> A dream that a lion had dreamed. . . .

> O Heart, be at peace because
> Nor knave nor dolt can break. . . .

> Ah, that Time could touch a form. . . .

> Aye, horsemen for companions. . . .

> What need you, being come to sense,
> But fumble in a greasy till. . . .

> My sleep were now nine centuries. . . .

> Because the mountain grass
> Cannot but keep the form. . . .

> Whereon I wrote and wrought. . . .
>
> She might, so noble from head
> To great shapely knees
> The long flowing line,
> Have walked to the altar. . . .

The language of a love lyric can even bear a legalistic conjunction:

> Whereas we that had thought
> To have lit upon as clean and sweet a tale. . . .

Yeats sometimes goes almost beyond English, as in the last line of 'That the Night Come', where the condensed subjunctive fetches the reader up with a full stop:

> She lived in storm and strife,
> Her soul had such desire
> For what proud death may bring
> That it could not endure
> The common good of life,
> But lived as 'twere a king
> That packed his marriage day
> With banneret and pennon,
> Trumpet and kettledrum,
> And the outrageous cannon,
> To bundle time away
> That the night come.

Or in 'The Living Beauty' he writes:

> Being more indifferent to our solitude
> Than 'twere an apparition,

where ''twere' has to bear the weight of 'if it were'. Grammar permits herself to be treated thus arrogantly only when the rest of the poem is more decorous.

The distinctive tone that Yeats's poetry gains during this middle period of his verse is due largely to the many turns of speech that become characteristic of him. In spite of his vaunted preference for normal syntax, a stylized word order was more characteristic of him:

And should they paint or write. . . .

Yet could we turn the years again. . . .

Who, were it proved he lies. . . .

Yet we, had we walked within
Those topless towers. . . .

I thought no more was needed
Youth to prolong. . . .

He disdains now to use adjectives following nouns, such as 'pavements grey' in 'Innisfree', but otherwise his habits of verbal arrangement bear little relation to detached theory.

To give his verse a ring of immediacy and colloquialism he is fond of clauses beginning with 'now':

'Maybe I shall be lucky yet,
Now they are silent', said the crane. . . .

For I am not so bold
To hope a thing so dear
Now I am growing old. . . .

Decided he would journey home,
Now that his fiftieth year had come. . . .

Clumsy auxiliary verbs would slow his pace too much, so Yeats habitually used 'had' to mean 'would have':

Yet we, had we walked within
Those topless towers
Where Helen walked with her boy
Had given but as the rest
Of the men and women of Troy,
A word and a jest.

The same consideration leads him to follow Irish practice in masking elaborate constructions behind 'for' rather than 'in spite of' or 'notwithstanding':

And yet for all that I could say. . . .

> All the wild witches, those most noble ladies,
> For all their broomsticks and their tears,
> Their angry tears, are gone. . . .

Another way of maintaining speed and suspense by withholding connectives is to insert an isolated phrase in a detached, ablative absolute relation to the rest of the sentence :

> Ah ! when the ghost begins to quicken,
> Confusion of the death-bed over, is it sent
> Out naked on the roads. . . .

> There cannot be, confusion of our sound forgot,
> A single soul. . . .

Or, to give an example from his later verse :

> How can I, that girl standing there,
> My attention fix
> On Roman or on Russian
> Or on Spanish politics ?

Many of his devices tease or entice the reader into granting the poet his assent. Such is the function of the word 'that' used as a demonstrative adjective ; it implicates the reader in common awareness of what the poet is talking about, as if the poet's world contained only objects which were readily recognizable :

> Sickness brought me this
> Thought, in that scale of his. . . .

> The time for you to taste of that salt breath
> And listen at the corners has not come. . . .

> While I, from that reed-throated whisperer
> Who comes at need. . . .

For the same reason, Yeats has a predilection for the word 'all', which encompasses everything in what purports to be a familiar world :

> All the wild witches, those most noble ladies,
> For all their broomsticks and their tears. . . .

Aye, and Achilles, Timor, Babar, Barhaim, all
Who have lived in joy and laughed into the face of Death.

I balanced all, brought all to mind. . . .

An especially apt example occurs in 'In Memory of Major Robert
Gregory', where the repetition of 'all' helps lend an aura of
universal genius to a young man who may have been only a
universal dabbler, and justifies the poet in his public sorrow :

> And yet he had the intensity
> To have published all to be a world's delight.
>
> What other could so well have counselled us
> In all lovely intricacies of a house. . . .[1]
>
> And all he did done perfectly. . . .
>
> Soldier, scholar, horseman, he,
> As 'twere all life's epitome. . . .
>
> . . . a thought
> Of that late death took all my heart for speech.

Simplified descriptions also reinforce the sense that this is a
known world. Aoife in 'The Grey Rock' is 'that rock-born,
rock-wandering foot'; his beloved in 'A Thought from Propertius' is pictured as 'The long flowing line',

> so noble from head
> To great shapely knees. . . .

With less metonymy, but as much stylization, the beggar in 'The
Hour Before Dawn' is

> A one-legged, one-armed, one-eyed man,
> A bundle of rags upon a crutch,[2]

anticipating the old man in 'Sailing to Byzantium' who is 'A
tattered coat upon a stick'. Landscape is similarly evoked by
only one or two particulars, and these symbolic :

[1] Yeats pronounced 'intricacies' with the accent on the second syllable.
[2] He afterwards altered the first line.

> I stumbled blind
> Among the stones and thorn-trees, under morning light. . . .

It is as if the poet had an agreement with his readers to get on with the essentials.

Yeats treads gingerly, and marvellously, between a distant and a familiar tone. He designs his poems with sudden beginnings, whether explosive or casual, and relies on unexpectedness to take the reader off guard. Special words and constructions recur to make the Yeatsian signature certain. Among these one of the more interesting is 'that'; we have seen him employing it as a demonstrative adjective to bring the reader into the charmed circle; it has also another effect, a loftier one, when it appears as a relative pronoun instead of 'who'. Yeats picked up this oddity from his father, but held to it because the hard dental in 'that' was one of the ways of patenting the emphatic, clear-headed personality who serves as speaker of the poems:

> Soldiers that gave, whatever die was cast. . . .

> Is there a bridle for this Proteus
> That turns and changes like his draughty seas?

> What's riches to him
> That has made a great peacock
> With the pride of his eye? [1]

On the other hand he avoided the appearance of over-assurance, understanding, with Jammes, that 'Les Vigny m'emmerdent avec leur dignité'. Probably for this reason he is addicted to affirming by repudiating the contrary position:

> There cannot be, confusion of sour sound forgot,
> A single soul that lacks a sweet crystalline cry.

> No government appointed him.

---

[1] Yeats's practice with the relative is opposite to that of Gerard Manley Hopkins, who, as W. A. M. Peters points out, usually omits it. But Yeats sought a calmer style than Hopkins could tolerate.

There's not a man can report
Evil of this place. . . .

There is not a fool can call me friend. . . .

We cannot pay its tribute of wild tears.

The habitual content of each with each
When neither soul nor body has been crossed.

I would be — for no knowledge is worth a straw —
Ignorant and wanton as the dawn.

Each of these statements repudiates a negative position so vigorously as to leave no possibility but affirmation in the reader's
mind.

The mixture of the distant and the familiar, of exalted diction
and homely images, can be seen at its clearest in one of his
epigrams, which he wrote with Schiller's and Goethe's *Xenien*
as well as Blake's epigrams in mind :

TO A POET, WHO WOULD HAVE ME PRAISE CERTAIN BAD
POETS, IMITATORS OF HIS AND MINE

You say, as I have often given tongue
In praise of what another's said or sung,
'Twere politic to do the like by these ;
But was there ever dog that praised his fleas ?

Dogs 'give tongue,' though it takes a surprised moment to
remember; the technical term is cut a little by the contraction in the
next line, 'what another's said or sung', although that colloquialism is in turn checked by the formal 'another' and by the com-
pression of the alternatives into the three words, 'said or sung'.
The phrase, "'twere politic', revives another archaic form, this
time in ironic mockery, while the last line is suspended at a high
level in the oratorical phrasing of the question, 'But was there
ever', before the poet suddenly allows it to drop and sting with
the homely image of the last five words. Yeats had to revise the
poem many times to make these effects clear.

Because his postures are never stiff, because his dignity suits

him well and is always passionately provoked, Yeats is able to
carry off fairly successfully even a *tour de force* like the concluding
poem of the *Responsibilities* volume (1914), where he writes a
fourteen-line poem in only one long, suspended sentence :

> While I, from that reed-throated whisperer
> Who comes at need, although not now as once
> A clear articulation in the air,
> But inwardly, surmise companions
> Beyond the fling of the dull ass's hoof
> — Ben Jonson's phrase — and find when June is come
> At Kyle-na-no under that ancient roof
> A sterner conscience and a friendlier home,
> I can forgive even that wrong of wrongs,
> Those undreamt accidents that have made me
> — Seeing that Fame has perished this long while,
> Being but a part of ancient ceremony —
> Notorious, till all my priceless things
> Are but a post the passing dogs defile.

The poem's careful workmanship is not altogether concealed.
Yeats utilizes the sonnet division into octave and sestet to divide
the subordinate and independent clauses of his sentence. He
makes the last lines of the octave and the first line of the sestet run
along easily so as to mitigate the difficult grammatical form of the
other clauses, and syntax and metrics combine with sense to
produce the violence of the concluding two lines. He prepares
the way for the blunt, passionate, and unpleasant image by the
twisted, almost tortured syntax that precedes it. Ezra Pound was
so impressed by the ending when he read it in 1914 that he said
Yeats had at last become a modern poet. But Yeats's modernity
was always of a traditional kind: he had borrowed the figure from
Erasmus.

Only occasionally does he assume in his lyrical verse a directly
oratorical role. 'September 1913' is an example, and even this is
more intricate than it first appears. Like many poems of the
middle and late periods especially, it uses to advantage the
rhetorical question. While some of Yeats's rhetorical questions,

like that at the close of 'Leda and the Swan', vary the type by posing unanswerable problems, here the answers are obvious :

> Was it for this the wild geese spread
> The grey wing upon every tide ;
> For this that all that blood was shed,
> For this Edward Fitzgerald died,
> And Robert Emmet and Wolfe Tone,
> All that delirium of the brave ?
> Romantic Ireland's dead and gone,
> It's with O'Leary in the grave.

The words 'for this' and 'all that blood' establish a contrast between the sordid present and a past heroic for the simplicity of its blood sacrifices. Yeats said that he thought in writing the lines of an old peasant who loved to roll such names over his tongue. The series of questions is powerful, but the questioner seems almost to forget that he is asking them in the triumphant summary, 'All that delirium of the brave'. But the word 'delirium', prepared for by the words 'all that' which imply that one customarily thinks of the heroic actions in this way, as well as that a single epithet will do for all, recalls the stanza from mere oratory. In the midst of his sounding periods, the poet finds time to set forth his personal attitude with remarkable honesty ; 'delirium' both ennobles their sacrificial deaths as heroic madness and imparts the more sober judgment that madness is still madness.

There is of course no reason why oratory should not be honest oratory, admitting all the complexities of the speaker's position, but in practice it usually is not. Yeats is one of the few poets who combine force and perceptiveness. His political poems, for example, are always complicated by his being above politics. In 'Easter, 1916' he celebrates the revolt of his compatriots but insists also on pointing out what seems to him to be its folly :

> And what if excess of love
> Bewildered them till they died ?

The word 'bewildered' is a thoroughly conscientious one here.

The poem has been castigated because it satisfied both the nationalists and the anti-nationalists, but Yeats, who had elements of both in his thought, expressed his whole position. In the same way, at the climax of 'Sailing to Byzantium', having set forth his scorn of nature, the protagonist asks to be gathered into the 'artifice of eternity' with full knowledge that the word 'artifice' has unpleasant connotations; because the natural world still holds some attraction for him, he does not entirely disavow them. The phrase, 'mere images', as applied to poetry in 'The Phases of the Moon', is another of these heavily loaded words, since it implies both 'merely' and, because of its Latin root, 'pure'. At the moment of greatest passion the poet manages to be critical too.

This complexity and honesty are characteristic of Yeats. It is partly because of the power of his style that he can afford qualifications of his position beyond the point where qualifications would have appeared possible. The many poems he wrote about the afterlife and heaven in later life are alike in that they never exclude an unexpected element of scepticism. In those poems where he comes closest to committing himself to a belief which he does not fully hold, he introduces a *caveat* at the crucial moment. In the climax of 'The Cold Heaven' he alludes to what 'the [holy] books say' with respect but not absolute credulity; in 'A Prayer for My Son' he refers to an episode of Christ's life with the remark, 'Unless the Holy Writings lie'; in 'All Souls' Night' heaven is 'the whole / Immense miraculous house / The Bible *promised* us'; and in 'On Woman' the prediction of rebirth is restrained by the reminder, 'If the tale's true'. This sense of a point beyond which assertions may not be made is one of the most contemporary aspects of Yeats's mind.

In the end, then, his rhetoric is made up of both firm assertiveness and subtle, complex qualifications. He knows the ways of oratory, and follows them, but only as far as they do not mitigate the honesty of his 'personal utterance'. By rhythm, syntax, and diction he recovers the traditionally authoritative manner of the poet, yet he does not forget that poetry must be an 'asylum for the affections' as well as the voice of powerful attitudes. His growth as an artist came about through the gradual strengthening, by style and other methods, of his poetic *persona*, who in the end is proud as well as humble, and may be 'shaken, but not as a leaf'.

CHAPTER VII

SYMBOLS AND RITUALS IN THE LATER POETRY

I. ANCHORAGES

OF Yeats's late work it may be said, as J. W. N. Sullivan remarked of Beethoven's final period, that nothing is abandoned and yet everything is changed. Impressive as many of the poems written before this period are, they are for the most part narrow in comparison with what he now writes. Human incompleteness and grandeur receive their most convincing expression, the one being removed from the amorous frustration of youth, the other from the defiant isolation of middle age. During the first part of the period, from Yeats's marriage in October 1917 until about 1933, there is a steady expansion of his world to include cosmic, public, political, and domestic themes. From 1934 until his death he returns to the same subjects with so much greater abandon and gusto that these years may be thought of as forming a distinct unit. Throughout more than two decades, poem after poem enlarges the area of his interest, knowledge, and attitudes, as if, having perfected his medium, he could make incursions upon regions which had previously thwarted his approach.

One of the most striking aspects of his mature poetry is its solidity, which comes in part from a strong sense of particular place. We are not in the woods, but at a blasted oak, not by the dim sea, but at the river that runs by the poet's house. Many protrusive objects appear too, often with iconic force. The most prominent of these is his great tower which, with its stairway, provides him with the titles of the two finest volumes of this period, *The Tower* (1928) and *The Winding Stair* (1933). It is drawn from the only real estate he ever owned, an old Norman tower at Ballylee near Lady Gregory's estate at Coole in western Ireland.   Yeats had longed for many years to buy it, and finally completed the purchase in 1916 ; after his marriage the following year he and his wife lived there for extended periods over several years, and it came to mean a great deal to him.   He wrote to Sturge Moore, who was designing the cover for *The Tower* volume :

> I am also sending you some photographs of the tower.   I need not make any suggestions, except that 'The Tower' should not be too unlike the real object.   I like to think of that building as a permanent symbol of my work plainly visible to the passer-by.   As you know all my art theories depend upon just this — rooting of mythology in the earth.

His conception of his work as rooted in the earth and destined to endure grew stronger during this period.   He set its key in a little verse, 'To be Carved on a Stone at Thoor Ballylee', the different versions of which point an amusing and significant contrast.   The earlier one, sent in a letter to John Quinn, ran :

> I, the poet, William Yeats,
> With common sedge and broken slates
> And smithy work from the Gort forge,
> Restored this tower for my wife George ;
> And on my heirs I lay a curse
> If they should alter for the worse,
> From fashion or an empty mind,
> What Raftery built and Scott designed.

Raftery, Yeats explained to Quinn, was 'the local builder', but in the final version he slips, along with Scott, from sight :

> I, the poet William Yeats,
> With old mill boards and sea-green slates,
> And smithy work from the Gort forge,
> Restored this tower for my wife George ;
> And may these characters remain
> When all is ruin once again.

The change makes the tower a more personal symbol.

For, although Yeats's tower had an existence in stone, it and the other towers that jut up into his verse are less masons' constructions than poets'. As such, they vary in meaning. In 'Ego Dominus Tuus', the first poem to mention the tower at Ballylee, and in 'The Phases of the Moon', written while the Yeatses were in residence there, the tower is, as in Yeats's letter to Moore, a symbol of his work, or, as he said in the latter poem, 'an image of mysterious wisdom won by toil'. Searching to root it in artistic tradition as well as the ancient earth, Yeats compares it to the tower of the Platonist in Milton's 'Il Penseroso', of Prince Athanase in Shelley, and to 'The Lonely Tower' in Samuel Palmer's picture of that name. Other facets of the symbol acquire emphasis in the poem called 'The Tower', where it is representative of the lonely but firm poet, of his Anglo-Irish nationalist and heroic tradition, and finally, through these associations, of the unconquerable and creative spirit of man. In 'Blood and the Moon', where we learn the tower has a ruined top, it is emblematic of the decay of modern nations and modern man on the one hand, and of man's still aspiring even if impeded creative impulse on the other. 'A Dialogue of Self and Soul' departs from these in making the tower emblematic of night and of a spiritual reality that spurns the earth. Yeats was aware that these meanings would play against one another and give his symbol something of the variability of a living man. He had mastered this technique in connection with the rose, but the tower was free of religious and mystical connotations.

Other poems are set in great houses, such as Lady Gregory's house at Coole, Lady Ottoline Morrell's house at Garsington, and his own (rented) eighteenth-century houses in Dublin's Merrion and Fitzwilliam Squares. They are sufficiently conspicuous in his work to have led some critics to protest as snobbish his preference for the society of titled women in aristocratic dwellings. Yet both Lady Gregory and Lady Ottoline Morrell were remarkable women; their houses were famous for a company of intelligence and taste; and Yeats's repugnance to the merely inherited glory of the rich, as opposed to the cultivated glory, is made perfectly explicit. He celebrates Lady Gregory's house because so many great Irishmen have visited there that it is a national monument, just as he endeavours to sanctify his tower, which had, as Norman towers go, a rather commonplace history, by joining Goldsmith, Swift, and Berkeley as fellow-tenants of it.

In his early verse there was much talk of mythical islands and woods, but now he writes of a mythical city, founded upon the city of Byzantium, with its dome of Santa Sophia, its marble dancing floor, its mosaics and golden work. Yeats adopts such symbols with his usual freedom ; although Byzantium is historically the holy city of Eastern Christendom, he makes it a secular city of the poetic imagination. The emperor and the lords and ladies to whom the wonderful golden birds sing have historical support, but Yeats releases them from the theological quarrels and civil wars that embroiled their turbulent lives.[1] He rebuilds the city to suit his own ideals, and chooses to find his own art reflected in its conventionalized designs and symbols. It is not Byzantium but new Byzantium.

II. 'A VISION'

Within the new Yeatsland the configuration of symbols and themes owes much to the strange phenomenon of Mrs. Yeats's automatic writing which her husband and his critics have made famous.[2] A few days after their marriage, Mrs. Yeats tried to distract her preoccupied husband by 'faking' automatic writing, and then discovered, to her astonishment, that she could write it without meaning to. The writing continued sporadically over

[1] Yeats's interest in Byzantium may have been awakened by the historian J. B. Bury, who was for a time his Latin master at the High School in Dublin and was probably already engaged in collecting materials for his Byzantine history. The word 'Byzantine' had a highly favourable sense for both Huysmans and Wilde, like 'Gothic' for Ruskin.

[2] The closest parallel in literary history is the *tables tournantes* on the island of Guernsey, which helped Victor Hugo in 1853 to consolidate his poetic scheme, and seemed to provide supernatural sanction for it. Yeats's experience did not quite match Hugo's, for the 'spirits' who seemed to be communicating through Mrs. Yeats often adopted the names of household pets (such as cats), while Hugo's extramundane visitants were Dante, Racine, Hannibal, 'and other heroes of that kidney'.

several years, but had to be sorted, organized, and completely revised before it could be published.

The reader of *A Vision* may have difficulty in accepting this account, even though masses of automatic writing exist to authenticate it, because the ideas in the book are not novel in Yeats's work. He had said them all before, in one way or another. Aside from particular symbols, the thematic basis is much the same as the one he developed in his youth. There are the cycles, the reincarnating souls, the possible escape from the wheel of time to a timeless state, the millennial reversal of civilizations that corresponds to the rebirth of individuals, the heroic, unconventional ethic, the unknown and problematical god, the battle between the spiritual and material worlds. All these are taken up and reworked.

Alongside them are other conceptions familiar to Yeats, though expressed in combinations that make them look new. The running antithesis in the book between Christian and Renaissance values was an application of his psychology to history, with character apportioned to the first and personality to the second ; it was also related to his early antithesis between Christianity and paganism, and to his contrast of the dried pips of Puritanism with the cornucopia of the Renaissance. What was new was the methodical tracing of the antithesis over more than 2000 years. The concern with the afterlife, and the proposition that during it the soul 'dreamed back' its lifetime experiences, stemmed naturally from folk-tales, spiritualism, Henry More, and Swedenborg, a group of authorities he had convoked in 1914 in an essay for Lady Gregory's *Visions and Beliefs in the West of Ireland*. The classification of types of human personality was also an ingrained habit in Yeats, and its particular form in *A Vision* owed much, as will become apparent, to his earlier pursuits.

That Georgie Hyde-Lees Yeats's automatic writing should have assumed so Yeatsian a form is not surprising. She had belonged to the same or similar occult organizations as her husband and had read many of the same books. She knew his work thoroughly, especially the most recent, such as *Per Amica*

Silentia Lunae (1917), a long essay which discusses the mask, the anti-self, and their supernatural counterpart, the daimon. And she spoke of these matters every day with a talkative husband. Consequently her mind, in a state which may be regarded naturalistically as partial self-hypnosis, could not escape focussing on the same subjects which beset it at conscious moments.

Mrs. Yeats's role was nevertheless important. For the material of the automatic writing emerged in an unpredictable way, and the possibility of disclosure of some entirely new truth lent excitement to speculations which might otherwise have proved wearisome even to an inveterate investigator like Yeats, as in fact they did to his wife. Then, too, the revelations were diversified; some cosmological insight would be associated with an intimate personal reminiscence of Mrs. Yeats, and with repercussions of their lives together, so that the notebooks were often extremely personal. This intimacy, and the unpremeditated character of the writing, were for Yeats a guarantee that he was not dealing with abstractions. It seemed likely that he had tapped what spiritualists call the subliminal mind, what Jung considers the racial unconscious, and what Henry More called *Anima Mundi*. While Yeats was uncertain of the precise depth of the revelations, as he sometimes confessed, he knew that Newton and Locke and the whole rationalist tradition had little or no part in the sporadic cacography of his sitting-room.

Although the themes were familiar to him, they never appeared without modifications which enlarged their import, and they rarely appeared except in the form of images. Here was a storehouse the like of which he had not been able to discover in a hundred trips to seances. *A Vision* is pictorial, at times even diagrammatic, but always unspeculative.

III. THE NEW SYMBOLS

The *Vision* is most accessible if regarded as a group of three symbols which mirror one another. The root symbol is a sphere inside of which whirl a pair of interpenetrating gyres or cones, or, as Yeats sometimes refers to them, vortexes. These are inextricably entwined yet perpetually at war with one another, now one and now the other triumphant in a series of regular, inconclusive battles.

YEATS'S LATE SYMBOLISM

The Great Wheel from *A Vision*, showing the twenty-eight phases from dark of the moon to full and back to dark, and the four symbols of flower, cup, fruit, and sceptre, which are related to the four elements.

With the sphere Yeats represents the unified reality beyond chaotic appearance or the experience of that reality. On consideration we realize that the sphere is the mature equivalent of the rose. It differs from the rose in that Yeats only occasionally mentions it in his verse; that is because it had come to seem a remoter ideal. The sphere is 'There' in the little poem of that name:

THERE

There all the barrel-hoops are knit,
There all the serpent-tails are bit,

> There all the gyres converge in one,
> There all the planets drop in the Sun.

The gyres, on the other hand, stand for the world of appearance, a world in which, as he says, 'Consciousness is conflict'. Wedded in antagonism, they symbolize any of the opposing elements that make up existence, such as sun and moon, day and night, life and death, love and hate, man and God, man and woman, man and beast, man and his spiritual counterpart or 'daimon'; on a more abstract level, they are permanence and change, the one and the many, objectivity and subjectivity, the natural and the supernatural worlds. With the gyres Yeats had a more excited and interesting picture of the universal conflict than, for example, two armies drawn up against one another would have afforded him; for the point of one gyre was in the other's base, as if a fifth column were operating in the very headquarters of the enemy. He concurred with Hegel that every thesis had implied in it an antithesis, and modified the notion that every movement holds the seeds of its own decay by identifying the seeds as those of a counter-movement. He was further confirmed in his symbol by the fact that it applied to his verse, which he realized with increasing clarity was guided by the principle of the containment of the utmost passion by the utmost control.

Like the sphere, the gyres are not often explicitly mentioned in his poems; they occupy a place equivalent to that of the cross in his early work, which appeared rarely also, because the opposition might be put less formally. But they furnish him with the title and subject of a late poem:

THE GYRES

> The gyres! the gyres! Old Rocky Face, look forth;
> Things thought too long can be no longer thought,
> For beauty dies of beauty, worth of worth,
> And ancient lineaments are blotted out.
> Irrational streams of blood are staining earth;
> Empedocles has thrown all things about;

Hector is dead and there's a light in Troy ;
We that look on but laugh in tragic joy.

What matter though numb nightmare ride on top,
And blood and mire the sensitive body stain ?
What matter ?   Heave no sigh, let no tear drop,
A greater, a more gracious time has gone ;
For painted forms or boxes of make-up
In ancient tombs I sighed, but not again-;
What matter ?   Out of cavern comes a voice,
And all it knows is that one word 'Rejoice !'

Conduct and work grow coarse, and coarse the soul,
What matter ?   Those that Rocky Face holds dear,
Lovers of horses and of women, shall,
From marble of a broken sepulchre,
Or dark betwixt the polecat and the owl,
Or any rich, dark nothing disinter
The workman, noble and saint, and all things run
On that unfashionable gyre again.

Such a poem makes clear the limits as well as the uses of *A Vision* :
'The Gyres' is not the product of the automatic writing, except
in its name for the symbols, but of all Yeats's experience. 'Old
Rocky Face' is the Delphic Oracle, who spoke through a cleft
in the rock, and is a proper muse for a prophetic poem. Yeats
brings the oracle into his neighbourhood by addressing it directly
with this familiar epithet, and then by ranging its supposed predilections, like those of his ghosts earlier, so that they will be
identical with his own. Although he celebrates the eternal recurrence of things, he is not pleased by the recurrence of all things,
but only of the things he likes, which are here traditional (therefore 'unfashionable' in this age) beauty and worth and a hierarchi-
cal dream of 'workman, noble, and saint'. The saint, often
treated by Yeats with less courtesy, is included as part of an
orderly society in contrast to the growing anarchic confusion of
the present. The description of the state of the world tallies,
even in its imagery, with that of the poems 'The Second Coming'
and 'Nineteen Hundred and Nineteen', but his exultation in the

face of tragedy in 'The Gyres' is not paralleled in those comfortless poems. It cannot be too much emphasized that he modified the symbols to suit the states of mind, irrespective of their consistency with *A Vision*. The gyres are his servants, not his masters. In the same way he treats Empedocles and Troy with a fine casualness as symbols of the present scene rather than as allusions to the past. All ages are equally present to his prophetic eye. Every element in the poem has appeared in his work before, but is recast to jibe with the Dionysian, ecstatic quality which he imparts by the exclamatory phrase, rare for him : 'The gyres ! the gyres !' and the repeated rhetorical question, 'What matter ?' These interjections mitigate the oracular tone of many of the statements and are the main force in the confrontation of past, present, and future. With fire and skill Yeats succeeds in transforming one's horror at the indifferent survival of evil as well as good into delight that good must survive as well as evil.

Yeats's ownership of his symbols is unchallengeable if we remember that the word 'gyre', and even 'cone' and 'vortex', did not appear originally in the automatic writing ; there the word used was 'funnel'. Yeats did not like 'funnel' and set out to find a better term. He noted that the double cone occurred in Swedenborg's *Principia*, which he was reading in 1914, but it had no central place in the Swedenborgian system. A single cone appears as a principal symbol in Henry More's poem, *Psychathanasia*, which Yeats must have read ; for More the cone represents the universe, with God as its base and the potentialities of matter as its point :

> Lo ! here's the figure of that mighty Cone,
> From the straight Cuspis to the wide-spread Base
> Which is even all in comprehension.

Yeats sometimes, as in 'Sailing to Byzantium', employed a single gyre instead of a double one, profiting perhaps from More's example.

Many occult writers have made use of cones, gyres, or vortexes. The vortex also occurs from time to time in Blake, but in a different way. None of Yeats's 'worthies' brought the symbol home to him so directly, however, as did Ezra Pound. In 1916 Pound and the sculptor Gaudier-Brzeska set up a new esthetic movement to which they gave the name of 'Vorticism'. Vorticism, of which Pound told Yeats, was intended to move away from the neutral, opaque, motionless images which the Imagist movement had theoretically fostered with Pound's blessing a few years before, and to restore or implant dynamism in the image ; a vortex, as Pound wrote John Quinn, was a 'whirlwind of force and emotion'. Pound's further explanation in his book on Gaudier presents the symbol more clearly :

> The Image is not an idea. It is a radiant node or cluster ; it is what I can, and must perforce, call a VORTEX, from which, and through which, and into which, ideas are constantly rushing. In decency one can only call it a VORTEX. And from this necessity came the name 'Vorticism'.

Such remarks of Pound may well have emphasized to Yeats the sexual basis of the symbol, and he had studied comparative mythology to too good purpose to be ignorant that such symbols have the most staying power. They would also preserve him from the dangers of abstract geometry. Some of the lines which he wrote in 1923 in 'The Gift of Harun Al-Rashid', a thinly veiled autobiographical poem, may be taken literally as well as metaphorically :

> The signs and shapes ;
> All those abstractions that you fancied were
> From the great Treatise of Parmenides ;
> All, all those gyres and cubes and midnight things
> Are but a new expression of her body
> Drunk with the bitter sweetness of her youth.

The more strange Yeats's symbols first appear, the more pains he takes to make them sound like household words. He surrounds the gyres with homely diction, often altering the more high-sounding names for them (gyres, cones, and vortexes) into a 'top', 'Plato's spindle', or 'bobbins where all time is bound and wound'; the winding movement is often represented as 'perning', a dialect word based on his recollection that at Sligo 'pern' was the spool on which thread was wound. Consequently, when he wrote in 'Demon and Beast' that he 'had long perned in the gyre, / Between my hatred and desire', or in 'Sailing to Byzantium' summoned the sages to 'perne in a gyre', that is, to whirl down from their more celestial part of the cone of the universe to his more natural part, he lightened esoteric symbolism by a word from peasant speech. That the peasant word was itself esoteric to his readers probably further endeared it to him.

He restated the symbol of the gyres and their transcending sphere in his second principal symbol, which was a representation of the opposition as between sun and moon. To avoid complications — and he was always trying to render the scheme as lucid as he could — Yeats put it entirely in lunar terms, with full moon and dark of the moon as the two contrary poles. These were depicted as phases fifteen and one respectively in the twenty-eight phases through which the moon passes each month. Any antinomial conflict can be registered in terms of the waning or waxing of the moon, just as it can be expressed in terms of the preponderance of one or the other gyre. Yeats preferred, however, to limit the lunar symbol to the description of the self as it shifts through a multitude of lives, in some of them tending towards the energetic personality, which Yeats calls 'subjectivity', of a Renaissance hero, and sometimes towards the sheering away of personality and the assertion of undistinguished equality, which he calls 'objectivity', of Christ or, he thinks, of Marx as well. One group exploits and extols the individual, and its counterpart suppresses and husks him. Self-fulfilment is related to the full moon and its neighbouring phases, while self-restraint is related to the dark of the moon. 'The typal man', Yeats writes in some early drafts of *A Vision*, 'lives through thirteen cycles, each of twenty-eight incarnations corresponding to the twenty-eight lunar mansions'; he later qualifies the statement by revealing that the two maximal phases when the moon is entirely full or dark are phases where the soul does not take on human form, but is a spirit in temporary refuge from the bustle of reincarnation :

> Twenty-and-eight the phases of the moon,
> The full and the moon's dark and all the crescents,
> Twenty-and-eight, and yet but six-and-twenty
> The cradles that a man must needs be rocked in :
> For there's no human life at the full or the dark.

The purpose of making the two extreme phases non-human was probably to keep the incompleteness of human life prominently displayed while at the same time demonstrating the nearness of supernatural life.

In the lunar symbol the equivalent of the sphere that transcends the gyres is the Thirteenth Cycle, sometimes known as the Thirteenth Cone or the Thirteenth Sphere. Here too reality inheres, and nothing can be known of it. Reality is also approximated, though not fully attained, in the four phases closest to full moon, where what Yeats (borrowing the phrase from his father) calls 'Unity of Being' is possible. In such unity the soul finds itself closest to its 'radical innocence'; it 'begins', he writes, 'to tremble into stillness, / To die into the labyrinth of itself!' [1] He develops the symbol most fully in 'The Phases of the Moon'. This is his most didactic poem, but even here he has none of *A Vision*'s dispassionateness. He introduces value judgments which give the poem its own colour ; the soul's incarnations are a heroic 'discipline' ; the spirits of the full moon are related to the lover's image of his beloved ; the objective phases are disparaged ; the poem is put in dialogue form, set in Galway, and its contents disingenuously represented as what the poet has not been able to discover.

The lunar symbol is more complex than that of the gyres. Moon and sun had been part of his early symbolism, but had occupied there a subordinate place. Yeats developed them steadily into greater prominence. In his *Autobiographies* he

---

[1] He shows little interest in that approximation of reality which occurs at phase one, presumably because it is the state of 'nothingness' of the saint rather than the state of 'everythingness' of the artist.

connected the symbolic meaning of solar and lunar with his work under MacGregor Mathers's tutelage in the Golden Dawn. '"Solar", according to all that I learnt from Mathers, meant elaborate, full of artifice, rich, all that resembles the work of a goldsmith, whereas "water" meant "lunar" and "lunar" all that is simple, popular, traditional, emotional.' These correspondences might be varied; in 'Lines Written in Dejection' (1915) the moon is 'heroic' and the sun is 'timid'. He called attention to the moon's phases, and related them solipsistically to the states of mind of the beholder, in *The Cat and the Moon*, a little play written shortly before his marriage. Such reflections were evidently habitual with him. He united to them the theory of astral influence used by astrologers, according to which character is marked out by the relative influences of the dominant planets which have presided over the individual's birth. Yeats simplified the astrological scheme by excluding the planets and considering only the moon, and was thereby enabled to evaluate his acquaintances and the men of the past, as had been his inveterate custom all his life, according to a simpler and more workable system. The source of the Thirteenth Cycle, as well as of the other twelve, was a reminiscence, in either his mind or his wife's, of Christ and the Twelve Apostles. To give God so mechanical a title was to ensure that He would be discussed only as 'it', never as a personal deity, least of all as a Christian one. God became thereby a feature of the Yeatsian cosmogony which like other features the poet's symbolic vocabulary might grasp and include. And the embodiment of divinity in so unprepossessing a term as Thirteenth Cycle stood in ironic and urbane contrast to Yeats's claims for the cycle's unlimited powers, as if one were to say, 'Ah yes, I have given Almighty God the name of "Thirteenth Cycle" in my scheme'.

The other restatement of the gyres has two parts. The first, which receives less attention, is the contraposition of the self and its spiritual opposite or daimon. The daimon is a kind of anti-self or mask elevated, so to speak, to a plane beyond the human. The human being is partial in comparison with the daimonic

fullness.[1]   In the second part, Yeats divided the self into two sets
of symbolic opposites, Will and Mask, Creative Mind and Body
of Fate.   These may be roughly translated as Imagination and
the Image of what we wish to become, and Intellect and the
Environment.   They are equivalent to fire and water, air and
earth, in the early symbolic scheme, but have much more complexity here.   Essentially their battle, for which Yeats had been
writing the bulletins throughout his work, was between what we
are and what we dream of becoming.   According to this theme,
first fully articulated in *The Player Queen*, a Caesar is buried in
every hunchback, a lecher in every saint.   It would be equally
valid to say that every hunchback has a Caesar for his daimon,
and every saint a lecher.   The daimon's faculties are exactly
opposite to those of his human counterpart.   Since the combination of internecine war within the self, and foreign war with the
daimon, made for impossible complications, Yeats was content in
all except one chapter of *A Vision* to trace the quaternion of the
soul and let the daimon fend for himself.

When the four faculties were in certain stages, when they
were in harmony rather than at odds, they might attain the
equilibrium of Unity of Being.   In this respect they resembled
Blake's Four Zoas, who in certain aspects could restore Albion,
the fallen man, to life.   Unlike Blake, Yeats avoided using his
special terms in his verse, and instead of finding the nomenclature
of the four faculties there, we find various contrasts which depend
on them but have a fresher look.   In 'Solomon and the Witch',
a poem written in 1918, not long after the automatic writing
began, some of Solomon's wisdom connects, at several removes,
with *A Vision* :

> 'A cockerel
> Crew from a blossoming apple bough
> Three hundred years before the Fall,
> And never crew again till now,
> And would not now but that he thought,
> Chance being at one with Choice at last,

[1] See below, pp. 236-8.

All that the brigand apple brought
And this foul world were dead at last.
He that crowed out eternity
Thought to have crowed it in again,
For though love has a spider's eye
To find out some appropriate pain —
Aye, though all passion's in the glance —
For every nerve, and tests a lover
With cruelties of Choice and Chance ;
And when at last that murder's over
Maybe the bride-bed brings despair,
For each an imagined image brings
And finds a real image there ;
Yet the world ends when these two things,
Though several, are a single light,
When oil and wick are burned in one ;
Therefore a blessed moon last night
Gave Sheba to her Solomon.'

In love, Solomon is saying, the lover's dream of his beloved and
her actual form are the same, and what he wills (Choice) is
exactly what he gets (Chance). This marriage is the equivalent
of the mystic marriage of *The Shadowy Waters*, but its physical
aspect is much more conspicuous, and the notion of its ending the
world is phrased as a witty conceit where the early play represented it as a genuine possibility. In this passage the Will, Mask,
and Body of Fate may be fitted in if anyone wishes, but the theme
antedates *A Vision* by many years.

With the four faculties, twenty-eight phases, and two gyres
in the foreground, and the sphere looming mightily behind them,
Yeats had the basic symbols for his book. There is no need to
explore the ramifications of the scheme in greater detail ; like
most schematizations, it bulges at the seams, and Yeats has to
knead history and human personality a good deal to make them
stay where he wants them. The logical shortcomings of *A Vision*
are not, however, of much consequence. The book ranged
together a group of symbols which had in common what the
earlier symbols, that clustered around a rose, lacked — a furious

movement. Man, as seen in it, is a creature for ever turning around a wheel during a single lifetime, and around a larger wheel in the course of a cycle of reincarnations. Even the afterlife is nothing but a projection of tumult beyond the grave and into new cradles, or, as Yeats sometimes pictures it, an unwinding of a bobbin which winds up again during life. Each lifetime is the scene of a tug-of-war between four 'faculties' of the human mind, the daimon, the dead, certain miscellaneous spirits, the Thirteenth Cycle, and other forces. This contest is so intricate, and its outcome so unpredictable, that what starts out in the first part of *A Vision* and in some of Yeats's poems as a deterministic system is re-framed by succeeding parts and other poems until it contains a large measure of free will. Yeats's father was accustomed to say that the poet should feel free to believe in marriage in the morning and not to believe in it in the evening, 'the important thing being not that he keep his mental consistency but that he preserve the integrity of his soul'; and his son felt similarly free to believe and disbelieve in free will until that Day of Judgment when chance would become one with choice at last.

The emphasis in *A Vision* falls heavily upon sublunary struggle, but from time to time it salutes translunar peace with the symbols of the sphere, the Thirteenth Cycle, and Unity of Being. Aware that he was no mystic and should not try to become one, Yeats also knew the importance of the furthest reaches of human experience or feeling, and felt that on four or five occasions of his life his 'body of a sudden blazed', and he had been released from conflict. And so his system, while its main allegiance is to Proteus, is also deferential to the god of stasis.[1]

Much of the argument of *A Vision* is clothed in a style more metaphorical than any used in English prose since the seventeenth century. If no reader has ever been converted to its doctrines, the reason is that one is never sure exactly what is

[1] In so prominent a place as the end of the introduction to the first edition of *A Vision*, Yeats admitted that there might be nothing for man but endless becoming : '. . . I murmured, as I have countless times, "I have been part of it always and there is maybe no escape, forgetting and returning life after life like an insect in the roots of the grass". But murmured it without terror, in exultation almost.'

being offered for acceptance or what attitude the writer wishes to elicit. Yeats varies greatly in the labels he applies to his book. It may be (1) direct revelation from remarkably loquacious spirits, imparted through his wife's automatic writing. This hypothesis is scarcely tenable, since he relentlessly doctored up the revelation, and since the spirits gave evidence of being well versed in his own earlier writings, and in books which he and his wife had read. Unconscious memory is a much less demanding explanation, and Yeats himself gradually relinquished the supernatural hypothesis. (2) It may be a system of historical and psychological classification. The difficulty here is that both history and psychology are over-simplified and stylized. As (3) a philosophy, its doctrines are often couched in too personal a language. Other labels lead in a different direction: it may be (4) 'a dream, and yet the nearest I can go to reality'; (5) a 'lunar parable'; (6) a myth or mythology; (7) a group of metaphors; (8) a symbolism or 'stylistic arrangement of experience'; or (9), in part at least, an 'exposition' of his poems. The title of the book does not help much in deciding among different labels, for the word 'vision' begs the question of whether a transcendental or merely a personal insight is involved.

A Vision can best be taken as a symbology, a study of symbols which sometimes stretches towards philosophy and at other times towards the condition of poetry. In so far as it was philosophical, Yeats felt compelled to apologize for it :

This book records 'A Vision', and its writer like the writers of all similar books in the past, when he uses some abstract term or definition, knows that they are incidental and temporary. He is even persuaded that whatever is so defined is taken out of experience as water is when we describe it as two atoms of hydrogen and one of oxygen, in momentary ignorance of the fact that it uses a little sunlight, or sediment, a little duckweed or a fish or two, and that spiritual realities especially can only be known in the animation of experience. . . .

The best part of the book is not the explanation of the symbols, but their application to psychology and history, where the 'animation of experience' dominates abstract definition. What we really have in these sections is a series of moods comparable to those in his verse, to which Yeats fits certain well-known individuals and periods of time.

That *A Vision* has inconsistencies he tacitly admits half-way through it, when he describes the temperament of his own phase as one that will deal with images rather than with ideas, and will synthesize them 'in vain, drawing with its compass-point a line that shall but represent the outline of a bursting pod'. But the inconsistencies are of less importance than the powerful sense of tumultuous life, and of the struggle to transcend it, which the book conveys. In some unused notes for the second edition Yeats suggests the book's importance for him :

I have now described many symbols, which seem mechanical because they are united into a single structure, and of which precisely because they are always the same story the greater number may have seemed unnecessary. Yet every symbol, except where it lies in vast periods of time and so beyond our experience, has brought me, as I think evoked for me, some form of human destiny, and the form once evoked appears everywhere, as my own form might in a room full of mirrors, for there is but one destiny.

It was his most splendid attempt to bring his mind to the state which Stendhal in another connection calls 'crystallization'.

IV. SYMBOLS IN THE POEMS

Important as *A Vision* is, it is in no sense a complete guide-book to Yeats's poetry. It provides him with a valuable system of symbols, but the attempt to interpret any poem solely in terms of the system will do it an injustice. Yeats was quite willing to hold *A Vision* in abeyance if his experience dictated some attitude not to be found in it. We need not wonder that, in spite of his promise in the book that the next era would be subjective and preferable to the present, the god of that era, who rises from the desert sands in the poem 'The Second Coming', is no beneficent Dionysus but a monster. The poet's vision of horror surmounts his vision of the cycles.   In the same way, his prose statements about Byzantium give no indication of the ambivalence to be found in 'Sailing to Byzantium'.   No one would suppose, on reading the extra-national *Vision*, that Ireland would occur so prominently in the poetry written contemporaneously with it ; nor would anyone expect that the saint, who stands near the 'objective' dark of the moon, would receive such favourable consideration in 'The Gyres'.

A Vision is not, then, a full background for his verse; it is drawn upon when it is needed, sometimes running counter to the verse, sometimes parallel, sometimes compounding with it.   In verse, as in prose, Yeats was searching to find adequate expression for the contest of self and soul, and the transcendence or equilibration of this contest.   His winding stair, which suggests the tortuous path of life, has a tower around it to suggest fixity ; these symbols are parallel to the gyres and sphere, and priority is impossible to assign.   Both themes have to be given play.   He has many ways of representing the contest :   he sets self against soul directly in 'A Dialogue of Self and Soul', more concretely in the encounters of Crazy Jane and the Bishop, or in the tree of 'Vacillation' which is half green leaf and half burning flame.   That tree is comparable to Yeats's old tree of life, but both sides of the tree have been shot through with energy since 'The Two Trees'.   He puts the conflict also in 'Sailing to Byzantium', more bluntly in an early draft than in the completed poem :

> Fish, flesh & fowl, all spring & summer long
> Extol what is begotten, born, & dies
> And man has made no monument to extol
> The unborn, undying unbegotten soul.

The contest is less ultimate than it appears :   Crazy Jane is no atheist ;   she merely finds all the religious terms applicable to physical union and human love.   According to her lights, she is more truly religious than the pompous bishop, just as the self in the 'Dialogue' is more truly blessed in the end than the soul, and the poet in 'Sailing to Byzantium' is not less interested in life but more capable of regarding it once he has been transformed into a singing bird.   There is always a means of escape from the prison of the antinomies, though it is not always grasped. Yeats takes up the theme of escape in a little unpublished poem, 'Wisdom and Knowledge (or John Hermit and His Friends)', which he wrote on March 24, 1929 :

> John Hermit stays at home for he
> Parcels out eternity.
>
> Tom Ratcatcher hoots at thought
> Till every rat in the world is caught.
>
> Biddy Cockle adds that still
> There are cockles in the shell.
>
> But were shells and tails in a row
> Man might know what man can know.

The hermit is the mystic who, by direct apperception of reality, avoids the antinomies.   Tom Ratcatcher represents action and the male, and Biddy Cockle, in a symbolism that occurs elsewhere in Yeats, mainly beauty and the female. If these two could be reconciled, man would have knowledge, a transcendence of opposites that in this poem differs from wisdom, also a transcendence, in being secular and in using earthly ingredients rather than dealing mystically in eternity.

In some notes for the first *Vision*, Yeats describes more fully than elsewhere the equilibrium of the Thirteenth Cycle.   There, he says,

. . . all whirling [is] at an end, and unity of being perfectly attained. There are all happiness, all beauty, all thought, their images come to view taking fullness, to such a multiplicity of form that they are to our eyes without form.   They do what they please, all [struggle] at an end, daimons and men reconciled, no more figures opposing one another in a demoniac dance, and it is these who create genius in its most radical form and who change the direction of history.

Two of his favourite symbols for this state, or a flashing glimpse of it, are the dance and the consummation of love ; they do not appear so often in *A Vision*, but are frequent in his poetry from 1917 on. By chance rather than decorum, Yeats, we have seen, waited almost until his marriage to write directly of sexual intercourse. It became a more and more constant subject in his work as he realized its symbolic possibilities. He wanted a symbol immanent in experience, expressing the most intense physical action, and yet transcending it. The heroine of his poem, 'Chosen', puts the case with excessive learning:

> If questioned on
> My utmost pleasure with a man
> By some new-married bride, I take
> That stillness for a theme
> Where his heart my heart did seem
> And both adrift on the miraculous stream
> Where — wrote a learned astrologer —
> The Zodiac is changed into a sphere.

But she understands the shift from Zodiacal illusion (the world of the gyres) to spherical reality. This claim for physical love is half urbanity, but in so far as intercourse is symbolic of the marriage of opposites it is high seriousness. The admixture of irony, however slight, and the insistence on a symbolic as well as an intrinsic value in the sexual experience, save Yeats from the too clamant sexuality of D. H. Lawrence.

A second major symbol, the dance, had a longer and more varied history in Yeats's verse. In *Oisin* and other early poems, dancing is the chief pleasure of the 'ever-living' ones. Yeats's later poems remove it from the other world. 'Nineteen Hundred and Nineteen' makes the dance display the endless movement of life in miniature:

> All men are dancers and their tread
> Goes to the barbarous clangour of a gong.

But it usually appears with a further significance. Yeats's friend, Arthur Symons, had remarked of the dance that it stood for 'possession and abandonment, the very pattern and symbol of earthly love. Here is nature (to be renounced, to be at least

restrained), hurried violently, deliberately, to boiling point. . . .'
This possibility of the symbol, that it might contain both self-
expression and self-renunciation, attracted Yeats to it.

The symbol usually appears in his poems with some such
resolved duality. In 'The Double Vision of Michael Robartes',
a girl is pictured dancing between a Sphinx and a Buddha, which
represent wisdom and love. She stands for a mid-point which
participates in the qualities of both :

> O little did they care who danced between,
> And little she by whom her dance was seen
> So she had outdanced thought.
> Body perfection brought,
>
> For what but eye and ear silence the mind
> With the minute particulars of mankind ?
> Mind moved yet seemed to stop
> As 'twere a spinning top.
>
> In contemplation had those three so wrought
> Upon a moment, and so stretched it out
> That they, time overthrown,
> Were dead yet flesh and bone.

Her dance is a solitary esthetic act, art so triumphant as to lend
an air of perpetuity, which is a kind of death, to movement. This
copulatory image of permanence and change, which Yeats elsewhere expresses as 'the stallion eternity' mounting the 'mare of
time', is central in his later poems. Another poem, 'Among
School Children', finds in the dance a fusion of personality and
abstract image :

> O body swayed to music, O brightening glance,
> How can we know the dancer from the dance ?

But the dancer is not necessarily alone. The symbol takes
another form in 'Crazy Jane Grown Old Looks at the Dancers' :

> I found that ivory image there
> Dancing with her chosen youth,
> But when he wound her coal-black hair

As though to strangle her, no scream
Or bodily movement did I dare,
Eyes under eyelids did so gleam ;
Love is like the lion's tooth.

When she, and though some said she played
I said that she had danced heart's truth,
Drew a knife to strike him dead,
I could but leave him to his fate ;
For no matter what is said
They had all that had their hate ;
Love is like the lion's tooth.

Did he die or did she die ?
Seemed to die or died they both ?
God be with the times when I
Cared not a thraneen for what chanced
So that I had the limbs to try
Such a dance as there was danced —
Love is like the lion's tooth.

To Crazy Jane the dance both represents the sexual act symbolic-ally and also is the sexual act itself. Like Wilde, who saw the lover as murderer, and beyond Baudelaire, who had declared that in love one person is always the executioner and the other the victim, Crazy Jane sees that both parties play both roles and that hatred is the key to love. Hence her fright and fascination.

These curious shifts in value take place in other symbols. The tree can be the 'great-rooted blossomer' of 'Among School Children' or the 'broken tree' of the old pensioner. The bone may suggest the meaninglessness of physical life, as in the 'slender needles of bone' of 'The Crazed Moon', or its strong roots, as in the tenacious memory of the 'bone upon the shore' in 'Three Things'. The sea-shell stands for the miracle of divine creation in 'Crazy Jane Reproved', but for the lovely emptiness of wealth in 'Meditations in Time of Civil War'. The moon is immutable perfection in 'Blood and the Moon' but mutable illusion in 'The Crazed Moon' and perhaps 'The Cat and the Moon'. Yeats allows nothing to petrify, and keeps his symbols

in movement from poem to poem.   Yet in each poem the symbol
is integral in its meaning and effect.

A letter from Yeats to Sturge Moore about the cover
design of *Four Plays for Dancers* (1921) will serve to point the
contrast between his late and early symbolic schemes.   Moore
had nailed a hawk on a board for his design, forgetting that the
hawk was emblematic of the mind or of logical thought.   Yeats
admonished him : 'Don't nail that hawk on a board.   The hawk
is one of my symbols, and you might rather badly upset the sub-
consciousness. . . . My main symbols are sun and moon (in all
phases), Tower, Mask, Tree (Tree with mask hanging on the
trunk), Well.'   To this list we may properly add the sphere and
gyres, the dance, and sexual union, and from it we may subtract,
because it appears so rarely, the well.   If these symbols are compared with those of the early work, the tree, the dance, and the sun
and moon are seen to be the chief survivals.   Each of these has
been altered : the tree is split down the middle, the dance is 'an
agony of trance', the sun and moon are divided into conflicting
phases.   The four elements survive as the four faculties (of
which the mask is one), and their intellectual opposition is clarified and heightened.   The fixed cross of the antinomies has become the whirling gyres, and only the sphere, which replaces the
rose, is permitted immobility.   The symbols, from being gentle,
are vortical.

V. RITUALIZING

Through symbols and myths Yeats sought to formalize his
view of life by binding it to the past and to the consciousness of
great numbers of men.   In his later work he also made much use
of ritual.   Ritual may be defined as a ceremonious performance
or recreation of a crucial, sanctified action ; it differs from myth,
a more inclusive term, in being inevitably ceremonious, crucial,
and sanctified.   Yeats had sporadically toyed with fertility ritual
in his play *The Green Helmet*, and elsewhere ; but he now cultivated this feature of his art with assiduity.

In choosing his rituals and ritual moments Yeats put aside Celtic materials in favour of those which had possessed more people and which, after Frazer, had been of central interest to comparative mythologists. The vegetation rituals surrounding Attis, Adonis, and Osiris, who, as Frazer demonstrated, were related gods, provided some of his subjects. But the whole atmosphere of the poetry of this period is ritualistic. We tread the sacred wood ; the golden bough hangs from the sacred tree ; Adonis has just been wounded by a boar ; the priest of Attis hangs his god's image from the tree ; Dionysus, Christ, and an unidentified beast-god are born ; Zeus begets children on Leda. The hero must fail unless he devours his predecessor's heart ; a heart is burned in resin as in an Aztec ceremony of sacrifice ; gods die to be resurrected.

These ancient patterns embrace modern subjects in Yeats's verse ; he never becomes a comparative mythologist collecting anthropological curiosities. As with his treatment of Helen of Troy earlier, and like Eliot after him, he reinterprets the past in terms of the present at the same time that he reinterprets the present in terms of the past. The second part of 'Vacillation' will serve as example :

> A tree there is that from its topmost bough
> Is half all glittering flame and half all green
> Abounding foliage moistened with the dew ;
> And half is half and yet is all the scene ;
> And half and half consume what they renew,
> And he that Attis' image hangs between
> That staring fury and the blind lush leaf
> May know not what he knows, but knows not grief.

In taking over the Attis ritual, Yeats arbitrarily changes the pine tree which was carried in the god's festival into a magical tree of which he had read in Lady Charlotte Guest's translation of the *Mabinogion*. He wants the tree to symbolize the worlds of the flesh and of the spirit. In the procession at the festival of Attis, it was customary for a priest to hang the god's image on the sacred tree, and Yeats here represents the poet as performing this ritual act.   But Attis is a god of a special sort, a vegetation god who castrates himself when Cybele, the earth mother, drives him to frenzy.   Yeats identified the poet with the priest, himself castrated in honour of his god, because like Thomas Mann he conceived of the artist as forced to sacrifice his life for the sake of his art.   For its sake he becomes one with Attis and in this union, which is also the union of body and soul, he experiences the ecstasy of seeing beyond the cross or gyres into the rose or sphere of things.

His portrayal of the Adonis legend is even more remarkable. The heroine of 'Her Vision in the Wood' has a sudden vision of the god's being slain by a boar :

> Dry timber under that rich foliage,
> At wine-dark midnight in the sacred wood,
> Too old for a man's love I stood in rage
> Imagining men.   Imagining that I could
> A greater with a lesser pang assuage
> Or but to find if withered vein ran blood,
> I tore my body that its wine might cover
> Whatever could recall the lip of lover.
>
> And after that I held my fingers up,
> Stared at the wine-dark nail, or dark that ran
> Down every withered finger from the top ;
> But the dark changed to red, and torches shone,
> And deafening music shook the leaves ; a troop
> Shouldered a litter with a wounded man,
> Or smote upon the string and to the sound
> Sang of the beast that gave the fatal wound.
>
> All stately women moving to a song
> With loosened hair or foreheads grief-distraught,
> It seemed a Quattrocento painter's throng,
> A thoughtless image of Mantegna's thought —
> Why should they think that are for ever young ?
> Till suddenly in grief's contagion caught,
> I stared upon his blood-bedabbled breast
> And sang my malediction with the rest.

That thing all blood and mire, that beast-torn wreck,
Half turned and fixed a glazing eye on mine,
And, though love's bitter-sweet had all come back,
Those bodies from a picture or a coin
Nor saw my body fall nor heard it shriek,
Nor knew, drunken with singing as with wine,
That they had brought no fabulous symbol there
But my heart's victim and its torturer.

The speaker, full of grief at her impotent old age, loses herself among the troop of women who mourn Adonis and sing maledictions upon the boar. But she differs from them in that her grief is not held in control by the stately processional. Her vision goes beyond theirs: the dead man looks at her with his 'glazing eye', and she shrieks and falls, recognizing that this is not the fabulous, symbolic god in whose death she might feel a genuine but detached grief, like that of an actor in a tragic play, but her own lover who is both torturer and victim as love itself is both bitter and sweet. This knowledge comes to her not as a similitude but as sudden, direct recognition. Pageants in Yeats have a way of turning into realities. The symbol strikes to the heart; while 'those bodies from a picture or a coin' of the ageless, repetitive chorus pass on unmoved, caught up in the legend which they re-enact in fitting, legendary style, immediate experience overwhelms her.

Christian rituals also prove malleable to Yeats's touch. The resurrection of Christ is the subject of one of his plays, but the real theme is not an orthodox celebration of the god but an affirmation of the cyclical renewal of spiritual forces through one god after another. Similarly, Christ's birth is represented ritualistically as that of a new and inferior Dionysus, vexing the world to nightmare by his rocking cradle. The poet's sympathy goes out to Joseph in 'A Stick of Incense', who prefers his gods to be born lustily from the mating of a god and woman rather than parthenogenetically. He sees the sacred drama of bearing a hero as like that of bearing a god :

What sacred drama through her body heaved
When world-transforming Charlemagne was conceived ?

What is common to his handling of all such ritual acts is his decided preference for supernatural events which have complex implications in the natural world. Conversely, he liked to find patterns of ritualistic repetition, implying something beyond nature, in natural events.

Among his ritualized poems none is more ingeniously contrived than 'All Souls' Night', which is on one level the invocation ceremony proper for November 2. The poet calls up one after another of his dead friends to drink from the extra glass on his table, and makes us think we are participating in a magical lark :

> Midnight has come, and the great Christ Church bell
> And many a lesser bell sound through the room ;
> And it is All Souls' Night,
> And two long glasses brimmed with muscatel
> Bubble upon the table.   A ghost may come ;
> For it is a ghost's right,
> His element is so fine
> Being sharpened by his death,
> To drink from the wine-breath
> While our gross palates drink from the whole wine.
>
> I need some mind that, if the cannon sound
> From every quarter of the world, can stay
> Wound in mind's pondering
> As mummies in the mummy-cloth are wound ;
> Because I have a marvellous thing to say,
> A certain marvellous thing
> None but the living mock,
> Though not for sober ear ;
> It may be all that hear
> Should laugh and weep an hour upon the clock.

The friends whom he proceeds to invoke are William Horton, Florence Farr Emery, and MacGregor Mathers. They had in common a mystical preoccupation with the other world which kept them from living comfortably in this one. After characterizing them in turn the poet seems, in his final two stanzas, to have forgotten that he had invoked them :

But names are nothing.   What matter who it be,
So that his element have grown so fine
The fume of muscatel
Can give his sharpened palate ecstasy
No living man can drink from the whole wine.
I have mummy truths to tell
Whereat the living mock,
Though not for sober ear,
For maybe all that hear
Should laugh and weep an hour upon the clock.

Such thought — such thought have I that hold it tight
Till meditation master all its parts
Nothing can stay my glance
Until that glance run in the world's despite
To where the damned have howled away their hearts,
And where the blessed dance ;
Such thought, that in it bound
I need no other thing,
Wound in mind's wandering
As mummies in the mummy-cloth are wound.

The poem ends and appears to have said nothing except that it
had much to say.   But in fact it has accomplished two things :
first, Yeats has pictured his dead friends unforgettably, so unforgettably that we are filled with sympathy for their partly pathetic,
partly ludicrous, yet partly heroic strivings to know what scarcely
can be discovered.   The second is more remarkable.   The next to
last stanza makes clear that the gross palates of the living miss the
wine's ecstatic essence which is available only to the dead.   What
Yeats has succeeded in doing is to create an atmosphere in which
the living are shown to be incomplete in comparison with the
dead, and each of his friends provides an apposite illustration
because each has spent his life trying to learn what the dead know.
With consummate subtlety he wins us to his point of view without
allowing us to suspect that he has expressed it.   A distinguished
critic has reproved Yeats for writing a magical poem, but the
poem has magic only in its façade.   And its object is not to praise

the dead for their superior knowledge. The other world appears to reveal the character of this one. In the guise of an invocation ceremony, Yeats utters a lament for human incompleteness.

This account of his rituals has necessarily called attention to the deliberate character of his art. Although he has powerful feelings to express, his poems are in no sense their 'spontaneous overflow'. The 'lyric cry' of Shelley is not his way. He gathers his intensity and force, which have hardly been equalled in modern verse, by creating, with the aid of symbol, myth, and ritual, patterns where thoughts and feelings find unexampled voice. There is nothing unplanned in his art ; its many surprises come from long preparation, like the discoveries of a great scientist.

Thus one of his most powerful ritualized moments is the rape of Leda by the swan, but the drafts of his poem about it are evidence that painstaking effort rather than a single flash of inspiration made it possible. If his mind had not constantly dwelled upon the rise and fall of civilizations, upon the 'divine influx' which began each new age, upon Leda as a parallel to Mary because her daughter, like Mary's son, changed the world, upon the terrible consequences of the begetting of Helen, he could never have written the poem. On the other hand, such preoccupations would have come to nothing if he had not decided to focus the poem upon the rape itself, in the description of which he could put all his passion, if he had not been familiar with the myth of Leda in literature and art, and if he had not found contemporary human feeling in the question on which the poem ends, whether power and knowledge can ever be united in life. And even when these elements had been joined, he had to revise again and again before he had submerged them in a completed poem. The first drafts, on which he worked in September 1923, are not vague like the first drafts of his early poems, but they are not sharply focussed :

> Now can the swooping godhead have his will
> Yet hovers, though her helpless thighs are pressed
> By the webbed toes ; and that all powerful bill
> Has suddenly bowed her face upon his breast.

> How can those terrified vague fingers push
> The feathered glory from her loosening thighs ?
> All the stretched body's laid in that white rush
> And feels the strange heart beating where it lies.
> A shudder in the loins engenders there
> The broken wall, the burning roof and Tower
> And Agamemnon dead. . . .
> > > Being so caught up
> Did nothing pass before her in the air ?
> Did she put on his knowledge with his power
> Before the indifferent beak could let her drop ?
> > > > > (Sept. 18, 1923)

Yeats evidently planned to centre the first quatrain on the god and the second on Leda. Only gradually did she assume more complete dominance of the scene if not of the situation :

> The swooping godhead is half hovering still
> Yet climbs upon her trembling body pressed
> By the webbed toes ; and that all powerful bill
> Has suddenly bowed her face upon his breast.
>
> The swooping godhead is half hovering still
> But mounts, until her trembling thighs are pressed
> By the webbed toes, and that all powerful bill
> Can hold her helpless body on his breast.
> How can those terrified vague fingers push
> The feathered glory from her loosening thighs ?
> All the stretched body's laid on that white rush
> And feels the strange heart beating where it lies.
> A shudder in the loins engenders there
> The broken wall, the burning roof and tower
> And Agamemnon dead.
> > > Being mounted so
> So mastered by the brute blood of the air,
> Did she put on his knowledge with his power
> Before the indifferent beak could let her go ?

Gradually the opening syntax became strained to give more dramatic shock :

> A swoop upon great wings and hovering still
> The bird descends, and her frail thighs are pressed
>
> A rush, a sudden wheel and hovering still. . . .

When the poem was first published in an ill-fated review, *To-Morrow*, in August 1924, Yeats had still not got the first lines as he wanted them :

> A rush, a sudden wheel, and hovering still
> The bird descends, and her frail thighs are pressed
> By the webbed toes, and that all-powerful bill
> Has laid her helpless face upon his breast.
> How can those terrified vague fingers push
> The feathered glory from her loosening thighs !
> All the stretched body's laid on the white rush
> And feels the strange heart beating where it lies ;
> A shudder in the loins engenders there
> The broken wall, the burning roof and tower
> And Agamemnon dead.
>   Being so caught up,
> So mastered by the brute blood of the air,
> Did she put on his knowledge with his power
> Before the indifferent beak could let her drop ?

But by 1925, in *A Vision*, he had at last brought the octave to the same perfection as the sestet :

> A sudden blow : the great wings beating still
> Above the staggering girl, her thighs caressed
> By the dark webs, her nape caught in his bill,
> He holds her helpless breast upon his breast.
> How can those terrified vague fingers push
> The feathered glory from her loosening thighs ?
> And how can body, laid in that white rush,
> But feel the strange heart beating where it lies ?
> A shudder in the loins engenders there
> The broken wall, the burning roof and tower
> And Agamemnon dead.
>   Being so caught up,
> So mastered by the brute blood of the air,

> Did she put on his knowledge with his power
> Before the indifferent beak could let her drop ?

The scene was now realized without the sacrifice of any of its implications for him. The new beginning lent an air of inevitability and destiny to the god's descent ; the historical results of the ritualistic begetting were epitomized in the images, at once physical and remote, of the beginning of the sestet ; and the personal, contemporary problem emerged in the final lines. The example gives evidence that to talk about Yeats's rituals, myths, and symbols, is to talk about his passions and ideas, in fact his whole being.

'I always feel', Yeats wrote to Sturge Moore, 'that my work is not drama but the ritual of a lost faith.' It is so in that it constantly returns to the past for support, but without slavishness, for it alters the past even as it re-creates it. The world of letters divides itself more and more readily in our time into those who regard the forms of life as ceaselessly changing and those who regard them as a series of repetitions or recurrences. Yeats sides vigorously with ritual rather than with helter-skelter change.

CHAPTER VIII

THE FINAL FORM OF EXPERIENCE

God guard me from those thoughts men think
In the mind alone ;
He that sings a lasting song
Thinks in a marrow-bone ;

From all that makes a wise old man
That can be praised of all ;
O what am I that I should not seem
For the song's sake a fool ?

I pray — for fashion's word is out
And prayer comes round again —
That I may seem, though I die old,
A foolish, passionate man.

YEATS, 'A Prayer for Old Age'

I. CULTIVATED EXTRAVAGANCE

WITH the abandon to which old age entitled him, and the control which a lifetime of painful development had made habitual, Yeats devoted his last years to sinking the shafts of his mines more deeply in the earth. In prose and verse, and sometimes in his life, he sought to violate standards of good behaviour which he had long known were superficial and self-betraying. Everything in life or letters that could be called 'outrageous' now delighted him. He embarrassed the Irish Academy by a speech announcing that, now that he had come to old age, he would become a butterfly, 'and fly, and fly, and fly'. But the other members should have realized that a Yeatsian butterfly is a symbol for natural, thoughtless life, and that even nature and thoughtlessness had been incorporated in his thematic and symbolic scheme, and were subject to rule. With the same outrageousness, Yeats made himself the first major poet to undergo a rejuvenation operation, and even dabbled for a brief period in the affairs of the parish fascist Blue Shirt organization of General O'Duffy. The astonishing result, not of these activities but of this frame of mind, was his final volumes of verse, *The King of the Great Clock Tower* (1934) and *Last Poems and Plays* (published posthumously in 1940), which rank with his best work.

Preoccupied with his desire to express what he felt to be a deepening sense of reality, Yeats sought sharper and sharper paradoxes to embody it. The poet's muses, he testified in his poem 'To Dorothy Wellesley', are the Furies. The absence of shock in his early work seemed to him one of its great defects, of which his new poems would not be guilty. An indication of his success is that for a time many critics responded to the final poetry chiefly by being shocked, finding his concern with sexuality unnatural and repulsive. To this charge T. S. Eliot replied that it is an honest expression of the mind of an old man when not 'subdued and disciplined by religion'. But for this defence Yeats would have challenged his advocate. The tenor of his work is that religion must embrace sexuality or be an empty dogmatism, life-destroying instead of life-furthering. He makes this point brazenly in 'A Stick of Incense', where Christianity is shown to have substituted a virgin womb and an empty tomb for the more inclusive phallicism of earlier religions. The result is that Saint Joseph is befuddled by the new creed and longs for the past, somewhat as in the poem 'The Magi' the old men were dissatisfied when their miraculous god died like a human being.

For propositions of this kind the Hermit Ribh serves Yeats as spokesman in *The King of the Great Clock Tower* volume. Ribh, the title of one poem declares, 'prefers an older theology', and, with the Smaragdine Tablet of Hermes Trismegistus rather than the Bible for authority, insists that even the gods participate in sexuality :

Natural and supernatural with the self-same ring are wed.
As man, as beast, as an ephemeral fly begets, Godhead begets Godhead,
For things below are copies, the Great Smaragdine Tablet said.

The same theme reanimates heaven in 'News for the Delphic

Oracle', a title whose amusing aggressiveness suggests the poem's content. Taking the oracle's description of Plotinus' arrival in the other world, which Porphyry has recorded, Yeats alters it by assigning heavenly copulation as wide a celestial area as that he allots to heavenly contemplation. His irony — for mockery plays a large part in these poems — reaches a climax in another lyric about Ribh, 'Ribh at the Tomb of Baile and Ailinn', where the hermit reveals that he reads his holy book in the light made by the physical contact of the two lovers who have become angels. The poem has the double function of bringing the angels, like the dead and the gods in the other poems, into a world corresponding to the human world, and of representing the monk, a half-serious parody of the poet, as detached from the reality which he describes, at the same moment both in and out of ecstasy, a scholar of the scene instead of a participant.

II. THE TENSIONS OF EAST AND WEST

But it would be a mistake to suppose that Yeats's last poems are the product merely of lustihood. His sexuality remains stylized and expressly symbolic. In old age he related it to another interest which, in a different poet, might have been purely intellectual, the attempt to establish the characters of Europe and Asia, and to bring together those elements that were reconcilable, while holding firmly apart those elements that were not. His study of the connections and disconnections of the two cultures began in boyhood. First he became convinced from Indian literature, and from the living proof of Mohini Chatterjee, that a man could live by doctrines wholly unacceptable to most Westerners. Then, under the influence of the Theosophical Society, which had headquarters at Adyar but most of its membership in Europe and America, and of Madame Blavatsky herself, Yeats dreamed of sowing the West with Eastern thought. Other literary men and artists shared his preoccupation. Laurence Binyon studied Chinese and Japanese painting ; Florence Farr and Sturge Moore studied Buddhism ; Ezra Pound and Arthur Waley translated

Japanese and Chinese; and in America T. S. Eliot applied himself to Sanskrit. Mainly through Pound's translations of the
Noh plays of Japan, Yeats discovered in 1914 the dramatic form
in which he was to couch almost all his remaining plays; in
Asian conventions he found a sense of life as ceremonial and
ritual, and of drama as august, formal, traditional. But his own
plays were adaptations, not copies, and attempted to infuse
Western passion into the narrow frame.

From about 1912 through 1915, Yeats felt his blood stirred,
as he said, by Rabindranath Tagore. Two qualities in Tagore's
work appealed to him : his poems were 'the work of a supreme
culture', yet seemed 'as much the growth of the common soil as
the grass and the rushes'; and he brought together purity and
passion in a way which seemed to Yeats un-European. The
Gitanjali or 'song offerings' for which Yeats wrote an introduction in 1915 were love poems but love poems of a special sort,
addressed to God. In them he discovered what European saints,
with the exception of St. Francis, lacked, and what Blake so
definitely possessed in far greater measure, a union of 'the cry of
the flesh and the cry of the soul'. In Tagore was no 'sanctity of
the cell and of the scourge', 'but a lifting up, as it were, into a
greater intensity of the mood of the painter, painting the dust and
the sunlight'. Tagore's attitude was summed up in the statement,
'And because I love this life, I know I shall love death as well'.
Eventually Tagore proved a disappointment to his admirers in
England as he grew prolix and revealed a want of English style,
but Yeats pondered the lessons of his work and kept an eye cocked
for other Eastern sages.

In 1931 he first met Shri Purohit, a swami who was visiting
England. At the time Purohit was working with Sturge Moore
on some translations, but after a quarrel Yeats took Moore's
place, and spent much time in the swami's company. Purohit
was a strange mixture of sensuality and asceticism in his personal
life, and philosophically seemed to occupy, like Tagore, some
intermediate place between a bias towards the soul and a bias
towards the body. He and Yeats went to Majorca for five

months in 1935 and translated the ten principal *Upanishads*, Yeats contributing the nuances of English prose to balance the swami's knowledge of Sanskrit. The poet also wrote an introduction to an autobiography written by Purohit's teacher, Bhagwan Shri Hamsa, and another to Purohit's translation of Patanjali's *Aphorisms of Yoga*. His poetry began to show signs of their association.

Yeats's view of Asia cannot be perfectly isolated, because it did not always mean the same thing to him. For the most part he conceived of Asia as having the positive values of simplicity, naturalness, prescribed duties, and tradition, and the negative attributes of formlessness, vagueness, immensity, abstractness, asceticism, and submissiveness which helped to make it the matrix from which everything has come. Europe, on the other hand, stood for history, measurement, flesh, metaphor, concreteness, and aggressiveness. Christianity, which, as Proclus said, brought with it a 'fabulous, formless darkness', was primarily Asiatic ; Greek and Roman civilization, and the civilization of the Renaissance, were primarily European.

His feelings towards Asia were mixed, and depended upon which aspects he was writing about. He was pleased to find that in 'The Song of Amergin', an ancient fragment of pagan Irish philosophy, the tone was Asiatic, and to feel that in ancient Ireland 'The old Irish poets lay in a formless matrix' (a word to which he now took a liking). Among modern Irish peasants, too, he saw 'much of Asia', and remembered that in his expeditions among the peasantry he and Lady Gregory had seemed to get down 'into some fibrous darkness, into some matrix out of which everything has come'. That the matrix was Asia, that his own culture was underlain by such a distant one, was part of the Asiatic fascination. In his introduction to the *Upanishads* he remarked that we have to discover in the East 'something ancestral in ourselves, something we must bring into the light before we can appease a religious instinct that for the first time in our civilization demands the satisfaction of the whole man'. It was as if Asia was part of the human soul and could therefore not be neglected. The conviction that the most ancient wisdom is probably the truest, which leads Eliot to quote the *Vedas* in *The Waste Land*, makes Yeats return again and again to Asia in his last years.

Nevertheless, only one poem, 'Lapis Lazuli', confronts Asia and Europe without representing them at odds with one another. This poem was written shortly after Yeats received a gift of a large piece of lapis lazuli 'carved by some Chinese sculptor into the semblance of a mountain with temple, trees, paths, and an ascetic and pupil about to climb the mountain'. He evidently began at once to think about its significance, and wrote to Dorothy Wellesley : 'Ascetic, pupil, hard stone, eternal theme of the sensual east. The heroic cry in the midst of despair. But no, I am wrong, the east has its solutions always and therefore knows nothing of tragedy. It is we, not the east, that must raise the heroic cry.' In the resulting lyric Yeats came to grips with the problem that makes our time so restless, the destruction of civilization which may be impending. In these circumstances have the poets the right to be gay ? Yeats proceeds to justify gaiety first in terms of the West and then of the East. The West is represented by the heroes of its tragedies :

> All perform their tragic play,
> There struts Hamlet, there is Lear,
> That's Ophelia, that Cordelia ;
> Yet they, should the last scene be there,
> The great stage curtain about to drop,
> If worthy their prominent part in the play,
> Do not break up their lines to weep.
> They know that Hamlet and Lear are gay ;
> Gaiety transfiguring all that dread.
> All men have aimed at, found and lost ;
> Black out ; Heaven blazing into the head :
> Tragedy wrought to its uttermost.
> Though Hamlet rambles and Lear rages,
> And all the drop-scenes drop at once
> Upon a hundred thousand stages,
> It cannot grow by an inch or an ounce.

This stanza is usually explained by references to prose passages in which Yeats maintains that 'The arts are all the bridal chambers of joy', but these too require explanation. His tragic heroes act upon an old theory of his : they play the tragic parts they have decided upon, and the moment of their actual death is the moment of their stage triumph, for death fuses them to their chosen image of themselves.[1] This is what they have aimed at and found, and in finding lost. This completion of their image is the moment of supreme joy, for at this moment, like the Norse god hung over an abyss as a sacrifice to himself, they simultaneously surrender and realize themselves, transcend their temporary being by becoming their timeless image, become immortal and die.

Now the poet turns to defend gaiety Asiatically. Seeing through the eyes of the three Chinese on the stone, he changes the perspective : we are no longer staring at a highlighted stage, but stand on a lofty mountain overlooking the world and the ages. From here the rise and fall of civilizations is no matter for pathos or female hysteria, but seems a necessary part of the scene. The three Chinese, like Nietzsche, find joy in eternal recurrence, a gaiety which rises stubbornly in the midst of full knowledge of sorrow :

> Every discoloration of the stone,
> Every accidental crack or dent,
> Seems a water-course or an avalanche,
> Or lofty slope where it still snows
> Though doubtless plum or cherry-branch
> Sweetens the little half-way house
> Those Chinamen climb towards, and I
> Delight to imagine them seated there ;
> There, on the mountain and the sky,
> On all the tragic scene they stare.

[1] There is a comparable idea in Gide, who comments in his *Journal* on January 3, 1892 : 'A man's life is his image. At the hour of death we shall be reflected in the past, and, leaning over the mirror of our acts, our souls will recognize *what we are*. Our whole life is spent in sketching an ineradicable portrait of ourselves. The terrible thing is that we don't know this ; we do not think of beautifying ourselves. We think of it in speaking of ourselves ; we flatter ourselves ; but later our terrible portrait will not flatter us. We recount our lives and lie to ourselves, but our life will not lie ; it will recount our soul, which will stand before God in its usual posture.'

> One asks for mournful melodies ;
> Accomplished fingers begin to play.
> Their eyes mid many wrinkles, their eyes,
> Their ancient, glittering eyes, are gay.

Under the tremendous pressure of the poet's mood, the lapis lazuli is made to yield the message of affirmation which he must have.

But Asia and Europe are usually less compatible. Europe could learn much from the East, but should not become Eastern. Yeats foresaw a dominantly Asiatic era to come with loathing. In Asia triumphant the vagueness and generalization which he had always hated would take on inter-continental proportions. Already in his last years he saw literature and life bent headlong towards the East. The school of Auden, Lewis, and MacNeice heralded an Asiatic era, he contended, for they had 'thrown off too much, as I think, the old metaphors, the sensuous tradition of the poets', and the masterpiece they might produce would be half-Asiatic. In the writings of Pound, Virginia Woolf, and Joyce, he thought he perceived a destruction of the conscious mind's intelligible structure, a loss of conscious control to the point almost of automatism,

. . . a philosophy like that of the *Samkara* school of ancient India, mental and physical objects alike material, a deluge of experience breaking over us and within us, melting limits whether of line or tint ; man no hard bright mirror dawdling by the dry sticks of a hedge, but a swimmer, or rather the waves themselves. In this new literature . . . man in himself is nothing.

He told Lady Gregory that the god of the new age would be a Buddha or Sphinx, both of them Asiatic symbols, for, as he had learned from Hegel, European civilization could not begin until Oedipus had destroyed the Asiatic sphinx which kept personality in bondage, and now the tables were to be turned, Oedipus himself to be destroyed. Against this fearful second coming Yeats called up the forces of Europe as if for some new Salamis. 'We must hold to what we have,' he asserted in *On the Boiler* (published after his death), 'that the next civilization may be born, not from a virgin's womb, nor a tomb without a body, not from a void, but of our own rich experience.' We must keep our 'freedom and form' lest the counter-Renaissance come 'not as an inspiration in the head, but as an obstruction in the bowels', as a self-abasing rather than self-ennobling influence. He had embodied the Asian point of view in the poem 'Meru', and he now wrote 'The Statues' as a European, performing an astonishing and masterful revaluation of past and present.

Yeats finds the genesis of Europe in the numbers of Pythagoras, which enabled the sculptors to carve their statues by exact measurements. He takes the occasion to defend an art which, like his own dramas, was said to lack character development :

> Pythagoras planned it. Why did the people stare ?
> His numbers, though they moved or seemed to move
> In marble or in bronze, lacked character.
> But boys and girls, pale from the imagined love
> Of solitary beds, knew what they were,
> That passion could bring character enough,
> And pressed at midnight in some public place
> Live lips upon a plummet-measured face.

That is, Greek boys and girls fell in love by seeing in each other's eyes the beauty of some statue of Phidias, which was itself not an emotional outpouring but the result of passion bounded by the most careful calculation :

> No ! Greater than Pythagoras, for the men
> That with a mallet or a chisel modelled these
> Calculations that look but casual flesh, put down
> All Asiatic vague immensities,
> And not the banks of oars that swam upon
> The many-headed foam at Salamis.
> Europe put off that foam when Phidias
> Gave women dreams and dreams their looking-glass.

The analogy to Yeats's own work was clear : it too concentrated system and number into what seemed like casual flesh. As he wrote to Ethel Mannin, his work was full of his 'private philosophy but there must [be] no sign of it ; all must be like an old faery tale'.   The artists, he declares, and not the Greek galleys at Salamis, defeated the Persian invaders by rejecting the formlessness of Asia.   As he said in prose,

There are moments when I am certain that art must once again accept those Greek proportions which carry into plastic art the Pythagorean numbers, those faces which are divine because all there is empty and measured.   Europe was not born when Greek galleys defeated the Persian hordes at Salamis, but when the Doric studios sent out those broad-backed marble statues against the multiform, vague, expressive Asiatic sea, they gave to the sexual instinct of Europe its goal, its fixed type.

In the third stanza of 'The Statues' Yeats describes how the Greek sculptors' image of man followed Alexander's armies into India. There it lost western energy and paradoxically gave a form to eastern passivity, which otherwise would have been formless. If Hamlet, nervous, desperate for knowledge, and full of self, embodies Europe, Buddha with empty eyeballs, rapt beyond passion or knowledge or self, embodies Asia.

> One image crossed the many-headed, sat
> Under the tropic shade, grew round and slow,
> No Hamlet thin from eating flies, a fat
> Dreamer of the Middle Ages.   Empty eyeballs knew
> That knowledge increases unreality, that
> Mirror on mirror mirrored is all the show.
> When gong and conch declare the hour to bless
> Grimalkin crawls to Buddha's emptiness.

Against this image of man, trivialized with a cat's name, and cringing before a god who denies form, comes the 'heroic cry' of the final stanza. In the Easter Rebellion of 1916, Patrick Pearse called on Cuchulain's spirit to rally the men fighting in the Post Office. This summons Yeats regarded as a summons not only of Cuchulain but of intellect, number, and measurement, the values of Europe, against the confusion of the modern world, which has become Asiatic everywhere:

When Pearse summoned Cuchulain to his side,
What stalked through the Post Office ? What intellect,
What calculation, number, measurement, replied ?
We Irish, born into that ancient sect
But thrown upon this filthy modern tide
And by its formless spawning fury wrecked,
Climb to our proper dark, that we may trace
The lineaments of a plummet-measured face.

His battle-cry to Irish poets in 'Under Ben Bulben' also insists
that 'Measurement began our might', and asserts that European
art from Egypt to Michelangelo had a goal of 'profane perfection'. It was threatened by the Persian fleet, then by Christianity
(which Yeats considers an Asiatic importation), and most recently
by other furious, levelling kinds of materialism, alike in being
without forms or ideals.

It is apparent that Europe and Asia were new representations
of the subjective and objective gyres, or rather, that they were
ways of regarding experience equivalent but not identical to
those that had gone before. Their importance to Yeats lay in
their being, unlike the gyres, established historical and geo-
graphical symbols. As he told Dorothy Wellesley, he felt that
one of the leading characteristics of all his verse except the earliest
was that it was inside history and time. Mallarmé had tried with
his metaphysical idea to escape from history, but Yeats, while
recognizing escape as an aspect of personality and reality to be
understood, had yoked his work to definite places and periods.

III. THE ULTIMATE STYLE

The brazenness and effrontery which gave increasing violence
to Yeats's later thought also affected his style. Once his definition
of style had been 'high breeding in words and in argument',
but he wanted now to achieve, within limits, occasional low
breeding.

His earlier stylistic liberations had never gone so far as to
permit the vocabulary he now developed, which included 'grand-
dad', 'belly', 'bum', 'rod', 'swop', 'swish', 'punk', 'bowels',
'randy', 'beanfeast', 'codger', 'leching', and 'warty'. Compound

words, which he had long avoided, now return to his verse, but the compounds are peculiar : 'man-picker Niam', 'great-bladdered Emer', 'leaf-sown, new-mown', 'pity-crazed', 'blood-dark', 'slumber-bound', or in the lines,

> Where but half-awakened Adam
> Can disturb globe-trotting Madam
> Till her bowels are in heat. . . .

The verse is full of arrogant imperatives and rhetorical questions, thicker than in the past. It has also an occasional exclamation, rare in Yeats's poetry :

> The gyres ! the gyres !   Old Rocky Face, look forth. . . .

> Hurrah for the flowers of Spring. . . .

> Ach, call me what you please !

> No !   Greater than Pythagoras. . . .

Incomplete sentences and unconventional grammar here and there lend immediacy and suddenness :

> Around me the images of thirty years. . . .

> No dark tomb-haunter once. . . .

> Many times man lives and dies
> Between his two eternities,
> That of race and that of soul,
> And ancient Ireland knew it all.

The continual thrusting beyond the rules is well suited to the unorthodox subject-matter.

Yeats also flouts more purely technical conventions. Like the Chinese artist, who paints bamboo shoots for ten years and wins the freedom of never having to look at a bamboo shoot again, Yeats knew that his long apprenticeship was over and that he had at last learned to his own satisfaction how to write. His mastery of his craft is nonchalant. Of the three sonnets in his last two volumes, the first, 'Meru', uses the standard Shakespearean rhyme scheme, but has as many as thirteen syllables in a line ; the second, 'A Crazed Girl', is still less orthodox, having only five rhymed lines, three of the remainder being altogether unrhymed and the other six connected only by assonance ; the third, 'High Talk', is in couplets and has lines fifteen syllables long. The mistake by which Yeats, in revising 'The Municipal Gallery Revisited', left one of the *ottava rima* stanzas a line short, could hardly have occurred at any other time in his life. Such unconscious carelessness was in keeping with his deliberate desire to give an impression of abandon. His rhyming is increasingly impatient ; the perfect rhyme is infrequent and usually employed for some special effect, imperfection of rhyme being almost the rule. He allows 'smooth' to rhyme with 'youth' and even, for a particular purpose, 'dance' with 'dance' in 'Sweet Dancer' ; another liberty he permits himself, which would have been out of the question a decade before, is to follow a couplet rhyming 'eye' and 'high' with one rhyming 'higher' and 'fire', as in 'High Talk'. Partly out of a desire to seem improvisatory and conversational, and partly out of a real nonchalance, he ends the twelve lines of 'Beautiful Lofty Things' with the following rhyming and unrhyming words : *head, crowd, out, back, tables, words, table, life, table, train, head, again.* He would not have permitted three lines ending in 'tables', 'table', and 'table' to remain in such close neighbourhood before *Last Poems.*[1] In general he prefers assonance and consonance to rhyme, probably because he secured in them effects more subtle and free ; in such devices, and in his syllabic variations on common rhythms, he took a satisfaction that must have been like that the aged Milton had in free verse, or, to take a contemporary example, like that which Eliot has in his line of four accents with the number of syllables indeterminate. But Yeats did not go as far as either of these, or as Blake either, and when, in his play *The Herne's Egg*, he experimented with Hopkins's sprung rhythm, he soon found himself returning to more traditional prosody.

[1] The ending of two successive lines of 'The Second Coming' (1919) in 'is at hand' is for a special incantatory purpose and not comparable.

The main characteristic of his late verse is a language that is confidently racy and apt, tolerates no dullness or flagging, and is capable of being exploited for both high and low subjects. This was an intensification of his previous medium, which even in his mellifluous early verse occasionally hit a note of great power, as in the last two of the three lines :

> But weigh this song with the great and their pride ;
> I made it out of a mouthful of air,
> Their children's children shall say they have lied.

The power was applied more steadily now, however, and to it he had gradually added a wit which became especially pronounced in his old age. Wit operates as a controlling force to give the poet his authority over even the most difficult subjects. He both beguiles and intimidates the reader with it. So, in the midst of matters of great moment, his attitudes are too rich to permit his earnestness to be unalleviated:

> Those that Rocky Face holds dear,
> Lovers of horses and of women, shall,
> From marble of a broken sepulchre,
> Or dark betwixt the polecat and the owl,
> Or any rich, dark nothing disinter
> The workman, noble and saint, and all things run
> On that unfashionable gyre again.

Perhaps only Yeats could venture to define the variety of darkness at this crucial moment in 'The Gyres' as 'betwixt the polecat and the owl'. With the same adroitness he neutralizes the 'hysterical women' in 'Lapis Lazuli', and thereby gives himself the right to contradict them :

> I have heard that hysterical women say
> They are sick of the palette and fiddle-bow,
> Of poets that are always gay,
> For everybody knows or else should know
> That if nothing drastic is done
> Aeroplane and Zeppelin will come out,

> Pitch like King Billy bomb-balls in
> Until the town lie beaten flat.

To begin with, the women are hysterical ; then, by omitting the articles before 'aeroplane' and 'Zeppelin', Yeats makes these mechanical demons sound exorcisable, and by comparing them to William of Orange's weapons at the Battle of the Boyne, with the king turned to 'Billy' and the bombs to 'bomb-balls' for pitching, he makes the hysteria of the women absurd. Detached from the poem, the reassurances he then offers are cold comfort, but in the context they are tenable and spectacular.

This rich, pungent language was now habitual with him. It demanded compact as well as felicitous phrasing, 'a strong driving force', he called it, in which passive verbs and undigested ideas could have no place. An excellent opportunity is afforded by some of his late revisions to see what he objected to and how he altered it. The revisions were not of his own work but of translations from the Irish made by Frank O'Connor. In Irish the poems were already simple, passionate, and often ironic ; O'Connor had kept their severe, unsentimental vigour. Occasional lines, however, seemed to Yeats either weak or out of key or somehow improvable, and he proposed a number of changes, some of which O'Connor accepted. The influence was reciprocal, since Yeats then borrowed from O'Connor phrases which turned into the lines,

> The lovers and the dancers are beaten into the clay. . . .

> Sing the lords and ladies gay
> That were beaten into the clay
> Through seven heroic centuries,

and

> His fathers served their fathers before Christ was crucified.

He also saw in the Irish poets a standard of directness and force close to his desire for his own verse. It is curious that, after using their work as background or subject-matter all his life, only in old age did Yeats begin to show any genuine resemblance to them. The evidence of the revisions is clear :

THE PRAISE OF FIUNN   (*Yeats's Revisions*)

Patrick you chatter too loud
   And lift your crozier too high
Your stick would be kindling soon,   It would lie low on the fire
   If my son Osgar were by.   If my son Osgar stood by.

    ·   ·   ·   ·

How could the Lord you praise   How could the God you praise
   And his mild priests singing a tune
Be better than Fiunn the fighter,   Be better than men of Fiunn,
   Generous, faultless Fiunn?   That faultless, generous man?

With never a spoken lie   By the honest strength of their hands
   Never a lie in thought   The Fenians' battles were fought,
In truth and the strength of their hands   With never a spoken lie,
   The Fenians' battles were fought.   Never a lie in thought.

There never sat priest in church   There never sat priests in church
   A tuneful psalm to raise   No matter what music there
Better spoken than these   Better spoken than these men
   Marred by a hundred frays.   For all their battle scars.

What you and your monks proclaim,   Whatever your monks have called
   The law of the King of Grace,
That was the Fenians' law
   His home is their dwelling place.   His place their dwelling place.

    ·   ·   ·   ·

OISIN   (*Yeats's Revisions*)

Yes and the teeth up here   Yes and these teeth up here
   Up in the ancient skull,   Up in this ancient skull,
Cracked the yellow nuts
   Tore the haunch of a bull.

    ·   ·   ·   ·

Yes and the eyes up here   Yes and these eyes up here
   Up in the ancient skull,   Up in this ancient skull,
Though they are dull tonight
   Once they were never dull.

    ·   ·   ·   ·

Yes and the legs below
  Nothing wearied them then,
Now they totter and ache
  A bundle of bones and skin.

Though now they race no more
  And all their glory is gone
Once they were quick to follow
  The shadow of golden Fiunn.

Yes and these legs below
  Nothing could weary them then,

Though they can run no more,

STORM AT SEA

A tempest on the plain of Lir
Bursts its frontiers far and near,
  And upon the mounting tide
  Wind and noisy winter ride—
Winter with his shining spear.

(Yeats's Revisions)

Breaks down its barriers far and near,

Winter throws a shining spear.

When the wind blows from the east
The wave is like a thing possessed,
  To the west it storms away
  To the wildest farthest bay
Where the light turns to its rest.

How are all those waves possessed,
  To the west they storm away

When the wind is from the north
The fierce and shadowy waves go forth
  While their crests snarl at the sky
  To the southern world they fly
To the confines of the earth.

Those dogs, the shadowy waves go forth
  And those dogs snarl at the sky

And the confines of the earth.

When the wind is from the west
Over waves of wild unrest
  To the east they thunder on
  Where the bright tree of the sun
Is rooted in the ocean's breast.

All those dogs that cannot rest
  To the east must thunder on

When the wind is from the south,
The waves, become a devil's broth
  Crash in foam on Skiddy's beach
  For Caladnets summit reach
And pound Limerick's grey-green mouth.

The waves turn to a devil's broth

.   .   .   .

O God who broods above the swell,
The storm and all its fears repel,
  Righteous captain of the feast,
  Save us from the killing blast
And guard us from tempestuous hell.

O God brooding above us all,

  Righteous captain of the blast,
  Save us from this killing beast
And from all else out of hell.
        [But Yeats suggests this stanza
                  be deleted.]

THE HERMIT'S SONG

(Yeats's Revisions)

A hiding tuft, a greenbarked yewtree,
  Holds the roof,
Dearest spot ! The oaktree guards me,
  Tempestproof.

  Spreads its roof,
An oak keeps this dear spot and me

. . . . .

Full of bounty, there's an apple
  Like an inn !
A fistful of a bush of hazel,
  Branching, green.

I can fetch an apple from a tree
  Like an inn
Or can fill my fist where hazels
  Block the scene.

A peaceful troop, a country gathering
  Pays a call,
And the foxes come to join them,
  Best of all.

Inquirers from the neighbouring country
  Pay a call,

To what feasts the woods invite me
  All about !
Water pure and herbs and cresses,
  Salmon, trout.

To what a diet the woods invite me

  Salmon and trout.

. . . . .

All a man could ask of comfort
  Round me grows
Haws and yewberries and strawberries,
  Nuts and sloes.

Hips and haws and strawberries,

And when summer spreads its mantle,
  There's a sight !
Marjoram and leeks and pignuts
  Green and bright.

Show green and bright.

. . . . .

Bees and beetles, nature's singers,
  Croon and strum,
Geese pass over, duck in autumn,
  Dark streams hum.

Bees and beetles, natural singers,

    .   .   .

In the year's most brilliant weather
  Heifers low
Through green fields, not harsh nor
    laboured,
  Tranquil, slow.

Through green fields, not driven and
    beaten,

    .   .   .

HUGH MAGUIRE

(Yeats's Revisions)

Too cold I think this night for Hugh,
I tremble at the pounding rain ;
  Alas that venomous cold
  Is my companion's lot.

Too cold this night for Hugh Maguire,

It is an anguish to my heart
To see the fiery torrents fall ;
  He and the spiky frost —
  A horror to the mind !

It brings an anguish to my heart

    .   .   .

Even the wild hare that haunts the
    wood,
Even the salmon in the bay,
  Even the wild bird, one grieves
  To think of now abroad.

One thinks of the hare that haunts the
    wood,
And of the salmon in the bay,

  To think they are abroad.

I mourn to think of Hugh Maguire
In a strange land at large tonight
  Flaunting the lightning's glare
  And clouds with fury filled.

Abroad in a strange land tonight
  Under the lightning's glare

Who in West Munster braves his doom,
And without shelter strides between
  The drenched and shivering grass
  And the impetuous sky.

In West Munster he braves his doom,

Cold on that tender blushing cheek
The fury of the springtime gales
  That toss the stormy bolts   That throw the stormy rays
  Of stars about his head.

I can scarce bear to conjure up
The smooth slope of his body crushed   The contours of his smooth body crushed
  This rough and gloomy night
  In its cold iron suit.   In their cold iron suit. ·

The gentle hand of rugged strife   The gentle war mastering hand
To the slim shaft of his cold spear
  By icy weather stitched —   Frozen by icy weather —
  Cold is the night for Hugh.

The low banks of the springtime streams   The low banks of the swollen streams
Are covered where the soldiers pass ;   Where the soldiers pass are swamped ;
  The meadows stiff with ice,
  The horses cannot feed.

And yet as though 'twould give him   And yet as though to bring him
    warmth   warmth
And call the brightness to his face
  Each limewhite wall becomes   A limewhite wall that he attacks
  A mass of billowing fire.   Sinks in a wave of fire.

The fury of the fire dissolves
The frost that sheets the tranquil eye,   The frost before his tranquil eye,
  And from his wrists the flame
  Thaws manacles of fire.

TO A BOY   (*Yeats's Revisions*)
·   ·

Words not salted with wit,   A word wit has not salted
  No nearer the heart than the lip   Is a word that stays at the lip
Are nothing more than wind,   And nothing more than wind,
  A puppy's insolent yelp.

·   ·   ·

STRAY VERSES   (*Yeats's Revisions*)

Love like heat and cold
  Pierces and passes soon,
Jealousy cleaves and clings   Jealousy pierces too
  Stuck to the marrowbone.   But stays in the marrowbone.

———

Conor, I vow   I vow that Conor
As little minds
Packing his poke
With Danish rings
As in the wood
At autumn's height   Than if they were apples
Tossing the russet   In the autumn wood
Apples down   God dropped on the ground
The king of Kings !   Where he stood.

Many of these creative alterations follow habits which Yeats had evolved long before, such as the eschewal of ''tis' or ''twould', the preference for 'this', 'that', or 'these' over the definite article, a special liking for expressions like 'hips and haws', and a reduction of inversions except where specially justified. There is a striking emphasis on verbs at the expense of other parts of speech, particularly of adjectives ; and on strong verbs at the expense of weak ones. He changes 'holds' to 'spreads', and 'becomes' to 'turns to', and changes 'Branching, green', to 'Block the scene'. The main direction is towards a freer flow and a stronger rhythm ; 'Salmon, trout' has to become 'Salmon and trout' to avoid the protrusive comma pause. 'A tuneful psalm to raise' was inverted and dull ; Yeats rewrote it as 'No matter what music there'. O'Connor's line, 'Dearest spot ! The oaktree guards me', was conventional ; with a quick turn of phrase Yeats made it nearly new, 'An oak keeps this dear spot and me' and compelled it to run without stopping into the following line, 'Tempestproof'.

The freer flow and stronger rhythm are concerns of Yeats in his own last poems. He winnowed out his subjunctives, made the suspension of his suspended sentences less breathtaking, and in every way established a plain-spoken world.

IV. BALLAD RHYTHMS

In simplifying his diction and style for the second time in his career, Yeats again found the ballad helpful. It led him to what he termed in his essay of 1902 on Spenser 'those great rhythms which move, as it were, in masses of sound'. It encouraged him to write in a bolder tone. He told O'Connor, 'You must always write as if you were shouting to a man across the street who you were afraid couldn't hear you, and trying to make him understand'. He could secure this effect by such ballad devices as making the syntax of successive lines the same, by writing in parallel groups of words or lines, and especially by verbal repetitions :

> All neighbourly content and easy talk are gone,
> But there's no good complaining, for money's rant is on.
> He that's mounting up must on his neighbour mount,
> And we and all the Muses are things of no account.
> They have schooling of their own, but I pass their schooling
>   by,
> What can they know that we know that know the time to
>   die ?
>   *O what of that, O what of that,*
>   *What is there left to say ?*

He carries over the same devices in subtler but still recognizable form in a poem that is not a ballad such as 'A Crazed Girl' :

> No matter what disaster occurred
> She stood in desperate music wound,
> Wound, wound, and she made in her triumph
> Where the bales and the baskets lay
> No common intelligible sound
> But sang, 'O sea-starved, hungry sea'.

His main borrowing from ballads was the refrain, which he had used fairly often in *The Winding Stair* (1933) but now inserted in about every third poem. The refrain occupies a strategic position. Frequently it takes the place of the emphatic symbols around which many of Yeats's poems were focussed, and like the symbol it is a focus of thought and emotion which is not explained. It embodies as a rule some traditional point of view.

Usually a Yeatsian refrain fulfils one of three functions. The first comes in poems such as 'John Kinsella's Lament for Mrs. Mary Moore' and 'The Three Bushes', where it epitomizes or jibes with the poet's theme and reinforces it by a more melodic corroboration than is possible in the rest of the stanza. Its relevance is not always immediately apparent; in 'Long-legged Fly' it at first seems mock-heroic or even bathetic :

> That civilization may not sink,
> Its great battle lost,
> Quiet the dog, tether the pony
> To a distant post ;
> Our master Caesar is in the tent
> Where the maps are spread,
> His eyes fixed upon nothing,
> A hand under his head.
> *Like a long-legged fly upon the stream*
> *His mind moves upon silence.*

But as the poem continues the refrain sets up a counter-sense ; it lends a fascinated intensity to the actions of genius, which individually must seem silent, slow, and trivial but in the end prove of the greatest consequence. The simile of the fly becomes steadily more apt each time it is repeated. In 'The Curse of Cromwell', the refrain which interrupts the recital of Cromwellian wrongs, and wrongs that have come after, is 'O what of that, O what of that, / What is there left to say ?', and these lines, which at first seem to remonstrate with the speaker for recalling old wrongs, are eventually seen to point out the indifference of the world to such wrongs and indignities ; by several reappearances, like glimpses of a train that approaches with an increasing roar, the refrain makes that indifference more galling and indefensible.

A second function of the refrain is to oppose instead of confirming the rest of the poem. Sometimes it does so by directly questioning what has been said, as when Plato's ghost, in 'What Then?', challenges the reality of the achievements about which the rest of the poem boasts:

> 'The work is done', grown old he thought,
> 'According to my boyish plan;
> Let the fools rage; I swerved in nought,
> Something to perfection brought';
> *But louder sang that ghost, 'What then?'*

Plato, whom Yeats now identified with his symbolic Asia, is a fitting spokesman to cast doubt upon the European world of appearances and events, of brilliant achievements and successes. Another instance is 'Colonel Martin', where the refrain, '*The Colonel went out sailing*', has literal meaning only in the first stanza, but by its later repetitions contributes an incongruous air of a child's harmless catch-tune to throw in glaring light a cruel and unhappy tale.

The third function of the refrain has mystery as its chief motive, although it may also combine with one of the other functions. '*How goes the weather?*', which is the burden of 'The O'Rahilly', suggests a password that O'Rahilly might have used, but we cannot be sure; and it also counterposes the trivial inquiry to the heroic actions of O'Rahilly during the Easter Rebellion. In 'The Apparitions', the area of mystery is wider:

> Because there is safety in derision
> I talked about an apparition,
> I took no trouble to convince,
> Or seem plausible to a man of sense,
> Distrustful of that popular eye
> Whether it be bold or sly.
> *Fifteen apparitions have I seen;*
> *The worst a coat upon a coat-hanger.*
>
> I have found nothing half so good
> As my long-planned half solitude,
> Where I can sit up half the night
> With some friend that has the wit

Not to allow his looks to tell
When I am unintelligible.
Fifteen apparitions have I seen;
The worst a coat upon a coat-hanger.

When a man grows old his joy
Grows more deep day after day,
His empty heart is full at length,
But he has need of all that strength
Because of the increasing Night
That opens her mystery and fright.
Fifteen apparitions have I seen;
The worst a coat upon a coat-hanger.

Yeats remarked in a late essay on Shelley that Shelley was unconsciously compelled to set up nightmare images to balance his
objects of desire. Here Yeats is doing the same thing. We might
infer that the worst apparition is the scarecrow image that the old
man has of his own death, a worse image than 'old clothes upon old
sticks to scare a bird' because its nothingness is emphasized by
the mechanical coat-hanger. Though this implication is not made
explicit, we know that the apparitions are related to the 'mystery
and fright' of approaching death, and contrasted with the old
man's joy; the poem's weirdness is due to the disembodied horror
of the image couched in mathematical precision.

The ballad form suited Yeats so well that he wrote a great
many poems in this *genre*, as he had not done since about 1890.
With Dorothy Wellesley he issued some of them, along with
hers, F. R. Higgins', and James Stephens', as *Broadsides* at the
Cuala Press. Mrs. Yeats began to worry that he would dissipate
his creative faculties in such work. But while some of them
might have given ground for anxiety — those, for example,
which relied on an easy patriotism, and the 'Three Marching
Songs', which oversimplified his political theories until they
sounded fascistic — most of the ballads conveyed complexity of
thought with simplicity of expression. They fulfilled his desire,
which became almost obsessive in old age, 'to think like a wise

man, but to express oneself like the common people'. In the narrative of 'The Three Bushes', for example, he found room for a symbolic dialogue of body and soul. He represented the hero of 'The Pilgrim' as pulled this way and that by drunkenness and by holiness, the flesh and the spirit, and evolving a curious middle ground. Even 'Colonel Martin', which purports to be merely a sardonic tale of an adulterous wife and her returning husband, is no plain ballad told only for the tale's sake, but serves as a perfect illustration of Yeats's conception of human nature. He did not write the poem until 1937, but he had told the story as early as 1910, when the *Evening Telegraph* of Dublin reported one of his lectures which contained it :

Mr. Yeats said the thing that was destroying the theatre in Ireland was the substitution of humanitarianism for artistic feeling. The business of art was the exposition of human nature in itself, making us delight in personality, in character, in emotion, in human life, when it is not troubled or persecuted by anything artificial. These things were being crushed away by all kinds of special interests. One man would spend his life in making money ; another man would spend his life on a mathematical problem. Human nature should not be merely endured ; it should keep its delight, its energy, and its simplicity. He believed that the countryman in Ireland, as the countryman who has kept his simplicity everywhere in the world, had kept his delight in human nature. In proof of this assertion the lecturer related a story which, he said, had been told him by a Galway shepherd, about a certain Colonel Martin, whose wife was unfaithful to him. Colonel Martin discovered his wife in the company of a wealthy neighbour. There were two revolvers on a table, but Colonel Martin did not like to take advantage of an unarmed man. He took other proceedings, and obtained two kegs of gold from the wealthy neighbour. He ordered his man, Tom, to put the kegs on the ass's back, and he went through the streets of Galway distributing the money amongst the poor. The wealthy man had men at every corner ready to attack Colonel Martin, but he could not attack a man who had been so good to the poor. At the end there was no money left, and the man, Tom, said his master would be in want before he died. And he was. That showed how the people delighted in a striking personality. It showed the mysterious love of that mysterious thing, human nature. When they could get free from the daily newspapers, from the rubbish, and get down to this rich soil, there could be a great artistic movement.

The Colonel, kind and cruel by turns, motivated by passions rather than Commandments, seemed to Yeats as to the Irish countryman more interesting and real than conventional heroes. This delight in caprice would have appeared reckless and unconscionable to Tennyson, but in Yeats it was a sign of imaginative gusto and acceptance of the fullness of life.

The atmosphere of the ballads and of the other last poems is not that of Milton, with 'calm of mind, all passion spent', or of Shakespeare, as he is usually considered to have manifested himself in his final plays. It is notable that Yeats did not share the usual notion of Shakespeare. 'The final reality of existence in Shakespeare's poetry is of a terrible kind', he told Stephen Spender, perhaps with his own in mind. His last poems have an effortless dignity and a blunt intolerance of any glossing over of the evils of the human condition. In 1926 he half ironically pictured himself as 'a sixty-year-old smiling public man', now he ironically assumed the role of 'the wild old wicked man'. This old man snorts, raves, prophesies, asserts, and mocks with less solemnity, less paraphernalia, and altogether, less ado than in the 'twenties and before. He concurs with Blake, 'Damn braces, bless relaxes'.

V. 'AN OLD MAN'S EAGLE MIND' AND ITS THEMES

But the energy is that of an old man, not of a young one. Over the poems lies, fittingly, the shadow of death. To match the tower which he had created years before to serve as symbol of his life he now creates a gravestone to commemorate his death in 'Under Ben Bulben', and writes his own epitaph for it. He is closer to friends in the grave than to the inadequate living. His thoughts often turn to religion and God, especially in *The King of the Great Clock Tower* volume, in which the Hermit Ribh replaces Crazy Jane as *persona*. This hermit's peculiar

religion is based as much on hatred as on love of God, and concentrates on the sensual rather than the spiritual side of celestial
life. Where Crazy Jane usually maintains that there is a spiritual
aspect to physical delight, Ribh defends the converse. In *Last
Poems* the wild old wicked man acknowledges the efficacy of
religious consolation but says he prefers 'the second-best', that
is, to 'forget it all awhile / Upon a woman's breast'. If Yeats
had lived he would have completed a second number of *On the
Boiler*, in which he proposed to attack all institutional religions.
But he would have attacked from the point of view of a partial
acceptor of all of them rather than of a sceptic.

In the way of old men, too, but also with a difference, Yeats
retraces the past, recapitulating everything. He returns to early
images, such as Oisin and Niamh whom he now ridicules, the
Countess Cathleen and Cuchulain whom he treats with sympathy, and to early friends and relatives. He reviews world
history in 'The Gyres', 'The Statues', and 'Under Ben Bulben',
and Irish history in a series of poems which centre on Parnell,
the Easter Rebellion ('The O'Rahilly', 'The Statues', 'Three
Songs to the One Burden'), and a new addition to the heroic
pantheon, Roger Casement.

Going over the past is always reinterpreting it too, now as
before. In 'The Circus Animals' Desertion' Yeats returns to
the theme of 'Byzantium', the relation of the images of poetry
to experience. He calls up some of his early characters partly to
show the imaginative power he then had, which he now feels is
lost, and partly to indicate how those characters arose out of his
life. He attests with bitterness what in 'Byzantium' he had
indicated with more liking, that poetic images grow in 'pure
mind' but have their origin in the welter of experience. Then,
under cover of lamenting the failure of his imaginative capacity,
Yeats exalts it once more as the pride of life. Other poems also
revisit old scenes. In 'The Municipal Gallery Revisited', a
nostalgic title, he celebrates his friends as he had frequently done
in the past; but now he widens the context to include Irish
history and art and letters in the same poem, so that all —

political and artistic heroes — appear as partners in the creation of an Ireland which the poets have imagined, 'beautiful and gay'. Perhaps even more daring is the way that, in 'Parnell's Funeral', the death of Parnell is described as if it were the death of some pagan god, and the ancient rite of eating the hero's heart to obtain his qualities is introduced metaphorically to explain the course of Irish history after Parnell's death.

In so recapitulating and amplifying old themes and recollections, Yeats does not spare himself. Always a man of conscience if not of conventional virtue, he reviews his life and asks himself directly, in 'The Man and the Echo', and indirectly elsewhere, remorseless questions :

> All that I have said and done,
> Now that I am old and ill,
> Turns into a question till
> I lie awake night after night
> And never get the answers right.
> Did that play of mine send out
> Certain men the English shot ?
> Did words of mine put too great strain
> On that woman's reeling brain ?
> Could my spoken words have checked
> That whereby a house lay wrecked ?
> And all seems evil until I
> Sleepless would lie down and die.

Other poems, 'An Acre of Grass', 'What Then ?', 'The Spur', 'Are You Content ?', and on a more cosmic level, 'Meru', rake over the poet's achievements, and man's, without finding any cause for satisfaction. As always Yeats asserted a consonance between the state of the world, the state of the Irish nation, and his personal plight. In the name of the past, which he casts into legend, or of an imagined standard, he berates the present ; and he alternately hopes for a revolution to turn the tide or damns the revolutionaries as 'beggars on horseback', since they do not fulfil his dream.

The quality which is always absent from the poems is smug-

ness. In the last poem he wrote, 'The Black Tower', he returned
to his old tower symbol, but made it a rampart in the last stages
of a battle, manned by resolute but hopeless men-at-arms. Only
their old cook, who catches 'small birds in the dew of the morn',
predicts that their king will yet come to relieve his garrison. The
cook may be fairly safely presumed to be the poetic imagination,
subsisting now (in old age) on small fare, and the men-at-arms
the practical, logical part of the mind, which considers its com-
rade, the cook, 'a lying hound'. The king is the epitome of all
dreams, and the enemy, who counsels expediency and 'realism',
the epitome of dream-shatterers. The tower's defenders may
be fools, an idea which haunts the hero of Yeats's late play, *The
Herne's Egg*, but they keep their oaths and will die steadfast.

A refusal to surrender anything is a common theme in Yeats's
last poems; their tenor is not Schopenhauerian even if the tower
is black. Whenever they question whether life has any meaning
or purpose, their own vitality and vehemence argue against their
doubts. Through the poems run the stalwart and daring horse-
man, the eagle (and Yeats was himself called 'the eagle' *en famille*),
tall dames, Malachi Stiltjack, and the great human figures carved
by Phidias and carved and painted by Michelangelo, all a little
more than life size. The old men in these poems sometimes
lament their loss of virility; they do not impugn virility's value.

Nor can they abide sentimentality. They know too much to
give way to easy feelings. The late poems of Michelangelo,
which also mourn physical decrepitude, are much less tough than
those of Yeats. A Yeats notebook, kept late in 1934, reveals
some unpublished love poems which indicate how a near-
sentimental theme grew hard and definite:

THEME FOR A POEM

All day you flitted before me
Moving like Artemis
I longed to clasp your knees in worship
When I sat down to rest you stood beside me as a child.
My eyes dimmed with tears
O beloved come to me when the night thickens

That I may hope [to end] in the bed's friendship
This heart-breaking inequality.

When old Pythagoras falls in love

Life was running out of these
Generous eyes on men you cast
I like other ageing men
Sat and gazed upon a past
In seeming all compounded of
Lost opportunities in love.

O how can I that interest hold !
What offer those attentive eyes ?
Mind grows young, this body old
When half closed that eyelid lies
A sort of sudden glory shall
About my stooping shoulders fall.

An age of miracle renew
Let me be loved as though still young
Or fancy that the story's true
When my brief final years are gone
Then shall be time to live away
And cram those open eyes with day.

Portrayed before his eyes
Implacably lipped,
It seemed that she moved,
It seemed that he clasped her knees.
What man so worshipped
When Artemis roved ?

He sat worn out and she
Kneeling seemed to him
Pitiably frail ;
Lover anxiety
Made his eyes dim
Made his heart fail

Then suffered he heart ache
Driven by love and dread

> Alternate will
> A winding pathway took ;
> In love's levelling bed
> All gyres lie still.
>
> (Dec. 27 [1934])

The comparison of the woman to Artemis, at first unconvincingly hyperbolical, is made more indirect and casual as the poem develops. The old man has no illusions about himself : her eyelid must be half-closed before 'a sort of sudden glory' may fall about his 'stooping shoulders'. He pretends to no certain belief in immortality, only wishing to 'fancy that the story's true'. The stilling of the gyres by love is a hard-bitten image without a shade of sentimentality. Yeats's manner here is as fully 'twentieth-century' as in his youth it had seemed 'nine-teenth-century'.

A poet so conscious of his place in literature and history might be expected to leave a testament. Yeats does not offer a set of fixed positions even at the end of his life. His contempt is clear for the 'unremembering hearts and heads' of the tradition-less *arrivistes* who more and more dominate the world. But 'in that endless research into life, death, God, that is every man's revery', he expresses himself with the indirection of a Zen Buddhist, and offers the conclusion, which must be examined later, that 'Eternity expresses itself through contradictions'. So in *On the Boiler* he rages against European culture: 'Of late I have tried to understand in its practical details the falsehood that is in all knowledge, science more false than philosophy, but that too false'. But he then modifies his stand : 'Yet, unless we cling to knowledge, until we have examined its main joints, it comes at us with staring eyes'. And if we drive it away, he says, we become Asiatic, that is, worshippers of what is undifferentiated. We must differentiate, but acknowledge the tentativeness of our results : 'I want to make my readers understand that explanations of the world lie one inside another, each complete in itself, like those perforated Chinese ivory balls'.

Against this background we can review some of his earlier

themes to discover whether they had, as a recent critic has suggested, through dint of repetition become beliefs. His essays in *Wheels and Butterflies* (1934) contain some of his most revealing testimony about his state of mind. His defence of reincarnation, for instance, is scarcely that of a believer :

I suggest to the Cellars and Garrets that though history is too short to change either the idea of progress or the eternal circuit into scientific fact, the eternal circuit may best suit our preoccupation with the soul's salvation, our individualism, our solitude.

Even on the assumption that the eternal circuit exists, he is still unwilling to assert finally that escape from it is impossible :

There is perhaps no final happy state except in so far as men may gradually grow better ; escape may be for individuals alone who know how to exhaust their possible lives, to set, as it were, the hands of the clock racing. Perhaps we shall learn to accept even innumerable lives with happy humility — 'I have been always an insect in the roots of the grass' — and putting aside calculating scruples be ever ready to wager all upon the dice.

Yet, while he admits uncertainty, he also insists that we must avoid at all costs the chaos of doubt. While there is considerable humour in his discussion of Ptolemy's Great Year of 36,000 ordinary years and its basis in the procession of the equinox, there is also serious purpose :

. . . Because of our modern discovery that the equinox shifts its ground more rapidly than Ptolemy believed, one must, somebody says, invent a new symbolic scheme. No, a thousand times no ; I insist that the equinox does shift a degree in a hundred years ; anything else would lead to confusion.

We must return to the rationale of such affirmations later.

His main preoccupation in the poetry of his last years was not with these subjects but with death. Two attitudes towards it especially engrossed him. The first is that death is man-made and illusory : 'The grave diggers', *On the Boiler* announces, 'have no place to bury us but in the human mind'. He puts this more spectacularly in 'Under Ben Bulben' :

Whether man die in his bed
Or the rifle knocks him dead,
A brief parting from those dear
Is the worst man has to fear.
Though grave-diggers' toil is long,
Sharp their spades, their muscles strong,
They but thrust their buried men
Back in the human mind again.

This passage is not to be taken as the whole-hearted view of Yeats, however, but only of 'Under Ben Bulben'. He was also working out another conception more difficult to explain, which we have observed in 'Lapis Lazuli'. His paraphrase, in a letter to Ethel Mannin of October 9, 1938, expands on it :

According to Rilke a man's death is born with him and if his life is successful and he escapes mere 'mass death' his nature is completed by his final union with it. Rilke gives Hamlet's death as an example. In my own philosophy the sensuous image is changed from time to time at predestined moments called *Initiationary* [sic] *Moments* (your hero takes ship for Bordeaux, he goes to the Fair, he goes to Russia and so on). One sensuous image leads to another because they are never analysed. At the *critical* moment they are dissolved by analysis and we enter by free will pure unified experience. When all the sensuous images are dissolved we meet true death. Franz will follow the idea of liberty through a series of *initiatory* moments — (1) Spain and then somewhere else but will never I think analyse the meaning of 'liberty' nor the particular sensuous image that seems to express it and so will never meet true death. This idea of death suggests to me Blake's design (among those he did for Blair's Grave I think) of the soul and body embracing. All men with subjective natures move towards a possible ecstasy, all with objective natures towards a possible wisdom.

What is important to notice is that the process of life and death is like the process of making a poem ; that too must begin with a series of sensuous images, which are dissolved at the critical moment by analysis, and the whole of image and idea formed as pure unified experience. The esthetic process becomes of the utmost consequence as a symbol of the life process, although the life process can also be taken as a symbol of the esthetic one.

All images can be dissolved only after the most painful and rigorous self-examination ; this moment of completeness, of perfection, of Unity of Being, is the moment of death. The dirty slate, says 'The Man and the Echo', has been cleaned off :

> There is no release
> In a bodkin or disease,
> Nor can there be work so great
> As that which cleans man's dirty slate.
> While man can still his body keep
> Wine or love drug him to sleep,
> Waking he thanks the Lord that he
> Has body and its stupidity,
> But body gone he sleeps no more,
> And till his intellect grows sure
> That all's arranged in one clear view,
> Pursues the thoughts that I pursue,
> Then stands in judgment on his soul,
> And, all work done, dismisses all
> Out of intellect and sight
> And sinks at last into the night.

Death is the final stage of the purgative process for the man who has dared to face himself. This thought girds the loins of the old man of 'The Apparitions', who speaks of death in sexual images and goes forth like Antony to meet darkness as a bride, with passion and befitting fear.

Life being a preparation for its end, Yeats saw his own approaching death as a necessary part of the heroic ritual. 'It seems to me', he wrote Lady Elizabeth Pelham a few days before he died, 'that I have found what I wanted. When I try to put all into a phrase I say "Man can embody truth but he cannot know it". I must embody it in the completion of my life.' There would soon be that dissolution of sensuous images for him ; the moment was almost come for what he elsewhere symbolized as the fusion of mask and face, of anti-self and self, of desire and attainment, of choice and chance, of image and idea. There would be no tragic illumination in the form of communicable knowledge, but heaven would blaze into his head.

Welcome as this conception of death was, Yeats was not one to leave it unquestioned even when his breath was failing him. As the man says to his echo in one of the last poems,

> O Rocky Voice,
> Shall we in that great night rejoice?
> What do we know but that we face
> One another in this place?

Brute honesty forced the poet to say this too. For his loyalty was not to a given conception of life or death, but to an art which would be always personal and honest, and would strive to put everything down.

CHAPTER IX

THE ART OF YEATS: AFFIRMATIVE CAPABILITY

Long have I swonk with anxious assay
To finden out what this hid soul may be,
That doth herself so variously bewray
In different motions.

HENRY MORE, *Psychathanasia*

I. VARIETIES OF THE IMAGE

GOETHE remarked, in a phrase Yeats liked to quote, that the poet must know all philosophy, but keep it out of his work. Yeats's notion was not to exclude philosophy, but to admit it on his own terms. He came to study it through its dingy back entrances, those cults which W. H. Auden has appropriately termed 'Southern Californian', and at first he saluted more reputable thinkers with something of the reluctance of an officer of another service. But in later life he investigated them carefully to find parallels between his thought and theirs. In the nineteen-twenties and 'thirties especially, he read fairly widely in Plato, Plotinus, Croce, Whitehead, Russell, Hegel, G. E. Moore, and others, searching out whatever he could find on the relation of the antinomies, on the connection between the sphere of reality and the gyres of illusory appearance, on subjectivism and kindred subjects.

During the middle 'twenties he carried on a controversy by correspondence with Sturge Moore and indirectly with G. E. Moore, the philosopher, whom Sturge often consulted before replying. To the brothers' annoyance, he took a resolutely incorrigible position in the argument, offering as his chief exhibit 'Frank Harris's cat'. As he explained, 'Ruskin, according to Frank Harris, saw a phantom cat at the end of the room and

stooped to fling it out of the window. That cat may have had
more significant form than the house cat, displayed all cat nature
as if it were the work of some great artist. . . .' Moore demanded
that he allow some distinction between an illusion and a fact;
Yeats as resolutely refused. In a letter of February 5, 1926 [?],
he strongly fortified his contention :

The Lit Sup this week — page 27 col 2 — divides possible beliefs
about the nature of the external world as follows —

(1) Everything we perceive 'including so called illusions exists
in the external world'. (Ruskin's cat and the house cat are real.)

(2) Nothing can exist that is not in the mind as 'an element of
experience'. (Neither Ruskin's cat nor the house cat is real.)

(3) There is a physical world which is independent of our minds —
'real' — but we can only know it through 'representations' that are
part of our minds and quite unlike it. . . .

(1) Always fascinated me for I learned it from a Brahmin [Mohini
Chatterjee] when I was eighteen and believed it till Blake drove it out
of my head. It is early Buddhism and results in the belief still living
in India, that all is a stream which flows on out of human control —
one action or thought leading to another. That we ourselves are
nothing but a mirror and that deliverance consists in turning the
mirror away so that it reflects nothing. The stream will go on but we
do not know.

(2) This is Zen Buddhism. Shen-hsiu said — so Waley's 'Introduction to the Study of Chinese Painting' page 221 — 'Scrub your
mirror lest the dust dim it' — I shorten the sentence — but Hui-nēng
replied 'Seeing that nothing exists how can the dust dim it'. Zen art
was the result of a contemplation that saw all becoming through
rhythm a single act of the mind.

Russell and his school cannot escape from the belief that each man
is a sealed bottle. Every man who has studied psychical science by
watching his own life knows that we share emotion, thought and
image. . . .

(2) This seems to me the simplest and to liberate us from all
manner of abstraction and create at once a joyous artistic life.

He chooses, it will be noticed, that interpretation of the external
world which gives the mind autonomy, while at the same time

insisting that no one's mind is isolated. His choice is largely pragmatic, the proof of the philosophy being its adaptability to poetry and its power to free the mind from abstractions. The first belief is too humiliating to man to be satisfactory ; it denies control of the mind over the objects it perceives and grants them independent existence. The third, says Yeats, 'has to meet all the arguments that have been pressed by idealists and realists alike against a "physical substratum" '. It, too, renders the mind half-helpless before an unfathomable external world. On the other hand, the second theory frees the poet, and the mind, from subservience ; the farthest-fetched illusions and fantasies are as valid as what others call sense data. While this theory seems to offer no differentiation among kinds of mental activity, it has the great merit of assuring full scope for unconventional ways of seeing and reporting.

He does not finally reject the first and third theories, or finally accept the second. He develops in his verse attitudes which are more subtly gradated. From them we may elicit a different classification, more personal to Yeats. He saw the problem somewhat in this way : in perception, we know, the image of an object is conveyed from the retina of the eye to the brain. This image may be taken as conforming quite closely to the perceived object. But such a view is naïve ; one need not be an idealist to appreciate that the image is always inadequate, partly because of failures of perspective, but also because of the peculiarities of our experience which affect our sight. Taking account of these objections, we may say of the image, in a second aspect, that it represents the object but does so with the superficial modifications induced by our angle of vision and our personal bias.

But it is also possible to hold that the objects are more than superficially modified, that they are, in fact, changed fundamentally so that they bear little resemblance to the objects as they might appear to a hypostasized neutral and impartial eye. For example, and the example is Yeats's, the mother can never see her son with detachment ; her imaginative perception alters, often almost beyond recognition, the object perceived. We may push beyond this third position to a fourth, and say that the imaginative eye not merely alters the object it perceives, but creates the object. For instance, the poet invents something which he calls love, and everyone rushes to try it out. The difficulty is to see how an image might be shared in common, instead of being limited to its creator. Why should there not be as many external worlds as there are imaginative men to create them ? Yeats recognized this problem. He conceived of a corporate imagination which he called *Anima Mundi* or *Spiritus Mundi*. It is this which creates and stores archetypes, and the man who is able to let his imagination fuse with this corporate imagination has all the images ever wrought by men available to him as well as the power to create new ones. Because *anima mundi* is corporate all men participate in it a little and can respond to its images.

Yeats was especially drawn to this fourth position, the most radical ; but he did not finally commit himself to it or to any one of the others. His steadfast commitment was rather to a concern with the tensions of all four positions. After 1917, and especially from 1924 on, the nature of the image is central to many of his finest poems.

II. IMAGES IN OPERATION

'Byzantium' is a dramatic example of Yeats's handling of the image, and a difficult one. At first the poet appears to distinguish between two meanings of the word. In the beginning stanza, 'The unpurged images of day recede'. These day-time images, which the poet so immediately dismisses, are apparently the ordinary objects of experience which make up the external world. Only at the end of the poem do we learn that they are made of the same stuff as the night-time images, one of which he now proceeds to invoke :

> Before me floats an image, man or shade,
> Shade more than man, more image than a shade.

Such images seem at first to be far removed from life, since they are identifiable neither with the living man nor his ghostly substitute.

How may the poet grasp these images, as he must do if his poetry is to go below the superficies of day ? Yeats answers with two powerful affirmations :

> For Hades' bobbin bound in mummy-cloth
> May unwind the winding path ;
> A mouth that has no moisture and no breath
> Breathless mouths may summon. . . .

Hades' bobbin is the soul, which comes from the underworld and eventually returns there until its rebirth. In life it winds up the mummy-cloth of experience, a funereal term used because in the poem life is paradoxically regarded as a surrender of the soul's freedom and therefore as a kind of imprisonment or death. On returning to Hades the soul unwinds the cloth — 'the winding path' of nature — like a bobbin unwinding thread. But, says the poet, even during life, at moments of 'breathless' inspiration, we escape from ourselves and our past and summon the deathless, lifeless image which 'has no moisture and no breath'.

> I hail the superhuman ;
> I call it death-in-life and life-in-death.

From the point of view of this life, such images are dead ; but from a more detached vantage-point, it is they that are immortal, and the living who have no genuine life.

In the next stanza the poet's eye fastens on another super-human image; by ecstatically defining it as 'miracle, bird, or golden handiwork', he locates it more precisely in the world of art. He thinks of it as having a bird's shape, and as either crowing like the cocks of Hades or scorning other birds and life. Yeats had learned from Eugénie Strong's *Apotheosis and After Life* that the cock, as herald of the sun, became 'by an easy transition the herald of rebirth' on Roman tombstones. Since in this poem he accepts reincarnation, he is distinguishing here between the birds that sing the common strain of the continuing cycle of human lives and those that scorn the cycle and sing only of escape from it ; here were the two directions of his own art.

There follows a sudden revelation of the process by which such images are hammered out, by the Byzantine smithies of the imagination, into their purest form :

> At midnight on the Emperor's pavement flit
> Flames that no faggot feeds, nor steel has lit,
> Nor storm disturbs, flames begotten of flame,
> Where blood-begotten spirits come
> And all complexities of fury leave,
> Dying into a dance,
> An agony of trance,
> An agony of flame that cannot singe a sleeve.

Begotten by the living, they have to be immortalized by fire. Some aspects of their perfected state are clarified in notes which Yeats made for *A Vision* two years before writing 'Byzantium' :

> At first we are subject to Destiny . . . but the point in the Zodiac where the whirl becomes a sphere once reached,[1] we may escape from the constraint of our nature and from that of external things, entering upon a state where all fuel has become flame, where there is nothing but the state itself, nothing to constrain it or end it. We attain it always in the creation or enjoyment of a work of art, but that moment though eternal in the Daimon passes from us because it is not an attainment of our whole being. Philosophy has always explained its moment of moments in much the same way ; nothing can be added to it, nothing taken away ; that all progressions are full of illusion, that everything is born there like a ship in full sail.[2]

By equating the perfection of the afterlife with every metaphysical perfection the philosophers have conceived and with the perfection of art wrought 'in nature's spite', Yeats avoids mere estheticism and justifies the description in 'Byzantium' which treats the passage of the spirits of the dead to the other world and their purification there as synonymous with the purgative process

---

[1] In his poem 'Chosen', Yeats writes : 'The Zodiac is changed into a sphere'.

[2] Compare 'Old Tom Again' : 'Things out of perfection sail, / And all their swelling canvas wear. . . .'

which a work of art undergoes. These processes are among
those which Yeats makes equivalent and symbolical of one
another.

But the fires of the imagination have a characteristic which
distinguishes them from the fires of this world : they burn and
do not burn.   They are all-powerful to purge images of any
experiential dross, but impotent to singe a sleeve. In a position
of prominence in the poem, the last line of the above stanza,
Yeats casts one of the many backward glances in his poetry,
directing it here towards the life of action that the spirit or image
is transcending.   At the very moment that he heralds the purgative process, he reminds us that the purgation can occur only
outside action, for there it has no power. The same reflection
causes him, at the end of the poem, to express not his admiration
for the completed work, as might be expected, but his wonder
at the spawning images, covered with the mire of experience, in
which the work began :

> Marbles of the dancing-floor
> Break bitter furies of complexity,
> Those images that yet
> Fresh images beget,
> That dolphin-torn, that gong-tormented sea.

Ecstatic before the perfection of the creative process, the poet
still yields a little to the fascination for the imperfect and unpurged images not yet arrived at Byzantium.

For Yeats is more the poet of the sea torn by sexuality and
tormented by time than the poet of the perfect moment. He frequently represents himself as on the verge of renouncing those
poetic vows which have kept him from the life of action, as in a
letter to Ethel Mannin of November 15, 1936, 'All my life it has
been hard to keep from action, as I wrote when a boy, "To be not
of the things I dream"'.   To write his poems he had reluctantly
'brayed my life in a mortar', he reported, when he was less than
twenty-four, to Katharine Tynan. His anxiety over this dilemma
lent poignancy to the otherwise glib antithesis, 'The intellect of

man is forced to choose / Perfection of the life or of the work'.
The same undercurrent, of a reaction from perfection, that
appears in 'Byzantium', appears in many other poems, notably
'Vacillation', 'The Grey Rock', and 'Meditations in Time of
Civil War'. In the last, after puzzling over whether he should
have devoted his life to poetry or to action, he concludes :

> . . . the abstract joy,
> The half-read wisdom of daemonic images,
> Suffice the ageing man as once the growing boy.

These lines were probably written with Wordsworth's 'Ode on
the Intimations of Immortality' in mind, and they illustrate the
difference between the two poets.   For Yeats claims no progression in philosophical insight from childhood to maturity ;
at neither period does the poet reflect calmly or with the 'philosophic mind'.   Daemonic images are with him in old age as in
boyhood.   And the word 'suffice' has a peculiar Yeatsian irony
about it : at no time in the poet's life have his images fully contented him, for his urge to action has always been thwarted by
his stronger impulsion to art.   This latent 'horreur des lettres' is
extremely un-Wordsworthian.

The distinction between day-time images, which may be
identified with the objects of the external world, and night-time
images, the objects of imaginative perception, recurs in part of
Yeats's poem, 'The Tower'.   The second section of the poem
tells of a peasant girl who was so highly praised for her beauty
by a song that farmers jostled one another at the fair to catch a
glimpse of her.   But, says the poet, it was the song which con-
ferred this beauty upon her, which drove men mad by rendering
the confusion or rather, fusion, of reality and imagination inextricable. The supreme art is one in which this fusion is accomplished, even though it may cause havoc in prosaic terms ('And
one was drowned in the great bog of Cloone'). Yeats does not
shirk the dangers because he recognizes the splendours of the
imagination.

In search of further authority he calls for advice upon Hanrahan. Hanrahan was a character of his own invention, and in treating him as an adviser Yeats implies first that Hanrahan, through being an image and unalloyed by actual experience, may know the secrets of *Anima Mundi* and of existence; and second, that the poet, by mustering up the creative power to describe Hanrahan's exploits and even his death, may with as much right follow him beyond the grave:

> Old lecher with a love on every wind,
> Bring up out of that deep considering mind
> All that you have discovered in the grave,
> For it is certain that you have
> Reckoned up every unforeknown, unseeing
> Plunge, lured by a softening eye,
> Or by a touch or a sigh,
> Into the labyrinth of another's being.

He asks Hanrahan, so experienced in love as to be called affectionately 'old lecher', whether the imagination is most possessed by the woman won or the woman lost. Clearly it is by the latter. Even the memory of an ideal image, lamentably not pursued, is enough to blot out the sun, and so to stand as another example, though again a painful one, of the passionate mind's dominion over a world that only seems to have independent existence.

The poet then dismisses Hanrahan to make way for an even more violent proposition. That rash imaginative power which could stir men beyond the possibilities of sight and touch, or create out of air beings like Hanrahan, who in turn are possessed by it, is the primal force which engenders the world. Now Yeats used Plato and Plotinus as his whipping boys, and attacked them as 'all transcendence'. Later he admitted that they did not deserve this designation, but he evidently considered it accurate enough to keep them as symbolic targets:

> And I declare my faith:
> I mock Plotinus' thought
> And cry in Plato's teeth,
> Death and life were not

Till man made up the whole,
Made lock, stock and barrel
Out of his bitter soul,
Aye, sun and moon and star, all,
And further add to that
That, being dead, we rise,
Dream and so create
Translunar Paradise.[1]

These remarkable declarations are not the blend of night-time
and day-time images, of moon and sunlight into 'one inextricable
beam', that Yeats desired earlier in the poem, but rather a forced
merger of all things into night-time images created by the human
imagination. In the poem 'Death', written two years later, he
would say again, 'Man has created death'. His subjectivism is
a dramatic cry of defiance against those who would denigrate
man or subject him to abstractions like death, life, heaven or hell,
God, Plotinus' One, Plato's Good or eternal ideas. Humanism
rushes to the point of solipsism ; rather than concede anything
to the opposition, it erects man as not only the measure but also
the creator of all things. Yeats utters his assertions in part
because they are not acceptable, out of an obstinacy which he
wants to be as mulish, and as heroic, as he can make it.

At the end of the 'twenties Yeats thought he had found an
ally for his most extreme positions in Berkeley. Before Berkeley
became Bishop of Cloyne he had 'proved', Yeats decided, that
'the world was a vision'. Only in pious, debilitated old age,
when ecclesiastical preferment had sapped his thought, did he
pretend that the vision was God's. To the young Berkeley,
Yeats announced with more vehemence than accuracy, the vision
was man's, as if man had built the world out of his imagination
and then contentedly started to live in it. Yet this position of
Yeats's prose is not one to which he rigidly adheres in his verse.

[1] In an early draft he had denounced the Hebrews as well as the Greeks :

I mock at Greek and Jew
Why could no Rabbi say
That Eternal Man
Rested the seventh day.

A declaration of 'Tom the Lunatic' differs from 'The Tower' and is closer to the older Berkeley than the younger :

> Whatever stands in field or flood,
> Bird, beast, fish or man,
> Mare or stallion, cock or hen,
> Stands in God's unchanging eye
> In all the vigour of its blood ;
> In that faith I live or die.

But Berkeley would not have so insisted upon the physical health of the images in God's eye, nor particularized their sex ; and, as always in Yeats, God's eye may be only a symbol of *Anima Mundi* or even, though he gives no such indication here, of Eternal Man. The finest image of any creature is the most genuine.

The qualifications in Yeats's Berkeleyanism must also be taken with respect to his Platonism and anti-Platonism, which emerge in other poems of the 'twenties and 'thirties especially. 'Quarrel in Old Age' in no way suggests that his beloved is unreal, or a creation of the imagination ; but it represents her image in her prime as a Platonic form, too beautiful ever to vanish:

> Where had her sweetness gone ?
> What fanatics invent
> In this blind bitter town,
> Fantasy or incident
> Not worth thinking of,
> Put her in a rage.
> I had forgiven enough
> That had forgiven old age.

> All lives that has lived ;
> So much is certain ;
> Old sages were not deceived :
> Somewhere beyond the curtain
> Of distorting days
> Lives that lonely thing
> That shone before these eyes
> Targeted, trod like Spring.

So much is not certain, but the poet's right to take his stand cannot be gainsaid without vulgarity. By main force he extrudes her into a purer world, refusing to accept, as if to do so would be a personal defeat, the change in her character and person. Of course, to Plato the highest beauty known to man in the world of appearance is only dross or at best, a stepping-stone, to the true beauty; to Yeats, however, the form of beauty is the highest beauty he has *seen* or imagined himself to have seen. What in Plato is an indescribable abstraction is in Yeats a woman's tangible image. The same rule holds in a slightly different case, 'Before the World Was Made', where Platonic theory is converted into a delightful defence of a woman's make-up :

> If I make the lashes dark
> And the eyes more bright
> And the lips more scarlet,
> Or ask if all be right
> From mirror after mirror,
> No vanity's displayed :
> I'm looking for the face I had
> Before the world was made.

This poem moves from the particular towards the archetypal, but even the archetypal beauty has particularity. Yeats humanizes the de-humanized essences of philosophy.

Images ride rampant through the work of this period. Some of the lyrics represent the triumph of the imagination over the external world as painful and short-lived at best. The theme of 'The Results of Thought' is the poet's recollection of his friends in their youth, and his contrast of their present ruin with their former vigour. Thinking of them, he restores their images which youth, 'that inhuman / Bitter glory', has destroyed :

> Acquaintance ; companion ;
> One dear brilliant woman ;
> The best-endowed, the elect,
> All by their youth undone,
> All, all, by that inhuman
> Bitter glory wrecked.

> But I have straightened out
> Ruin, wreck and wrack ;
> I toiled long years and at length
> Came to so deep a thought
> I can summon back
> All their wholesome strength.

In the final stanza he is so taken with his dream that he dismisses the present, senile shapes of his friends as negligible, even suggesting that he does not know them in such disguises :

> What images are these
> That turn dull-eyed away,
> Or shift Time's filthy load,
> Straighten aged knees,
> Hesitate or stay ?
> What heads shake or nod ?

The poem's effect comes from the reader's understanding that the speaker is battling to the last against the irresistible, vainly but grandly spitting, as in the revised 'Lamentation of the Old Pensioner', 'in the face of time'. 'Girl's Song' affords a good contrast, for it finds the cleavage between youth and age grounds for tears rather than heroism :

> I went out alone
> To sing a song or two,
> My fancy on a man,
> And you know who.
>
> Another came in sight
> That on a stick relied
> To hold himself upright ;
> I sa᠁nd cried.
>
> And that was all my song
> When everything is told,
> Saw I an old man young
> Or young man old ?

This time imagination has less power.

The most moving of Yeats's many fine poems about the images in the mind's eye and those in the external world is 'Among School Children', which he wrote in 1926. The last three stanzas of the poem have evoked some controversy. In them Yeats speaks of the powerful theories of Plato, Aristotle, and Pythagoras, only to dismiss them because the theories, great as they were, proved powerless to avert the philosophers' own decrepitude and death. Power and knowledge, as he had said in 'Blood and the Moon' and implied in 'Leda and the Swan', cannot exist together. Yet there is one escape from mortality : when our eyes are blinded by affection, passion, or piety, like those of a mother, of a lover, or of a nun, we see images which are independent of life or fact. Such images, like Attis' image in 'Vacillation' or the image of the work of art in 'Byzantium', are changeless, and heaven can be nothing else but the state to which they seem to allude. Because they do not depend upon observation, and in fact flout the evidence of the senses to which decay and mortality are real, they are 'self-born':

> Both nuns and mothers worship images,
> But those the candles light are not as those
> That animate a mother's reveries,
> But keep a marble or a bronze repose.
> And yet they too break hearts — O Presences
> That passion, piety or affection knows,
> And that all heavenly glory symbolise —
> O self-born mockers of man's enterprise ;
>
> Labour is blossoming or dancing where
> The body is not bruised to pleasure soul,
> Nor beauty born out of its own despair,
> Nor blear-eyed wisdom out of midnight oil.
> O chestnut tree, great-rooted blossomer,
> Are you the leaf, the blossom or the bole ?
> O body swayed to music, O brightening glance,
> How can we know the dancer from the dance ?

In such images at such moments time and appearance are destroyed. Nevertheless there is grief at the moment of triumph.

For in life the body is bruised to pleasure soul, beauty comes only from despair at its lack, and wisdom is tainted by the toil with which it is gained. Yeats's irony gathers in the word 'where' at the beginning of the last stanza : labour blossoms in images, in heavenly glory if there is any (the poet is not entirely committed to it here), and, through the ecstatic character of the last few lines, in the poem itself. But the ecstasy comes from desperate sorrow over the inadequacy of the tenacious world of appearance. No one admires sight so much as the blind, and only the incomplete can so appreciate a contrary state.

In his last poems Yeats bears down firmly on the inadequacy of the real world when compared to the image of the ideal. Not finding a contemporary equal to the heroes of old times puts Crazy Jane in tears :

CRAZY JANE ON THE MOUNTAIN

I am tired of cursing the Bishop,
(Said Crazy Jane)
Nine books or nine hats
Would not make him a man.
I have found something worse
To meditate on.
A King had some beautiful cousins,
But where are they gone ?
Battered to death in a cellar,
And he stuck to his throne.
Last night I lay on the mountain,
(Said Crazy Jane)
There in a two-horsed carriage
That on two wheels ran
Great-bladdered Emer sat,
Her violent man
Cuchulain sat at her side ;
Thereupon,
Propped upon my two knees,
I kissed a stone ;
I lay stretched out in the dirt
And I cried tears down.

But Yeats is not Swift; such despair is nowhere near absolute. The force of Crazy Jane's emotions, her exaltation of powerful images once seen and her evocation of them in the poem, save her from chronic melancholy.

III. DEATH AND LAST THINGS

The claim which Yeats makes for the vitality of mental images brings him steadily back to a consideration of the image of death. Some of his attitudes towards it have already been examined. He does not always say, as in 'The Tower' and 'Death', that death is a man-made creation. In fact, his three poems on Robert Gregory's death might have been written by members of three different religious denominations. The first, 'Shepherd and Goatherd', is a dialogue in which the shepherd portrays Gregory's life, while the goatherd traces the progress of the soul after death. On the other hand, no mention of an afterlife relieves the sorrow of the second poem, 'In Memory of Major Robert Gregory'. At the request of Lady Gregory, Yeats did not publish the third poem, '"Reprisals"', addressed to Major Gregory, but in it he makes powerful use of the ghost rather than the soul of the dead man, and concludes by urging Gregory to lie still in his tomb and be utterly dead. The first two poems focus on the dead man's virtues, and the third on the poet's rage over the Black and Tans, so that in none of them is the philosophical theme of the nature of death the dominant one.

'REPRISALS'

Some nineteen German planes, they say,
You had brought down before you died.
We called it a good death.   Today
Can ghost or man be satisfied ?
Although your last exciting year
Outweighed all other years, you said,
Though battle joy may be so dear
A memory, even to the dead,
It chases other thought away,
Yet rise from your Italian tomb,

Flit to Kiltartan cross and stay
Till certain second thoughts have come
Upon the cause you served, that we
Imagined such a fine affair :
Half-drunk or whole-mad soldiery
Are murdering your tenants there.
Men that revere your father yet
Are shot at on the open plain.
Where may new-married women sit
And suckle children now ?   Armed men
May murder them in passing by
Nor law nor parliament take heed.
Then close your ears with dust and lie
Among the other cheated dead.[1]

The poet, a Buddhist one moment, a stoic the next, and a spiritualist the next, can look at death as well as other images with changing eyes.

While Yeats frequently takes the position, as in the last of the Gregory poems, that this world, lamentable though it is, exists, he sometimes suggests, with Blake or the Hindu seers, that this world is a fiction, and death mere fantasy.   So he declares, in 'Old Tom Again' :

Things out of perfection sail,
And all their swelling canvas wear,
Nor shall the self-begotten fail
Though fantastic men suppose
Building-yard and stormy shore,
Winding-sheet and swaddling-clothes.

This is the opposite position to that of 'The Tower', where life

[1] An earlier version of the poem began :

Considering that before you died
You had brought down some nineteen planes,
I think that you were satisfied,
And life at last seemed worth the pains.
'I have had more happiness in one year
Than in all other years' you said ;
And battle joy may be so dear
A memory even to the dead
It chases common thought away. . . .

and death are real precisely because 'fantastic men' have imagined them so.   Yeats's attitude is even more Eastern in 'Meru', named for India's holy mountain.   According to this poem, man's life is nothing but illusion ; and reality, if like the Hindu ascetic we could attain it, would turn out to be desolation.   The reflection that at the end of all human enterprise was nothing was not new in his work ; in some papers of 1914 about spiritualism, he had even suggested that the unconscious mind might be beguiling us into a belief in immortality :

> We ask ourselves, are we in the presence of a dream ? Is there a world-wide conspiracy of the unconscious mind, of what Maxwell calls 'the impersonal mind' that speaks through dreams, to create a false appearance of spiritual intercourse, a seeming proof of the soul's survival after death ; a renewed fabrication by nature of an old falsehood necessary perhaps to the order of the world ; perhaps, in the end, necessary even to the continuance of human life ?

This view, that man needs mythologies and fictions in order to live, is altered in 'Meru' to the exciting theme that man is never satisfied unless he destroys all he has created :

> Civilization is hooped together, brought
> Under a rule, under the semblance of peace
> By manifold illusion ; but man's life is thought,
> And he, despite his terror, cannot cease
> Ravening through century after century,
> Ravening, raging, and uprooting that he may come
> Into the desolation of reality :
> Egypt and Greece, good-bye, and good-bye, Rome!
> Hermits upon Mount Meru or Everest,
> Caverned in night under the drifted snow,
> Or where that snow and winter's dreadful blast
> Beat down upon their naked bodies, know
> That day brings down the night, that before dawn
> His glory and his monuments are gone.

In spite of the poem's location and declarative tone, it is personalized so as to fit no other man's religion or philosophy.   Its principal emphasis is not on the illusory character of life, but on man's courage and obligation to strip illusion away, in spite of the terror of nothingness with which he will be left. A good commentary on the poem is contained in a letter from Yeats to Sturge Moore about a related subject :

Science is the criticism of Myths, there would be no Darwin had there been no Book of Genesis . . . and when the criticism is finished there is not even a drift of ashes on the pyre. Sexual desire dies because every touch consumes the myth, and yet a myth that cannot be so consumed becomes a spectre. I am reading William Morris with great delight and what a protection to my delight it is to know that spite of all his loose writing I need not be jealous for him. He is the end as Chaucer was the end in his day, Dante in his, incoherent Blake in his. There is no improvement, only a series of sudden fires, each though fainter as necessary as that before it. We free ourselves from obsession that we may be nothing. The last kiss is given to the void.

This view of sexual love is unusual in Yeats : it is that the lovers' dreams of one another's perfections are dissipated in the course of physical contact, and the self demands that they be so dissipated. It craves to be obsessed by the ideal, the dream, the image, the myth, and it also — such is its paradoxical nature — craves to be freed from obsession.

'Meru' does not specify whether the nothingness of reality is simply a total blank, or whether it is Nirvana, which Yeats elsewhere describes as 'Blackout : Heaven blazing into the head'. In some curious notes for the second edition of *A Vision*, where reality was symbolized by the sphere, Yeats points out that we cannot know the nature of reality :

I have never knowingly differed from my Instructors, but one saying of theirs long tempted me to do so. 'Consciousness', they said, 'is conflict' ; that in itself was clear ; mind without images must be unconscious ; but if consciousness is indeed conflict must not the phaseless sphere from which all comes and to which all returns and source of all value be unconscious, and annihilation, as some say the early Buddhists thought, end all our effort ? I have come to see, however, that their conflict resolves itself into the antinomies of Kant and that we must say of the ultimate reality as the early Buddhists themselves said, 'We do not know that it exists, we do not know that it does not exist', and as the early Buddhists did not, that we can express it by a series of contradictions.

To paraphrase this difficult statement, Yeats implies that ultimate reality, whether or not it exists, has a function in man's view of his condition, and is an important part of mental life which cannot be ignored. Since man cannot see except by perceiving differences, he can represent reality, which must be opposite to all he knows and therefore single and indivisible, only by a series of contradictions. To this theory of contradictions we must return, but it may be noted at once that Yeats was enabled by it to encompass in his scheme both the existence and non-existence of the sphere, and its possible attributes of dark nothingness or heavenly light.

IV. IMAGES AND DAIMONS

Yeats's researches in later years often attempted, more learnedly than in his youth, to loosen the grip of the external world. He frequently returned to the view that things have no existence except as a series of relations. 'We know nothing but a stream of souls', he wrote, perhaps with Berkeley's remark in mind, 'Nothing properly but persons, *i.e.* conscious things, do exist, all other things are not so much existences as manners of the existence of persons'. Contemporary philosophers interested him because they were concerned with similar analyses of the external world. He wrote Mrs. Shakespear that Whitehead's philosophy was close to his own, especially in its contention that 'What we call physical objects of all kinds are "aspects" or "vistas" of other "organisms" — in my book the "body of Fate" of one being is but the "Creative Mind" of another. What we call an object is a limit of perception.' The world becomes increasingly a mental construct, not of one man but of all men. 'We create each other's universe.' He was endeavouring, as always, to find a metaphor for binding the world together, and late in life he formed a schematization which was more explicit than the chapter, 'The Completed Symbol', in *A Vision*.

It is embodied in a series of 'Seven Propositions' which he never published. These astonishing propositions, instead of looking at life by comparing it with a more perfect world, like most of Yeats's writings, look at the more perfect world, the world of the daimons, by comparing it with life. Notwithstanding the change in perspective Yeats keeps his familiar themes intact. The first two propositions assert (1) the insubstantiality of time and space, thus continuing Yeats's lifelong revolt against 'the despotism of fact', and (2) the substantiality of individual differences even in the daimonic world, thus confirming his reiteration of the value of personality.

(I) Reality is a timeless and spaceless community of Spirits which perceive each other. Each Spirit is determined by and determines those it perceives, and each Spirit is unique.

(II) When these Spirits reflect themselves in time and space they still determine each other, and each Spirit sees the others as thoughts, images, objects of sense. Time and space are unreal.

Images have here only a parity with thoughts and objects of sense, all being relations of spirits.

The next two propositions are deterministic :

(III) This reflection into time and space is only complete at certain moments of birth, or passivity, which recur many times in each destiny. At these moments the destiny receives its character until the next such moment from those Spirits who constitute the external universe. The horoscope is a set of geometrical relations between the Spirit's reflection and the principal masses in the universe and defines that character.

(IV) The emotional character of a timeless and spaceless spirit reflects itself as its position in time, its intellectual character as its position in space. The position of a Spirit in space and time therefore defines character.

Connecting the emotions with time, and the intellect with space, is probably purely arbitrary. Yeats's interpretation of the horoscope has the virtue of regarding it as a description, rather than a determiner, of character. He next turns to human life :

(V) Human life is either the struggle of a destiny against all other destinies, or a transformation of the character defined in the horoscope into timeless and spaceless existence. The whole passage from birth to birth should be an epitome of the whole passage of the universe through time and back into its timeless and spaceless condition.

That is, in life the being either combats other reflections of the spiritual world, whether people or circumstances, or, more radically, combats space and time themselves. This is the distinction which Yeats so frequently made, between two ways of life and two kinds of art, the first concerned with the world of change, the second with transcending it to changelessness. In the second sentence he means, among other things, that, growing old, one should more and more be concerned with the second form of struggle, leading out of space and time, like the old man in 'Sailing to Byzantium'.

The sixth proposition relates the spirits to the symbols of gyre and sphere :

(VI) The acts and nature of a Spirit during any one life are a section or abstraction of reality and are unhappy because incomplete. They are a gyre or part of a gyre, whereas reality is a sphere.

This is the explanation of the line sung by the spirits in *The King of the Great Clock Tower*, 'Mortal men our abstracts are'. By using the term 'incomplete', Yeats steers away from any Christian notion of sinfulness. In his final proposition, he dilates upon the essential freedom of the spirits ; he had speculated himself into determinism in (III) and (IV), and now he speculates a path out of it :

(VII) Though the Spirits are determined by each other they cannot completely lose their freedom. Every possible statement or perception contains both terms — the self and that which it perceives or states.

Instead of subject and object we have spirit and spirit. Beside their brightness the natural, physical, material world is tentative, precarious, and shadowy.

V. THE DUTY OF AFFIRMATION

Yeats's poetry is bound together by one unchanging conviction, the desirability of intense, unified, imaginative consciousness. But apart from this central pillar it reveals a series of points of view, sometimes parallel and sometimes divergent. What are we to make of his various attitudes towards reality, truth, life, death, and imagination? The question is of special moment because he kept increasingly as his career progressed to the ideal of writing poems of insight and knowledge which he had marked out for himself in youth. His position hovered for a time near that of Keats, who held that he was 'certain of nothing but of the holiness of the Heart's affections and the truth of Imagination — What the imagination seizes as beauty must be truth'. Keats would undoubtedly have added, if pressed, that beauty does not open her doors to the cheap, the temporary, or the false. The quality of the great writer, he maintained on one occasion, was '*Negative Capability*, that is, when a man is capable of being in uncertainties, mysteries, doubts, without any irritable reaching after fact and reason'. Yeats's conception of his art moved beyond this theory, because his verse depended, more than Keats's, on presenting a complete picture of the self, and to do so became full of reaching after fact and reason.

To explain and confirm his practice Yeats evolved a hypothesis which is closer to defining the situation in which the modern poet finds himself than negative capability. It might be described as *affirmative capability*, for it begins with the poet's difficulties but emphasizes his resolutions of them. Rejecting Keats's cry for 'a life of Sensations rather than of Thoughts', Yeats considered it the poet's duty to invade the province of the intellect as well as of the emotions. Neither the intellect nor the emotions can be satisfied to remain in 'uncertainties, mysteries, and doubts'; they demand the more solid fare of affirmations.

Yeats expressed himself on this crucial matter in a journal entry of January 1929. He had been talking about it at Rapallo with Ezra Pound, and Pound had apparently urged, with Hume, that even causation cannot be proved, since we can only be sure of a sequence, and that scepticism is therefore the only possible attitude for a responsible poet. Yeats felt that scepticism constricted the mind as much as pliant submission :

Ezra Pound bases his scepticism upon the statement, that we know nothing but sequences. 'If I touch the button the electric lamp will light up — all our knowledge is like that.' But this statement, which is true of science, which implies an object beyond the mind and therefore unknown, is not true of any kind of philosophy. Some Church father said, 'We can never think nor know anything of the Gospel' ; some Arian, 'I know God as He is known to Himself'. The Church father had like Ezra a transcendent object of thought ; his arose out of self-surrender, Ezra's out of search for complete undisturbed self-possession. In Eliot, and perhaps in [Wyndham] Lewis, bred in the same scepticism, there is a tendency to exchange search for submission. Blake denounced both nature and God considered external like Nature as mystery ; he was enraged with Wordsworth for passing Jehovah 'unafraid', not because Jehovah is mystery but because the passage from potential to actual man can only come in terror. 'I have been always an insect in the roots of the grass' — my form of it perhaps.[1]

As the cure for scepticism he does not propose belief :

I agree with Ezra in his dislike of the word belief. Belief implies an unknown object, a covenant attested with a name or signed with blood, and being more emotional than intellectual may pride itself on lack of proof. *But if I affirm that such and such is so, the more complete the affirmation, the more complete the proof, and even when incomplete, it remains valid within some limit. I must kill scepticism in myself, except in so far as it is mere acknowledgement of a limit,* gradually, in so far as politeness permits, rid my style of turns of phrase that employ it. Even the politeness should be ejected when charm takes its place as in poetry. *I have felt when re-writing every poem — 'The Sorrow of Love' for instance — that by assuming a self of past years, as remote*

[1] See above, p. 162.

*from that of today as some dramatic creation, I touched a stronger passion,
a greater confidence than I possess, or ever did possess.* Ezra when he
re-creates Propertius or some Chinese poet escapes his scepticism.
*The one reason for putting our actual situation into our art is that the
struggle for complete affirmation may be, often must be, that art's chief
poignancy.* I must, though [the] world shriek at me, admit no act
beyond my power, nor thing beyond my knowledge, yet because my
divinity is far off I blanch and tremble.

He is caught between the meaningless beliefs which the mob continually casts up before him, and the struggle to affirm on his
own, individuality being a vital test of the affirmation's quality.
The struggle is the more desperate because its sanction, his
divinity — the sphere or world of completeness — is far-off and
known only slightly. In this situation the poet receives help
from tradition, which provides roots when scepticism parades
its rootlessness as modernity :

We, even more than Eliot, require tradition and though it may
include much that is his, *it is not a belief or submission, but exposition
of intellectual needs.* I recall a passage in some Hermetic writer on the
increased power that a God feels on getting into a statue. I feel as
neither Eliot nor Ezra do *the need of old forms, old situations that, as
when I re-create some early poem of my own, I may escape from scepticism.*
For years past I have associated the first unique [?] impulse to any kind
of lyric poetry that has the quality of a ballad ('The Tower', for instance) with an imagination of myself awaiting in some small seaside
inn the hour of embarking upon some eighteenth or seventeenth
century merchant ship, a scene perhaps read of in boyhood, that
returns with simpler rhythms and emotions. Nor do I think that I
differ from others except in so far as my preoccupation with poetry
makes me different. The men sitting opposite me, in the Rapallo
restaurant where some days ago the sound of a fiddle made me
remember the old situation, are to my eyes modern but only a per-
verted art makes them modern to themselves. *The 'modern man' is a
term invented by modern poetry to dignify our scepticism.*[1]

Old forms and situations give the poet dignity and reassurance.
His individuality is not anarchic, but is founded on the re-enact-

[1] My italics.

ment of an ideal. His mind cannot bear what is raw and sanction-less ; it must anastomose with the past.

Yeats's journal entry is so closely packed that it must be amplified. In his youth he had defended his thematic and conceptual variations from poem to poem on the grounds that he was depicting a series of moods or states of mind. He now extended this notion by demanding an art of affirmations, by which he meant positive statements which were the active expression of a man, distinguished from beliefs or ideas which were outside structures to which the man submitted himself.

This demand is not the same as his youthful dictum that 'truths of passion' might be 'intellectual falsehoods'. Nor is it precisely Vaihinger's theory of convenient fictions, as Donald A. Stauffer has suggested, for the affirmations were not fictional for Yeats. Nor is it identical with the polemicism of Blake and Shaw, or the madness of Blake's Ezekiel who was mad as a refuge from unbelief, although these are compatible with it. It can be taken in two ways. In a world where no sort of truth is common, and where complete truth is impossible, incomplete truths must be put forward as the best we have. The poet must himself undertake what Coleridge required only of the reader, the willing suspension of disbelief. Even though incomplete, his affirmations are 'valid within some limit', as Newton's laws, although superseded by Einstein's, are still applicable to certain classes of phenomena. Of course, they are formulated with none of the scientist's cold detachment.

But the entry should be understood in a more specifically Yeatsian sense. Man, as the 'Seven Propositions' expounded, is a being who is always incomplete and yet who is always partially transcending his incompleteness. His affirmations at any given moment will contain, therefore, a measure of incompleteness and of completeness. This measure is what Yeats means by a limit.

His attitude towards scepticism is not entirely defined, but he was working towards some such generalization as this : in so far as scepticism prevents positive statement, it is a danger to art.

Such scepticism feeds parasitically upon the beliefs of others, and cannot satisfy the mind. But in so far as scepticism is one of the obstacles which the poet masters in the course of his attempt to transcend the limits of his incompleteness, it may render his positiveness, wrung from him partly in spite of himself, more poignant, and more noble because marked with the scars of battle. It is the wind resistance which makes flight possible. In poems which scepticism has affected, the specific affirmation is often of less central consequence than the struggle with the incompleteness of the human situation ; the poet labours to speak his whole mind, yet — such are his human limitations — even his most fervent utterances will reflect the incompleteness he cannot wholly overcome.

Yeats requires an art based upon affirmations, then, by representing it as the expression of the fundamental urge of living beings, to transcend themselves. It is necessary because, just as the artist finds in tradition an 'exposition of intellectual needs', so his art secures its value also by satisfying needs, his own and those of his readers, as fully as possible. 'Truth', he told his father in youth, is 'the dramatic expression of the most complete man', not a set of doctrines. In a diary of 1908, he pointed out, 'We taste and feel and see the truth. We do not reason ourselves into it.' The only philosophy admissible in a play, he wrote in 1909, was 'the mere expression of one character or another'. He writes more fully in a letter to his father of September 12, 1914 :

I think with you that the poet seeks truth, not abstract truth, but a kind of vision of reality which satisfies the whole being. It will not be true for one thing unless it satisfies his desires, his most profound desires. Henry More, the seventeenth century Platonist whom I have been reading all summer, argues from the goodness and omnipotence of God that all our deep desires must be satisfied, and that we should reject a philosophy that does not satisfy them. I think the poet reveals truth by revealing those desires.

Art, then, to be genuine, must include those affirmations which will help to form 'a vision of reality which satisfies the whole being'.[1]

Yet if such affirmations are only incomplete and limited expressions of the truth, how can they compose a vision of reality? Yeats answers, first, that the vision of reality which the poet gives us may be psychological; that is, it may be a vision of total human personality, and if so, the expression of divergent points of view and an awareness of the limits of each would contribute to the totality. He is close here to I. A. Richards, who argues in *Science and Poetry* that the test of a statement in a poem is not its truth but its effectiveness in releasing or organizing our impulses and attitudes. But Yeats, while he agrees with the therapeutic function of art, believes that it has also a revelatory function. He holds that the total expression of human personality must include our partial transcendence of our incompleteness, our intimations of a state which is not incomplete. To the extent that it furnishes these, the artist's vision of reality has an element of objective truth as well as of social and personal usefulness.

There are moments in Yeats's later life when he speaks of reality a little differently, when he has less confidence that our affirmations are even approximations of truth. At these moments he implies that reality is entirely distinct from human experience, that we cannot transcend our incompleteness. If it is so distinct, how can we establish any contact with it? Yeats suggests that we can express it through a series of contradictions. Here he is

---

[1] The danger of abstraction in art, with its consequent frustration instead of satisfaction of desires, was at the bottom of an unpublished poem, 'Art Without Imitation', written late in Yeats's life. He suggests, rather cryptically, that an art based as mathematics is based on abstractions would castrate its subjects and make them unfit for love and life :

> Old Mathematics plied the shears,
> He has the fragments in his bag,
> And trundles it about and swears
> Nature may fling off every rag
> And hardly find a single painter
> To beg her picture for his book,
> Or who is fitted for the quainter
> Operation of sweet love.
> How could he answer look for look
> And after clip being clipped enough?

closer to Kierkegaard than is usually supposed. The principle involved is that the more sharply we represent the contradictions of life, the more urgently we invoke a pattern of the reality which must transcend or include them. The poet cannot penetrate to this reality directly, but he can give a sense of the jaggedness and anfractuosity which it must encompass. Through focusing in themes and symbols the contradictory attitudes to which the world of appearance gives rise, attitudes which entrance his mind without securing its final allegiance, the poet presents reality as if by antithesis.

The conception of affirmative capability provides, in short, that poetry must centre on affirmations or the struggle for affirmations, that it must satisfy the whole being, not the moral, intellectual, or passionate nature alone, and that it must present a vision of reality. Our backs against the wall, we cannot decide whether reality is adequately described by our intimations of a state of completeness, or whether it is describable only as the opposite of all that we can see and imagine. In either case the artist must be its interpreter. Affirmative capability does not free him from the responsibility of intellectual search or understanding of experience, as negative capability might seem to ; rather it forces him to live, as well as to write, in such a way that his consciousness will be inclusive. Any narrowness, any adherence to a given affirmation beyond the moment that it satisfies the whole being, any averting of the eye, destroys the vision.

The conception of affirmative capability is particularly suited to a time when there is no agreement over ultimate questions, when we are not even sure exactly what we think on matters that are so crucial and yet so obscure. It is suited to a time when man is not regarded as a fixed being with fixed habits, but as a being continually adapting and readapting himself to the changing conditions of his body and mind and of the outside world. We can keep silence altogether, but if we speak out we must do so in terms of some such hypothesis as affirmative capability.

In a speech he gave to the British Association in September 1908, Yeats put his position with great eloquence :

We [artists], on the other hand, are Adams of a different Eden, a more terrible Eden perhaps, for we must name and number the passions and motives of men. There, too, everything must be known, everything understood, everything expressed; there, also, there is nothing uncommon, nothing unclean; every motive must be followed through all the obscure mystery of its logic. Mankind must be seen and understood in every possible circumstance, in every conceivable situation. There is no laughter too bitter, no irony too harsh for utterance, no passion too terrible to be set before the minds of men. The Greeks knew that. Only in this way can mankind be understood, only when we have put ourselves in all the possible situations of life, from the most miserable to those that are so lofty that we can only speak of them in symbols and in mysteries, will entire wisdom be possible.

Beside this nobility and largeness of mind, the lives of most of Yeats's contemporaries seem no more than 'the struggle of the fly in marmalade'.

VI. YEATS OUT OF CONTEXT

What emerges from a consideration of Yeats's whole poetic career is an impression of its seriousness and importance. All his work, in both poetry and prose, was an attempt to embody a way of seeing. That way is close to that of Blake and the romantics, but not identical with theirs. Like Blake, Yeats conceives of the imagination as the shaping power which transforms the world; but coming a century later, he has a tough-minded appreciation of the world's intransigence. He has little hope of building Jerusalem even in Ireland's green and pleasant land, and for him as for Keats, one function of art is to freeze life's inadequacies so as to render them harmless and beautiful. More than Keats or Coleridge, more perhaps even than Blake, he defends the imagination with the defiance of a man who sees himself as preventing the incursions of chaos. Yet his poetry is as much offensive as defensive. It fights its way beyond the frontiers of common apprehension, and brings previously untamed areas of thought and feeling under strong rule.

In modern poetry Yeats and T. S. Eliot stand at opposite poles. For while both see life as incomplete, Eliot puts his faith in spiritual perfection, the ultimate conversion of sense to spirit. Yeats, on the other hand, stands with Michelangelo for 'profane perfection of mankind', in which sense and spirit are fully and harmoniously exploited, and 'body is not bruised to pleasure soul'. So strongly does he hold this view that he projects sensuality into heaven to keep heaven from being ethereal and abstract. He presents this faith with such power and richness that Eliot's religion, in spite of its honesty and loftiness, is pale and infertile in comparison.

Yeats's richness, or better, his magnificence of tone, comes partly from the sumptuous images of his work, partly from the different levels of diction and the intricate rhythms at his command. His sense of decorum never fails him because he knows through long testing the value of everything ; and this power to estimate things at their true worth contributes to his talent for general statement. To paraphrase his own comment on Goethe, he sought to experience and tried to express moments acceptable to reason in which our thoughts and emotions could find satisfaction or rest.

In his endeavour to express these moments, he changed many elements of his verse, yet his identity is stamped upon them everywhere. His symbols keep altering, but the later symbols, in spite of their increased animation when compared to the earlier, are mature equivalents rather than new departures. His heroes also remain recognizable through many transformations ; in his later writings they do not abdicate their thrones or take up island apiculture or go mad, but that is because they become aware of their essential isolation even when performing some communal role, and because their internal battle depends only slightly on external circumstance. They remain uncommon men, uncommon in their nobility, charismatic in the power with which they excite emulation and focus intellect and emotion. The heroes of the later verse are simply the heroes of the early verse who have, like their creator, matured.

The principles of growth and of stability keep constant watch on one another in Yeats's poetry. He was a many-sided man who by dint of much questioning and inner turmoil achieved the right to speak with many voices and to know completely the incompleteness of life. And if, as seems likely, his works will resist time, it is because in all his shape-changing he remains at the centre tenacious, solid, a 'marble triton among the streams'.

APPENDIX, CHRONOLOGY, AND NOTES

The following abbreviations and short titles are used in the Appendix and Notes :

AU   W. B. Yeats, *Autobiographies* (London, Macmillan, 1926, and New York, Macmillan, 1927).

CP   Yeats, *The Collected Poems of* (London, Macmillan, 1950, and New York, Macmillan, 1951).

Essays   Yeats, *Essays* (London, Macmillan, 1924, and New York, Macmillan, 1924).

FD   Yeats, unpublished first draft of his *Autobiographies* written in 1916–17.

Vision (1925)   Yeats, *A Vision* (London, T. Werner Laurie, 1925).

Vision (1937)   Yeats, *A Vision* (London, Macmillan, 1937, and New York, Macmillan, 1938).

Henn   T. R. Henn, *The Lonely Tower* (London, Methuen, 1950, and New York, Pellegrini & Cudahy, 1952).

Hone   Joseph Hone, *W. B. Yeats, 1865–1939* (London, Macmillan, 1942, and New York, Macmillan, 1943).

Jeffares   A. Norman Jeffares, *W. B. Yeats, Man and Poet* (London, Routledge, 1949, and New Haven, Yale, 1949).

Man and Masks   Richard Ellmann, *Yeats : The Man and the Masks* (London, Macmillan, 1949, and New York, Macmillan, 1948).

Letters   Allen Wade, ed., *The Letters of W. B. Yeats* (London, Rupert Hart-Davis, 1954, and New York, Macmillan, 1955).

ltr.   letter.

unp.   unpublished.

Except where confusion might result, Yeats's name is omitted before works written by him. When English and American editions are not identical, page references are given first to the English edition, then in parenthesis to the American edition.

TOWARDS A READING OF THE POEMS

THE commentaries that follow seek to clarify some obscurities in the poems and to throw light on Yeats's methods of composition. Along with analysis and paraphrase, they therefore make use of collateral material, published and unpublished, when this is of help.

'The Cap and Bells' (written 1893)

Yeats's note on this poem in *The Wind Among the Reeds* is misleading : 'I dreamed this story exactly as I have written it, and dreamed another long dream after it, trying to make out its meaning, and whether I was to write it in prose or verse. . . . The poem has always meant a great deal to me, though, as is the way with symbolic poems, it has not always meant quite the same thing.' Actually the wording was much changed after the poem's first publication in the *National Observer* : Yeats removed a bad line from the seventh stanza, 'The night smelled rich with June', altered the third stanza which had previously read, 'She drew in the brightening casement, / She snicked the brass bolts down', and made other alterations.[2] While the significance of the poem may have changed for him, its immediate meaning was less obscure than it has been represented. The jester, after first sending the queen the trappings of common romance, finally offers the cap and bells which are his alone, and she, obdurate before the familiar and grandiloquent gifts of heart and soul, yields when the jester sends what is most essential and individual in him. That Yeats recognized this meaning in the poem is suggested by the fact that in later lectures he would read 'The Cloths of Heaven' as an example of 'How not to win a lady', and 'The Cap and Bells' as an example of how to win one.[3]

---

[1] *The Wind Among the Reeds* (London, Mathews, 1899), pp. 94-5.
[2] *National Observer*, XI (March 17, 1894), 453-4.
[3] Hone, 152 (159), 321 (343).

'*King and No King*' (written December 7, 1909)

This puzzling poem is based on Beaumont and Fletcher's play of the same title, in which King Arbaces falls in love with his sister Panthea.[1] Tortured by guilty love, he tells her :

> I have lived
> To conquer men, and now am overthrown
> Only by words, brother and sister.   Where
> Have those words dwelling ?   I will find 'em out,
> And utterly destroy 'em ;   but they are
> Not to be grasped : let 'em be men or beasts,
> And I will cut 'em from the earth ;   or towns,
> And I will raze 'em, and then blow 'em up :
> Let 'em be seas, and I will drink 'em off,
> And yet have unquenched fire left in my breast ;
> Let 'em be anything but merely voice.   (IV, iv.)

But at the play's end Arbaces discovers he is an adopted child and therefore 'No King', so able now to marry Panthea and thus become King in fact.

Yeats's parallel and contrast are a little awkward.   The power of the word was a frequent theme in his poetry from 'The Song of the Happy Shepherd' in his first volume ;   he follows Arbaces in pointing out how much more powerful is a word than what sounds powerful, noise and cannon.   Arbaces' scruple over incest is like Maud Gonne's vow, taken 'in momentary anger', presumably not to live with Yeats. But 'Old Romance' offers Arbaces a solution which the modern lovers are denied.

The phrase, 'I that have not your faith', refers to Maud Gonne's conversion to Catholicism shortly before her marriage.[2]

'*The Mountain Tomb*' (written August 1912, at Colleville,
France, where Yeats was staying with Maud Gonne)

The Rosicrucian myth has it that Father Rosenkreuz or Rosicross, the brotherhood's patron 'saint', achieved perfection at the time of his death.   The proof was that, when his tomb was reopened a hundred and twenty years afterwards, his body lay miraculously undecayed. Yeats, who knew the myth well because it was involved in the most

---

[1] Allan Wade tells me that Yeats gave him this hint about the poem.
[2] Jeffares, 141.

important of the several initiations of the Golden Dawn,[1] took it over to illustrate one of his recurrent views. He represents Rosicross's disciples as having mixed feelings about their master's death : on the one hand, they rejoice at his attainment of perfection, and celebrate it by a pagan wake, with drinking and love-making. If their conduct seems lacking in decorum, it must be remembered, as Yeats remarked in an early draft of *Per Amica Silentia Lunae*, that the brothers of the Rosy Cross 'claimed not holiness but wisdom' ; they might have said with Blake, 'Go put off holiness and put on intellect'. Their wisdom accepts the body as well as the soul. Yet, on the other hand, they lament — and their sorrow becomes dominant in the final stanza — that he has been taken from them, and that they can neither bring him back to life nor participate in the universal wisdom that he has attained in death.

The role of the smoking cataract is at first puzzling, because it changes. In the first stanza the disciples accept the cataract as a part of the general bustle and excitement at Rosicross's perfect death. But at the end of the poem, it becomes a reminder of life's continuing violence, and the everlasting taper is a sardonic commentary on the continued inadequacy of the world of time. As Yeats says with more explicitness in 'Blood and the Moon', 'Wisdom is the property of the dead, / A something incompatible with life'.

'The Wild Swans at Coole' (written October 1916)

When this poem was first published in the *Little Review* in June 1917, the fifth stanza came after the second. By putting the third stanza at the end Yeats emphasized his personal deprivation in time, and made possible the symbolic reading that his awakening would be his death, a paradox well within his intellectual boundaries.[2]

'The Collar-Bone of a Hare' (written July 5, 1915)

While the theme of contrasting the ideal and real worlds is common in Yeats, the image of the collar-bone of a hare is unusual. *The*

[1] In this initiation, known as the Path of the Portal because it led from the Outer to the Inner Order, the initiate lay down in the tomb, like Rosicross; but the Golden Dawn emphasized his rising up again as a rebirth of his spirit. Yeats takes only that part of the myth which he needs for his symbolic parable.

[2] See also Donald A. Stauffer, *The Golden Nightingale* (New York, Macmillan, 1949), 48-79.

Celtic Twilight reveals that he borrowed the strange, spontaneous image from the Irish peasantry :

A peasant of the neighbourhood once saw the treasure. He found the shin-bone of a hare lying on the grass. He took it up ; there was a hole in it ; he looked through the hole, and saw the gold heaped up under the ground. He hurried home to bring a spade, but when he got to the rath again he could not find the spot where he had seen it.[1]

The change from shin-bone to collar-bone was perhaps for metrical reasons.

'The Scholars' (written April 1915)

The second stanza gave Yeats much trouble. In *Poetry*, February 1916, this read :

> They'll cough in the ink to the world's end ;
> Wear out the carpet with their shoes ;
> Earning respect, have no strange friend,
> If they have sinned nobody knows :
> Lord, what would they say
> Should their Catullus walk that way ?

He was not satisfied with the revision of the poem which made the first four lines of the last stanza begin with 'all', feeling perhaps that their rhetoric was too easy. In his 1928 diary he wrote down another version in which he changed from the third person to direct address :

> Shuffle there, cough in the ink,
> Wear out the carpet with your shoes,
> Think what all good people think,
> Youth could sin, but old age knows.
> Lord, what would you say
> Did your Catullus walk that way ? [2]

But he did not alter the published version, which had a better ring to it.

Yeats did not always take so frowning a view of scholarship. A poem written three and a half years later declared, 'Truth flourishes where the student's lamp has shown'.[3]

---

[1] *The Celtic Twilight* (London, Bullen, 1902), 147. The story first appeared as part of an essay, 'Irish Fairies', in 1890.   [2] Unp. MS.
[3] 'The Leaders of the Crowd' (written 1918–19), CP, 207 (182).

'The Double Vision of Michael Robartes' (written 1919)

Yeats usually conceived of the two extremes of his own nature, and of human nature in general, as the utmost development of the self on the one hand, and its obliteration on the other. Man might seek his 'profane perfection' by exploiting all his faculties to the full, or his spiritual perfection by sheering them away. Michael Robartes' double vision is based upon this opposition, for Robartes is caught between the two extremes, and his satisfaction at the end of the poem comes from his having been able to visualize them so precisely even though he belongs neither to one extreme nor the other.

The scene of the poem is Cashel, in Tipperary, which is associated with Cormac mac Cuilleanaín, the picturesque bishop-king of Munster in the tenth century, and with Cormac mac Carthy, king of Munster in the twelfth century, who restored the chapel which is now the 'ruined house'. Its present ruin is symbolic of the modern world in the same way that the 'half-dead' tower is symbolic of it in 'Blood and the Moon'. Robartes' [1] first vision occurs when the moon is dark, a state which symbolizes the blotting out of self. He sees the spirits of this state, who are will-less, helpless, abstract, deader than the dead. Rapt in his vision of them, Robartes declares he has never had free will but has always been a doll controlled by these doll-like forms, who are themselves controlled by some further demiurge.

But this determinism is only the first part of the double vision, and is best understood as the state of mind which Robartes experiences at one of the two extremes. The other comes in the second part, and is made up of three images of the self at its fullest development. Yeats's choice of Sphinx, Buddha, and dancing girl for these images has proved troublesome [2] because in other works he uses them differently. They represent here aspects or powers of the mind raised to a super-human degree. The sphinx is the intellect, gazing on both known and unknown things ; the Buddha is the heart, gazing on both loved and unloved things ; and the dancing girl, most important of all, is primarily an image of art. She dances between them because art is neither intellectual nor emotional, but a balance of these qualities.[3]

[1] For Robartes, see Man and Masks, 238 (234-5). He is here a persona of the visionary.

[2] Henn's interpretation, 179-80, that the dancing-girl is Iseult Gonne, that Homer's Paragon is Maud Gonne, and that the Sphinx and Buddha are West and East, is misleading.

[3] 'Introduction' to Patanjali, Aphorism of Yoga (London, Faber, 1938), 18.

The dancer, more than the two images beside her, reconciles body and mind, dreaming and thinking, and like them, she is full of life although dead. In 'Byzantium' also Yeats describes the image of art as 'dying into a dance, / An agony of trance', and as combining 'death-in-life and life-in-death', and in *A Vision* he describes the poem and the painting as participating in this state.[1]

The third part of the poem derives from the second, and deepens the contrast with the darkness of the first part. Robartes declares that he has long struggled to bring to consciousness, as the poet to composition, 'that girl' and the conception of art she implies. She is not to be identified with anyone he has actually seen or known, he cautions us, for she has appeared only to his 'unremembering nights'. She comes from *Anima Mundi*, the reservoir of images, and not from experience, yet the power of the image is such that Robartes feels as though he had been 'undone' by Helen of Troy, that is, as though he had had the most shattering of experiences. At the poem's end he recovers from the vision and makes his moan because he is himself caught, not between pure intellect and pure emotion, but between the less attractive antinomy of self-exaltation and self-obliteration. Yet he gives thanks for having been permitted to transcend his moment in time if only for the instant of vision.

'An Image from a Past Life' (written September 1919, at Thoor Ballylee, the first poem to be written there)

In the notes to the Cuala Press edition of *Michael Robartes and the Dancer* (1920), Yeats explains that the poem is based on the thought that our lives are haunted by memories of past lives, and that in some circumstances one may see 'the forms of those whom he has loved in some past earthly life, chosen from *Spiritus Mundi* by the sub-conscious will, and through them, for they are not always hollow shades, the dead at whiles outface a living rival'. These forms are known as Over Shadowers or, if the imagination doctors them up, as Ideal Forms. Yeats says that the woman in the poem sees the Over

---

[1] *Vision* (1937), 135-6. In *Plays and Controversies* (London, Macmillan, 1923, and New York, Macmillan, 1924), 217-18, Yeats speaks of this poem as being concerned with 'a supreme moment of self-consciousness, the two halves of the soul separate and face to face'. His remarks on pp. 207-8 of *Vision* (1937) are in a different context. In *Vision* (1925), 213, he quoted the first section of 'The Double Vision' as a prophecy of the future darkness.

Shadower or Ideal Form ('whichever it is') that is passing through the man's mind without his being conscious of it.[1]

The poem is better understood as an attempt, not completely successful, to create a mysterious, fearful image of amorous anxiety, and Yeats gives the image vitality by showing its effect, the rousing of the jealousy of the living woman. This active competition between living and dead is common enough in Yeats's verse ; compare his long narrative poem, 'The Two Kings', and his play, *The Only Jealousy of Emer*. He may have taken the theme for the poem from Tagore's 'In the Dusky Path of a Dream', which he included in the *Oxford Book of Modern Verse* ; it begins, 'In the dusky path of a dream I went to seek the love who was mine in a former life'.

'The Second Coming' (written January 1919)

The notion that a new god comes at regular intervals to replace the old god is a familiar one in Theosophy ; every cycle is said to have its special deity. Frazer and other comparative mythologists hold, however, that the same divinity often passes from one culture to another, where he is given a new name and otherwise adjusted to suit local and temporal conditions. Yeats was equally versed in both theories, but for the purpose of his poetry found the cyclical god of the Theosophists more suitable. His poems are thick with allusions to the coming of some god, or of some change in the world's complexion, and in his early and middle periods he usually longs for the impending transformation. So in 'At Galway Races' he delights in the prospect that 'the whole earth' will 'change its tune'.

But 'The Second Coming' differs from previous prophecies in envisaging the new god's arrival with horror. The first World War and the Black and Tan War seemed foreshadowings, and, if these were not enough, Mrs. Yeats's automatic writing constantly impressed the word 'terror' upon him. In entitling his poem 'The Second Coming', Yeats took over a device which he had used in his early story, 'The Adoration of the Magi', where he gave Christian parallelism to a prediction of the return of the old pagan gods by calling the three old men who receive the new revelation 'magi'. The title of the poem is even more shocking, for it depends upon a fusion of Christ's prediction in Matthew 24 of his second coming, and St. John's vision of the coming of the beast of the Apocalypse, or Antichrist.

[1] Pp. 28-30.

Yeats rightly considered this one of his most important poems, and quoted it in 1938 to Ethel Mannin as proof that he was not indifferent or callous towards the rise of fascism. 'Every nerve trembles with horror at what is happening in Europe : "The ceremony of innocence is drowned".' [1] He also quoted it in his *Autobiographies* in 1922 to sum up the 'growing murderousness of the world',[2] and it underlies the sentence with which he ended *The Trembling of the Veil*, 'After us the Savage God'.[3] The two editions of *A Vision* paint a pleasanter picture of the new god than might be expected, and are not wholly consistent with the poem. According to *A Vision*, the new god will usher in a subjective era in which, as during the Renaissance, personality will be fully expressed instead of downtrodden as now. 'As Christ was the *primary* [objective] revelation to an *antithetical* [subjective] age, He that is to come will be the *antithetical* revelation to a *primary* age.' [4] 'When our historical era approaches . . . the beginning of a new era, the *antithetical* East will beget upon the *primary* West and the child or era so born will be antithetical.' [5] In less technical language, Yeats explains in a note to *Michael Robartes and the Dancer* :

All our scientific, democratic, fact-accumulating, heterogeneous civilization . . . prepares not the continuance of itself but the revelation as in a lightning flash, though in a flash that will not strike only in one place, and will for a time be constantly repeated, of the civilization that must slowly take its place. This is too simple a statement, for much detail is possible.[6]

But unlike these prose passages, 'The Second Coming' gives no hint of the redeeming or even salutary qualities of the new dispensation.

The details of the poem offer some difficulty. The image of the falcon who is out of the falconer's control should not be localized, as some have suggested, as an image of man loose from Christ ;

---

[1] *Man and Masks*, 282 (278).   [2] AU, 238-9.   [3] AU, 430.
[4] *Vision* (1925), 169.
[5] *Vision* (1937), 257; note also the quotation of the poem on 263. In *Wheels and Butterflies* (London, Macmillan, 1934, and New York, Macmillan, 1935), 103 (93), Yeats writes that from about 1903 he was always imagining 'at my left side just out of the range of the sight, a brazen winged beast that I associated with laughing, ecstatic destruction', and that he afterwards described it in 'The Second Coming'. But the image had to lose its wings and be invested with horror before it went into the poem. See also *Man and Masks*, 96 (93).
[6] Dundrum, Cuala, 1921, 34.

Yeats would not have cluttered the poem by referring to Christ both as falconer and as rocking cradle further on. Essentially the falcon's loss of contact implies man's separation from every ideal of himself that has enabled him to control his life, whether this comes from religion or philosophy or poetry. It is also, in more general terms, his break with every traditional tie. 'The blood-dimmed tide' refers primarily to the terrible destructive forces that are unleashed at the end of an era, and has special reference to war.[1] While 'The ceremony of innocence' carries an allusion to the purification rite of baptism, ceremony is used mainly in its meaning of ceremoniousness. For, as Yeats says in a poem of the same period, 'A Prayer for My Daughter' (1919), the soul is innocent only when it recognizes no force but its own and is completely self-sufficient. Ceremony is its way of protecting itself against the vulgarity of the streets; once ceremony is obliterated, the best men have nothing to hold them above the tide.

The first stanza prepares the way for the ominous event of the second stanza. Until the beginning of the thirteenth line the reader can still hope that the Second Coming will be Christ's beneficent although awesome reappearance. But with the word 'troubles' and the description of the image this hope is converted to fear. Whatever the new dispensation can bring, it inspires only a sense of horrible helplessness to avert what no man can desire. That the image comes from *Spiritus Mundi*, the storehouse of images, is important because it indicates that the image is not a personal one, that he has not deliberately thought it up but has had it forced into his consciousness. He is 'inspired', not by a god, but by an equally irresistible and all-knowing power.

Although he refers to the image as a 'shape', and intends the indeterminate label to increase its portentousness, he makes clear that it is, or is like, the Egyptian sphinx, which is male (unlike the Greek sphinx). This beast has been in stony sleep for two thousand years, and even now it seems to be moving as if in nightmare towards birth and awakening. 'The rocking cradle' of Christianity has at last made

---

[1] 'The blood-dimmed tide' is an image which recurs in Yeats's verse to describe turbulent life, usually but not always pejoratively. He speaks of 'that raving tide' in 'The Phases of the Moon', of 'blood on the ancestral stair' in 'Blood and the Moon', of 'odour of blood when Christ was slain' in 'Two Songs from a Play', of 'the fury and the mire of human veins' and 'the flood' in 'Byzantium', and of 'this filthy modern tide' in 'The Statues'.

way for its opposite, for Christianity has reached its utmost bound.[1]
Movements call up their opposites like 'Ille' in 'Ego Dominus Tuus',
whether willingly or unwillingly. While Yeats is not fond of Christianity, and regards its suppression of individual personality as having
led to the present anarchy, yet at the end of the poem he envisages
something far worse. The final intimation that the new god will be
born in Bethlehem, which Christianity associates with passive infancy
and the tenderness of maternal love, makes its brutishness particularly
frightful.

'Two Songs from a Play' (written 1926 except for last stanza, which was first published in 1931)

These songs have an extraordinary effect even when imperfectly
understood. They come from the play *The Resurrection*, in which the
pattern of the death and resurrection of Christ is treated as if it were
an enactment under a new guise of the death and resurrection of
Dionysus. Yeats, delighted by cyclical rounds, was struck by the
fact that both gods had died and been reborn in March, when the sun
was between the Ram and the Fish, and when the moon was beside
the constellation Virgo, who carries the star Spica in her hand. Virgo
is usually connected with Astraea, the last goddess to leave the world
after the golden age ; Virgil prophesied in the Fourth Eclogue that
she would return and bring the golden age again, and the passage was
commonly read in later centuries as a prophecy of the coming of Mary
and Christ, the former as Virgo, the latter identified with Spica as the
Star of Bethlehem.

The Golden Bough provides the key to the first stanza. Dionysus,
like Christ, was the child of a mortal and an immortal, of Persephone
and Zeus. Because of the jealousy of Hera, the Titans tore him to
pieces, but Athena snatched his heart from his body and bore it on
her hand to Zeus. Then Zeus put the Titans to death and, according
to one version, swallowed the heart and begat Dionysus afresh upon
the mortal Semele.[2] Athena, who is traditionally represented as
'clear-eyed' or 'grey-eyed', is the 'staring virgin' of Yeats's poem.
The word 'staring' has reference also to her acting as if in a trance

---

[1] Compare the triumph of fact which calls up its opposite, myth, in *Vision* (1925), 212.
[2] James G. Frazer, *The Golden Bough* (London and New York, Macmillan, 1922,
one-volume edition), 388-9. I am indebted to Marguerite Jupp for most of the astro-
nomical and mythological details of this interpretation.

and performing what is foreordained. The Muses sing of Magnus Annus, that is, of a new cycle, because the ritual of the god's death and rebirth is the necessary beginning for a cycle ; and if they see God's death as 'but a play', it is because they know that these events will recur many times.

The second stanza begins with Virgil's prophecy, which Yeats had first referred to in 1896 in 'The Adoration of the Magi'. His words there are close to those of the poem : 'After you have bowed down the old things shall be again, and another Argo shall carry heroes over sea, and another Achilles beleaguer another Troy'.[1] He cited it again in *Samhain* in 1904,[2] in *Discoveries* in 1906,[3] and then quoted it more exactly in the 1925 version of *A Vision* :

'The latest age of Cumaean Song is at hand ; the cycles in their vast array begin anew ; Virgin Astraea comes, the reign of Saturn comes, and from the heights of Heaven a new generation of mankind descends. . . . Apollo now is King and in your consulship, in yours, Pollio, the age of glory shall commence and the mighty months begin to run their course.'[4]

But Yeats differs from Virgil, and from Shelley, whose variation of the Fourth Eclogue in *Hellas* he knew, in prophesying another age rather than a great age, in accentuating cyclical upheaval rather than future prosperity. Like Gibbon, he held that Christianity destroyed the Roman Empire and that in many ways the destruction was regrettable ; and consequently he could not join in the Virgilian eagerness.[5]

The last three lines of the second stanza daringly assert a parallelism and even identity between the three pairs, Astraea and Spica, Athena and Dionysus, and Mary and Christ, who all merge into 'that fierce virgin and her star'. Lady Gregory, in her journal for May 24, 1926, gives an earlier version of this stanza which uses the name of the constellation instead of 'virgin' :

And I hear Yeats 'purring' next door, and he has just come in and said, 'I meant this to be a poem of Christianity and it has come like this :

> Another Troy must rise and set —
> Another Argo's painted prow
> Drive to a flashier bauble yet.

[1] *The Tables of the Law ; and The Adoration of the Magi* (Stratford, Shakespeare Head, 1904), 28, 31. He calls it the *Fifth* instead of the *Fourth* Eclogue.
[2] *Collected Works* (Stratford, Shakespeare Head, 1908), IV, 154.
[3] *Essays*, 359.   [4] P. 152.
[5] Jeffares, 270, relates Yeats's poem to *Hellas* ; the differences are important, however.

The ancient kingdoms are appalled,
They dropped the news [reins ?] of peace and war
When Virgo and the Mystic Star
Did to the fabulous darkness call.' [1]

Both songs refer to a 'fabulous, formless darkness', a phrase which Yeats borrowed from the neo-Platonic philosopher Proclus, who so described Christianity. The elaborate Graeco-Roman culture is forced to yield before the turbulence which came out of Asia.[2] Yeats gives Babylon the role of ushering in Christianity because the astronomers there, who plotted the stars, helped to reduce man's status in relation to the universe by promulgating the inhuman abstractions of science.[3] Afterwards it was but a step to what John Stuart Mill considered Christianity's passivity, or what the Greek in Yeats's play calls its 'self-surrender' and 'self-abasement'.[4] Platonic tolerance had been self-sufficient enough to regard all gods as supernatural and perhaps illusory, and in any case as being separate from men. The reason that Christ's death is so confounding is that its 'odour of blood' means not only that it was a real death, but also that the mutually exclusive 'privacy' of gods and men cannot be maintained, for Christ was both god and man.[5]

The last stanza was not included in the first publication of 'Two Songs', and in its last two lines does not follow very well from the rest of the play. While it takes up the theme of the passing of Platonic tolerance and Doric discipline, its insistence upon such qualities, and in fact upon all things, as man-made is slightly out of key with the insistence of the rest of the two songs on divine miracle. Lines 3 to 6 grew out of a passage in the *Autobiographies* : 'Our love letters wear out our love ; no school of painting outlasts its founders, every stroke of the brush exhausts the impulse. . . .' [6] But the final two lines add a new note of reverence for man, who goes on with his creation notwithstanding the impermanence of it. They recall two lines that Yeats had quoted in an essay on 'The Symbolism of Poetry' in 1900 :

[1] Lady Gregory's *Journals* (London, Putnam, 1946), 263. Lennox Robinson, ed.
[2] He refers to the turbulence of Christ's death in 'The Magi'. Christ is usually represented in his work, for example, in 'The Statues', as a manifestation of Asia.
[3] For this implication of Babylon, compare *The Hour-Glass* in *Responsibilities* (London and New York, Macmillan, 1916), 153, and *Vision* (1925), 181.
[4] *Wheels and Butterflies*, 121 (108).   [5] *Ibid.* 121 (108), 128 (114-15).
[6] P. 388.

> And all man's Babylons strive but to impart
> The grandeurs of his Babylonian heart.[1]

But these lines are more glorifying than his own. He probably had in mind also a passage in 'Vacillation' written in 1931 or 1932 but perhaps already taking shape :

> From man's blood-sodden heart are sprung
> Those branches of the night and day
> Where the gaudy moon is hung.
> What's the meaning of all song ?
> 'Let all things pass away.'

Here the knowledge that man makes all things out of himself leads to the cry for all things to pass away, while in 'Two Songs' the knowledge that all things pass away brings the poet to the opposite position of exalting man's might as maker and his foolish yet heroic persistence in the face of transience. The author of Ecclesiastes might have written the first six lines of the last stanza, but not the last two. Yet the whole stanza is suffused with melancholy, for the final affirmation offers pride but little comfort.

'Fragments' (I first published 1931, II first published 1933)

Blake considered Locke largely responsible for imprisoning man in the cage of the five senses by making the mind a passive receptacle for sensations, and constantly excoriated him for it. Yeats followed Blake in this happy over-simplification, and in his first fragment conceived a mock-creation, in which God's Caesarean operation is performed on Locke rather than Adam and brings forth not Eve but the spinning-jenny. He wrote in *Wheels and Butterflies* :

I can see in a sort of nightmare vision the 'primary qualities' torn from the side of Locke, Johnson's ponderous body bent above the letter to Lord Chesterfield, some obscure person somewhere inventing the spinning-jenny, upon his face that look of benevolence kept by painters and engravers, from the middle of the eighteenth century to the time of the Prince Consort, for such as he. . . .[2]

In other words, Locke turned the world to abstraction and mechanism and away from the unified consciousness (the Garden) which had grown up during the Renaissance.

[1] *Essays*, 195.   [2] P. 27-5 (22) ; see also p. 104 (93).

The second fragment holds that the first was no idle fancy, but came from a medium's mouth, from nothing, from the forest loam, from dark night. As in 'The Second Coming', Yeats wishes to deny that he is expressing a mere personal opinion. There he described the source of his image as *Spiritus Mundi*, here he gives it no name but emphasizes its mysterious, unfathomable, and powerful nature. 'The crowns of Nineveh' may possibly be traced to a poem of O'Shaughnessy that Yeats quoted or alluded to many times, in which the claim is made for the poets,

> We built Nineveh with our sighs,
> And Babel itself with our mirth.[1]

The same force which produced Nineveh with its dynasties, the same imaginative reservoir which holds the crowns as symbols of man's ancient accomplishments, has enabled the poet to sum up four centuries in an epigram.

'On a Picture of a Black Centaur by Edmund Dulac' (written September 1920)

This gnomic poem reflects Yeats's satisfaction over the progress of his art and over the revelations of his wife's automatic writing. The centaur can be identified with the help of other passages in his work. He remarked in *The Trembling of the Veil*, written about 1922, 'I thought that all art should be a centaur finding in the popular lore its back and its strong legs',[2] and the conception of art as double-natured is common.[3] In this poem, however, the centaur is not so much art in general as his muse or imagination. It connects with a recurrent image of Pegasus, who appears in 'Coole Park and Ballylee, 1931' as 'that high horse', in 'The Fascination of What's Difficult' in 1909–10 as 'our colt', and as a horse on which the poet's 'wits have taken a fantastic ride' in a poem of 1919, 'Under Saturn', which also has reference to Yeats's life after his marriage.

A poem couched so completely in symbols does not lend itself easily to prose explanations; but, in blunt paraphrase, it is a review

---

[1] *Pages from a Diary Written in Nineteen Hundred and Thirty* (Dundrum, Cuala, 1944), 54; compare *Essays*, 194. [2] AU, 236.
[3] He prophesies, for example, 'the day when Quixote and Sancho Panza long estranged may once again go out gaily into the bleak air'. Note to *The Unicorn from the Stars* in *Collected Works* (1908), III, 221.

of intellectual and poetic activity. Remembering how he had always been attracted by the '*au-delà*', in spite of the warnings of his friends and of his own mind, he blames his imagination for leading him to the borders of consciousness beyond which all is dangerous and out of control. The wood is the area outside normal or everyday experience, and its horrible green parrots are the baleful fascinations which this other world exerts upon the poet. That he describes them so pejoratively now is due to the fact that they have persecuted him and prevented his living a common life or writing in ordinary ways. Instead his works have been stamped down into the mud of this border region, so taboo to the rationalism of his age. The danger of such imaginative horseplay had been evident to him from the first; he had always known that wholesomeness lay in the area of conventional experience, far from the wood.

But because he was driven almost to obsession by the pressures of a mysterious life that was unknown to him, and yet lacked the clairvoyant power to investigate them directly, he had to have recourse to traditional wisdom ('old mummy wheat'). He collected this wisdom in the 'mad abstract dark', a darkness which is not to be confused with the more natural darkness of the 'forest loam' and 'dark night' mentioned in 'Fragments', from which all truths come. What results he obtained came with the utmost laboriousness, as he indicates in the image of the grinding of mummy wheat grain by grain and its slow baking.

But now he has wine instead of bread, wine which comes from a barrel he has found. This wine, which he elsewhere refers to as 'the frenzy that the poets have found in their ancient cellar',[1] is natural, instinctive, close to the sources of life. Instead of spending tedious hours in the bakery, he now has access to spontaneous insight. It is the same miraculous potion which the seven sleepers of Ephesus drank, and Yeats interprets their sleep as a kind of bedding down in reality.

The way is now prepared for the curious paradox of the final quatrain, where the imagination is bidden to sleep a Saturnian or Ephesian sleep, and yet is expected to keep unwearied eyes upon the horrible green birds. Yeats means that it should participate in the instinctive, spontaneous experience (which he connects with sleep) that is now open to him, for there it can best observe the wood beyond

[1] *The Unicorn from the Stars and Other Plays* (New York, Macmillan, 1908), viii.

normal consciousness. There is now no more talk of danger, for the imagination is in firmer control. And the poet makes a handsome amends for the almost recriminatory tone of the first two quatrains; he declares, with literal as well as figurative truth, that he has loved his imagination better than his soul. As he had asserted in 'The Grey Rock' and would say later in 'Vacillation', he had put perfection of the work before perfection of the life.[1]

'Veronica's Napkin' (written 1929)

This poem contrasts two kinds of religion, of art, or of thought, the first based on transcendence of life, the second on participation in it. Veronica's napkin, wiped on Christ's face and carrying his image, represents the second, while the constellations represent the first. The image of the 'needle's eye', which Yeats used again in 'Supernatural Songs', grew out of a belief that infinity might be represented by something infinitely small as well as by something infinitely large.[2]

'Symbols' (written October 1927)

'Consciousness is conflict', and life is for ever incomplete. The three couplets deal with wisdom, power, and love respectively, and illustrate these Yeats axioms. Wisdom comes to the hermit who is blind, power is in the sword which a fool wields, and love, which one might hope would resolve the antinomies, deepens them by uniting beauty and folly. The poem can be compared to On Baile's Strand, where the two 'combatants who turn the wheel of life' are a strong, foolish man and a powerless, clever blind man.

'The Nineteenth Century and After' (written January–March 2, 1929)

Yeats wittily borrowed for his title the name of the review The Nineteenth Century, which had to change its name at the end of the century to The Nineteenth Century and After. 'I have come to fear', he wrote Mrs. Shakespear on March 2, 1929, 'the world's last great poetic period is over.'[3] An early version of the poem put it in the

---

[1] An amusing account of the composition of the poem is given by Cecil Salkeld in Hone, 326-8 (348–50).
[2] For his interest in this idea, see Hone, 327 (349).   [3] Letters, 759.

first person singular rather than plural, and did not limit its application to letters :

> Though the great men return no more
> I take delight in what I have
> The rattle of pebbles on the shore
> Under the outgoing wave.[1]

He had intended that this poem should form the third in what he called a 'lyrical sequence', the first two being 'At Algeciras — A Meditation upon Death' and 'Mohini Chatterjee', but gave up the plan.

'Three Movements' (written January 26, 1932)

In his diary on January 20, 1932, Yeats noted, 'The Passion in Shakespeare was a great fish in the sea, but from Goethe to the end of the Romantic movement the fish was in the net. It will soon be dead upon the shore.' [2]

'At Algeciras — A Meditation upon Death' (written January 23, 1929)

Yeats, in bad health at Algeciras, wrote from there to Lady Gregory on November 13, 1927 :

Today there has been rain but yesterday and the day before bright sun ; and today, now that the rain has stopped, the butterflies are lighting on the roses in the hotel garden. At sunset some hundred or so white herons will come flying from beyond Gibraltar and go to sleep in some dark trees.[3]

The birds' journey evidently impressed him as symbolic of life and death, and he remembered it later in conjunction with a well-known passage from Newton :

I do not know what I may appear to the world; but to myself I seem to have been only like a boy, playing on the sea-shore, and diverting myself, in now and then finding a smoother pebble or a prettier shell than ordinary, whilst the great ocean of truth lay all undiscovered before me.

'Mohini Chatterjee' (written January 23–February 9, 1929)

The manuscript indicates that the second stanza came to Yeats as

---

[1] Unp. MS. [2] Unp. diary. [3] Unp. ltr.

an afterthought, and did not form part of the poem as he first wrote it. He wrestled with the beginning of the second stanza for some time before hitting upon what he wanted.   One draft began,

> A stranger with strange eyes
> Murmured in my youth
> These or words like these.

and a later one read :

> In my callow days
> Mohini Chatterjee
> Spoke these, or words like these :
> I add in commentary,
> 'Once more shall lovers have
> All a peacock's pride —
> Grave is heaped on grave
> That they be satisfied —
> Soldier soldier face
> In grim strategic thought ;
> Birth treads birth a pace,
> That the last round be fought
> And thunder time away
> That birth and death may meet
> Or, as great sages say,
> Man dance on deathless feet.'
>
>   (February 9, 1929)[1]

Shifting the military image to the metaphor of the cannonade of births, as Yeats finally did, helps to make the poem one of his most powerful.[2]

'*Vacillation*' (written November 1931–March 5, 1932)

On June 30, 1932, Yeats commented to Mrs. Shakespear on his *Collected Poems*, which he was preparing for publication : 'The swordsman throughout repudiates the saint, but not without vacillation.   Is that perhaps the sole theme — Usheen and Patrick — "So get you gone Von Hugel though with blessings on your head" [?]'[3] The statement is a considerable over-simplification, even if we know that by the swordsman he meant the self or personality, and by the

---

[1] Unp. MS.   [2] See above, pp. 44-7.   [3] *Man and Masks*, 276 (272).

saint the moral character or soul.[1] For his poetry is made up of a great many examples of what may be called lay sanctity. Crazy Jane has a martyr's steadfastness about her cult of the body, and regularly insists that it is also a cult of the soul. What Yeats does is not so much to repudiate the saint as to absorb him. He accepts the saint's point of view but regards it as partial.

Even the sense of beatitude is not the saint's exclusive preserve, as Yeats made clear at the end of 'A Dialogue of Self and Soul', and reaffirmed in the fourth section of 'Vacillation'. The latter is a description of an experience of his own during the first World War, of which he was reminded by a similar experience in November 1931. The first experience is described in *Per Amica Silentia Lunae* (1917):

At certain moments, always unforeseen, I become happy, most commonly when at hazard I have opened some book of verse. . . . Perhaps I am sitting in some crowded restaurant, the open book beside me, or closed, my excitement having over-brimmed the page. I look at the strangers near as if I had known them all my life, and it seems strange that I cannot speak to them : everything fills me with affection, I have no longer any fears or any needs ; I do not even remember that this happy mood must come to an end.[2]

Of the second experience he wrote Mrs. Shakespear on November 23, 1931:

The night before [your] letter came I went for a walk after dark and there among some great trees became absorbed in the most lofty philosophical conception I have found while writing 'A Vision'. I suddenly seemed to understand at last and then I smelt roses. I had realized the nature of the timeless spirit. Then I began to walk and with my excitement came — how shall I say — that old glow so beautiful with its autumnal tint. The longing to touch it was almost unendurable. The next night I was walking on the same path and now the two excitements came together. The autumnal image remote, incredibly spiritual, erect, delicate featured, and mixed with it the violent physical image: the black Mass of Eden. Yesterday I put my thoughts into a poem which I enclose, but it seems to me a poor shadow of the intensity of the experience.[3]

---

[1] The words have this sense in 'A Dialogue of Self and Soul'.
[2] *Essays*, 533.
[3] *Letters*, 785.

What must be noticed is that the experience was physical as well as spiritual, a mixture characteristic of Yeats's brand of sanctity. He had not had many such moments, although like William James he made them his constant study. That he returned to the earlier experience rather than portraying the later was probably due to its remarkable contrast of commonplace surroundings and the blazing body.

Shortly after writing the fourth section he decided to make it part of a 'lyric sequence'. He had grown tired of the Crazy Jane poems and wanted to work on a loftier plane. At first he called the sequence 'Wisdom', and, though he transferred the title to another poem later, he kept the notion that he was exposing his mature point of view in 'Vacillation'. A letter to Mrs. Shakespear of December 15, 1931, announces: 'I have begun a longish poem called "Wisdom" in the attempt to shake off "Crazy Jane" and I begin to think that I shall take to religion unless you save me from it'.[1] Her answer evidently amused him, and in his reply of January 3, 1932, he picked a sentence from it to start out with:

You will be too great a bore if I get religion [she had written him]. I meant to write to you this morning (it is now 3 : 15) but thought of that sentence of yours, and then wrote a poem which puts clearly an argument that has gone on in my head for years. When I have finished the poem I began yesterday I will take up the theme in greater fullness.[2]

His manuscript book reveals how much trouble he had with the phrasing of this poem, the seventh section of 'Vacillation'. Its first version ran:

HEART AND SOUL

Soul

Find Heaven's reality not things that seem.

Heart

I am a singer and I need a theme.

Soul

Ezekiel's coal, and all shines out anew.

Heart

No imagery can live in heaven's blue.

[1] *Letters*, 788. [2] *Letters*, 789.

Soul

Knock on this door, all wisdom waits within.

Heart

Shakespeare and Homer sang original sin.[1]

This was presumably written on the morning of January 3. By mid-afternoon he had arrived at the version which he sent Mrs. Shakespear:

Soul

Search out reality; leave things that seem.

Heart

What be a singer born and lack a theme?

Soul

Ezekiel's coal and speech leaps out anew.

Heart

Can there be living-speech in heaven's blue.

Soul

Knock on that door, salvation waits within.

Heart

And what sang Homer but original sin.[2]

The next day he wrote, 'Leave the "And" out of last line of poem. Have vacillated all day. Not "And what sang" but "What sang".'[3] His use of the word 'vacillated' in his letter perhaps suggested the change of title. His manuscript book shows that he continued to be dissatisfied with the last line:

Homer and Shakespeare	sang original sin		
But granddad Homer	„	„	„
What sang Homer but		„	„
What theme had Homer but		„	„
Shakespeare and Homer	„	„	„
What theme had „	„		„	„ [4]

The letter of January 3 promised to take up the theme in greater fullness, and elaborated:

I feel that this is the choice of the saint (St. Theresa's ecstasy, Gandhi's smiling face): comedy; and the heroic choice: Tragedy (Dante, Don

Quixote). Live Tragically but be not deceived (not the Fool's Tragedy). Yet I accept all the miracles. Why should not the old embalmers come back as ghosts and bestow upon the saint all the care once bestowed upon Rameses. Why should I doubt the tale that when St. Theresa's tomb was opened in the middle of the Nineteenth Century the still undecayed body dripped with fragrant oil. I shall be a sinful man to the end, and think upon my death bed of all the nights I wasted in my youth.[1]

Many of these phrases were taken up in the final section (VIII) of the poem, which for a time contained also the lines :

> And all such things delight me, and yet I swear that I
> Must keep my heart unchristian, like Homer live and die.[2]

The composition of 'Vacillation' can be traced closely through his manuscript book and correspondence. Originally section I had a title, 'What is Joy', and its next to last line read : 'If these have named it right'. Section II at first had the title, 'The Tree', and then, 'The Burning Tree'. A draft of the fourth and fifth lines reads :

> For ignorance and knowledge fill the scene
> But no not half for each is all the scene
> What one consumed the other can renew.[3]

Yeats at first had sections II and III as one unit, and in later versions their stanza forms remain the same. Section IV was first entitled 'Joy' and then 'Happiness'. Section V was first 'Remorse' and then 'Conscience'; two early versions of its second stanza read :

> Blunders of thirty years ago
> Or said or done but yesterday
> Or what I did not say or do
> But that I thought to do and say
> A word or sound and I recall
> Things that my conscience and my vanity appall.
>
> A thousand things upon me weigh
> Things done some thirty years ago
> Or things I did not do or say
> But thought that I would say or do

---

[1] *Letters*, 790.   [2] Unp. MS.   [3] Unp. MS.

There's not a day but I recall
Things that my conscience or my vanity appall.[1]

The last three sections were on first publication entitled 'Conquerors', 'A Dialogue', and 'Von Hügel'.[2]

In structure the lyric sequence is fairly loose, and moves from side to side as well as forward. It begins by posing the question of what joy can be. For the antinomies rage till the moment of death, and death is no reconciler. What the body calls death the heart, which sees everything in terms of feelings, considers to be remorse for the failure to resolve the antinomies. There would seem to be no place for joy in this scheme at all.

Sections II and IV offer answers to the question, 'What is joy?' The first is more cryptic; it describes a tree mentioned in the *Mabinogion*.[3] Half fire and half green leaf, the tree is symbolic of soul and body. Yeats transplants it from Wales to Asia Minor, and relates it to the worship of Attis, the vegetation god at whose yearly festival in March his devotees castrated themselves. To hang the image of Attis between the two sides of the tree was to give up one's hopes for normal experience and to become one with the god, thereby achieving a reconcilement of the antinomies.[4] He who sacrifices himself in this way 'may know not what he knows' because such knowledge is not susceptible of intellectual formulation, but he knows the ecstatic state of not-grief, which may be called joy.[5]

Section III opens with instructions which turn out to be ironic, since the goals they recommend are mere 'Lethean foliage'. In the midst of money-getting or other ambitious schemes, one must keep in mind an opposite scheme of values; and, especially from one's fortieth year, one must prepare for death and build works worthy enough to make possible a proud, laughing entrance to the tomb. But the sixth section stands against the third: man, who creates everything, both the antinomies and their reconciling image (night and day, and the 'gaudy moon'), wills the extinction of his own

[1] Unp. MS.

[2] *Words for Music Perhaps* (Dublin, Cuala, 1932), 5-7. Sections II and III form a single section in this version.

[3] 'The Celtic Element in Literature', *Essays*, 217.

[4] See above, pp. 171-2.

[5] 'A poet creates tragedy from his own soul, that soul which is alike in all men. It has not joy, as we understand that word, but ecstasy, which is from the contemplation of things vaster than the individual and imperfectly seen, perhaps, by all those that still live.' *Dramatis Personae* (London and New York, Macmillan, 1936), 89 (96).

monuments. There is a weariness that comes at the moment of triumph or glory. Yeats had once noted down Heraclitus's fragment no. 43: 'Homer was wrong in saying "Would that strife might perish from among gods and men". He did not see that he was praying for the destruction of the universe; for if his prayers were heard all things would pass away. . . .' [1] But here he takes Homer's part.

Sections IV and V picture joy and remorse respectively. Besides the joy of artistic creation which is implied in section II, there is also the possibility of momentary secular blessedness, which Yeats had mentioned in 'Demon and Beast'. In the seventh section the soul takes its cue from the line, 'Let all things pass away', and urges the heart to leave things that seem. But the heart makes the sensible protest that to do so would be to abolish poetry, which from Homer on has concerned itself with original sin, not with sinlessness. Isaiah's coal (Isaiah 6 : 6-11) would wash away iniquity but leave nothing to write about.

The final section takes up this theme more earnestly, with the Catholic mystic Von Hügel as Yeats's straw man. Although Christianity offers a palatable afterlife, the poet, while sharing its faith in miracles, [2] prefers the restlessness of his more pagan or Homeric ideal, which holds with what seems most welcome out of the tomb rather than in it. The lion and honeycomb come, of course, from Judges 14 : 5-18 ; but Yeats diverts them to make the lion a symbol of the ancient strength and 'healthy flesh and blood' [3] of the poets, whose mouths drop honey rather than jeremiads.

The poem ends, then, by celebrating the unchristened living rather than the holy dead, but it bows politely to orthodoxy in Von Hügel and to annihilation ('Let all things pass away'), and insists not only on the heroic virtues of 'proud, open-eyed and laughing men' but also on the value of transcending life through art and lay visions.

'Crazy Jane and the Bishop' (written March 2, 1929)

The first appearance of Jack the journeyman in Yeats's work

[1] Unp. MS.

[2] Yeats writes to Sturge Moore on February 2, 1928, 'By the bye, please don't quote him [G. E. Moore] again till you have asked him this question: How do you account for the fact that when the Tomb of St. Teresa was opened her body exuded miraculous oil and smelt of violets? If he cannot account for such primary facts, he knows nothing.' Quoted Henn, 149.   [3] 'Owen Aherne and His Dancers', CP, 248 (217).

is in a little play he wrote in 1902, *The Pot of Broth*, where the tramp sings :

> There's broth in the pot for you, old man,
> There's broth in the pot for you, old man,
>> There's cabbage for me,
>> And broth for you,
> And beef for Jack the journeyman.

> I wish you were dead, my gay old man,
> I wish you were dead, my gay old man,
>> I wish you were dead
>> And a stone at your head,
> So as I'd marry poor Jack the journeyman.[1]

In a note, Yeats gives the song this provenance : 'The words and the air of "There's Broth in the Pot" were taken down from an old woman known as Cracked Mary, who wanders about the plain of Aidhne, and who sometimes sees unearthly riders on white horses coming through stony fields to her hovel door in the night time'.[2] Twenty-seven years later he returned to Cracked Mary, combining her apparently with another old woman who lived near Lady Gregory, 'the local satirist and a really terrible one'.[3] He changed the name from Cracked Mary to Crazy Jane because of possible invidious religious implications.

The refrain line, 'The solid man and the coxcomb', gradually shifts its meaning so that instead of Jack's being, as the bishop said, a coxcomb, he is the solid man, and the bishop the true coxcomb. Yeats hit upon this idea late in the poem's composition, as early versions of the first and third stanzas disclose :

> Bring me to the chapel wall
> That at midnight I may call
> *O the safety of the grave* ;
> A blasting curse out of the sky,
> Ere the one or tother die
> None so old as he and I :
> *There the learned man and the knave.*

[1] *The Hour-Glass, Cathleen Ni Houlihan, The Pot of Broth : Being Volume Two of Plays for an Irish Theatre* (London, Bullen, 1904), 65-6.
[2] *Ibid.* unnumbered page following 82.
[3] Ltr. to Mrs. Shakespear, November 1931, *Letters*, 786.

The bishop's body is a foul
Worm-rotten, weather-worn toad stool
O the safety of the grave
Nor hides in rusty black
A belly rounder than his back
But a straight birch tree my Jack
There the learned man and the knave.[1]

The change of scene from the chapel wall to the blasted oak made the malediction more exciting, and also established an appropriate kinship between Cracked Mary, now an old woman, and the blasted tree.

'*Crazy Jane Reproved*' (written March 27, 1929)

Whether Crazy Jane is reproving herself, or, as is more likely, someone else is reproving her, she is being told to choose lovers with attractions more subtle than those of roaring, ranting Jack the journeyman. Great storms, and Jupiter's appearance to Europa as a bull, are merely divine *rhetoric*, while heaven has to take immense pains in creating a delicate shell. She should choose her lovers with these truths in mind. This interpretation is supported by Yeats's *Autobiographies* :

. . . politics, for a vision-seeking man, can be but half-achievement, a choice of an almost easy kind of skill instead of that kind which is, of all those not impossible, the most difficult. Is it not certain that the Creator yawns in earthquake and thunder and other popular displays, but toils in rounding the delicate spiral of a shell ? [2]

The refrain was originally 'Fol de diddle, fol de diddle'. Yeats modified it and used it again in 'The Pilgrim'. In this poem it can be either a judgment on rhetoric or Crazy Jane's retort to the reproof ; the poem admits of both possibilities.

'*Crazy Jane on God*' (finished July 18, 1931)

Confronted by the transitoriness of the passions of her lovers, Crazy Jane asserts in her refrain that nothing is ever lost, and illustrates her contention by the army which suddenly sees an old ruined house

[1] Unp. MS.

[2] P. 307. For the shell image, see also AU, 337, and *Four Plays for Dancers* (London and New York, Macmillan, 1921), 28, where the shell is produced by the storm instead of being contrasted with it.

lit up from door to top. She finds in the intensity of experience a
guarantee of permanence. The refrain, 'All things remain in God',
embodies an idea that Yeats sought to confirm in all the philosophers,
especially Berkeley; but it probably came to him first from Madame
Blavatsky. Twenty-five years after the event he wrote, in 1914, in
Lady Gregory's *Visions and Beliefs*: 'I was once at Madame Blavatsky's when she tried to explain predestination, our freedom and God's
full knowledge of the use that we should make of it. All things past
and to come were present in the mind of God and yet all things were
free.'[1] In the poem he wished to relate the philosophical idea to
experience.

He remembered that the 'timeless individuality or daimon' of
Plotinus, similar to his own *Anima Mundi* and to God in this poem,
'contains archetypes of all possible existences whether of man or
brute', and argued from this, in *Wheels and Butterflies*, that 'the Irish
countrywoman did see the ruined castle lit up . . .'.[2] The image was
a favourite one of his later verse. The converse of Crazy Jane's
house is the house that fades in 'The Curse of Cromwell':

> I came on a great house in the middle of the night,
> Its open lighted doorway and its windows all alight,
> And all my friends were there and made me welcome too;
> But I woke in an old ruin that the winds howled through. . . .

At the climax of his next to last play, *Purgatory*, a burnt house is
suddenly lit up and its dead occupants appear as if they were still alive.
He probably had in mind in all these passages the ruined castle near
Castledargan House, about six miles from Sligo town, which he
refers to by name in a song of *The King of the Great Clock Tower*:

> O, but I saw a solemn sight;
> *Said the rambling, shambling travelling-man;*
> Castle Dargan's ruin all lit,
> Lovely ladies dancing in it. . . .
> Yet all the lovely things that were
> Live, for I saw them dancing there.[3]

The image of the army is probably founded on the fact that the
original 'Cracked Mary' sometimes saw 'unearthly riders on white

[1] Lady Gregory, *Visions and Beliefs* (New York and London, Putnam, 1920), I, 277.
[2] Pp. 36-8 (32-3).
[3] *The King of the Great Clock Tower* (New York, Macmillan, 1935), 12. I owe the
location of Castledargan's ruin to John V. Kelleher.

horses'.[1] In the poem, however, the army is not unearthly but its collective vision is or appears to be ; the explanation of the vision is that the house in its unruined state remains 'in God'. Together the second and third stanzas are Crazy Jane's parable to show why she makes no moan but sings on.

'Crazy Jane Talks with the Bishop' (written November 1931)

The meaning of lines 3 and 4 of the second stanza is, 'My friends have departed from my bed or died, but the truth that "fair needs foul" is not contradicted either by copulation or death. For the foul grave is the repository of fair lovers, and sexual love is itself both fair and foul, full of pride and bodily lowliness.'

The lines, 'For love has pitched his mansion in / The place of excrement', are probably based on a line in Blake's *Jerusalem* : 'For I will make their places of love and joy excrementitious'.[2] Blake's dictum at the beginning of *The Marriage of Heaven and Hell*, 'Without contraries is no progression', is also close to Crazy Jane's point of view.

An early draft of this poem read :

> When that church crowd had gone
> I caught the Bishop's eye ;
> Have you so foul a tongue said he
> Those veins are running dry
> Think on a heavenly mansion
> Bid the rest go by.
>
> When fair and foul were with me yet
> They seemed the same said I
> My friends are gone but that's a truth
> Nor grave nor bed denied
> Learned in bodily lowliness
> And in the heart's pride.
>
> When love is most a perfect whole
> Its nature is most rent
> What lover could have kept those eyes
> That are on heaven bent
> Had he not found love's mansion in
> The place of excrement.[3]

---

[1] See above, p. 275, n. 2.   [2] Jeffares, 272.   [3] Unp. MS.

The final two lines were the last to be settled. Even after the rest of the poem was perfected, these read :

> Nothing is a perfect whole
> That has not been rent.[1]

With the change of the next to last line to 'For nothing can be sole or whole', the poem, to use Yeats's metaphor, came right with the click of a closing box.

'His Bargain' (written 1929)

Against the view of life as a mere whirling spindle,[2] with one Platonic year following another in a never-ending circuit, so that eternity dwindles into mere repetitiousness and the infidelity of ordinary lovers seems part of the natural order of things, the poet sets up his fidelity to his own beloved as beyond all such whirling. He borrows the last five lines from the one hundred and seventy-third poem of Hafiz's *Divan*, a favourite passage. He first quoted the poem in a speech in *Diarmuid and Grania*, which he and George Moore wrote together in 1902 : 'Life of my life, I knew you before I was born, I made a bargain with this brown hair before the beginning of time and it shall not be broken through unending time'.[3] He quoted it again in *Discoveries* (1906).[4] But it is stronger in 'His Bargain' because of the contrast of two views of the world and of love.

'After Long Silence' (written November 1929)

Yeats had Mrs. Shakespear in mind when he wrote this poem, although the theme of aged yet powerless wisdom as against young yet ignorant power was a habitual one. A letter to her of December 16, 1929, from Rapallo, said : 'When I first got here I was fairly vigorous though sleepy and wrote that little poem of which I showed you the prose draft'. The prose draft occurs in a diary :

[1] Unp. MS.

[2] The whirling image is a frequent one. Yeats writes, 'So the Platonic Year / Whirls out new right and wrong, / Whirls in the old instead', in 'Nineteen Hundred and Nineteen' ; 'the whirling Zodiac' in 'Chosen' ; 'whirling round / The one disastrous Zodiac', in 'The Two Kings' ; 'all whirling perpetually', *Vision* (1925), 149.

[3] *Diarmuid and Grania* (*Dublin Magazine*, XXVI, April–June 1951), 21. William Becker, ed.   [4] *Essays*, 359.

SUBJECT

Your hair is white
My hair is white
Come let us talk of love
What other theme do we know
When we were young
We were in love with one another
And therefore ignorant.[1]

'*I Am of Ireland*' (written August 1929)

One night at Yeats's home Frank O'Connor read aloud an early fourteenth-century English lyric :

I am of Ireland
And of the holy land
    Of Ireland.
Good sir, pray I thee,
For of *saint charité*,
Come and dance with me
    In Ireland.[2]

Yeats took fire at once from the words, snatched wildly for a piece of paper, and gasped, 'Write, write'. The result was 'I Am of Ireland', in which the woman's lines were at first very close to the original :

'I am of Ireland
And the Holy Land of Ireland
Good sir' cried she
'By St. Charity
Come dance with me in Ireland' [3]

But the woman in Yeats's poem is not only of Ireland, she is Ireland ; and she summons all men to follow the ideal Ireland which she represents. Time, she reminds them, is passing, and yet nothing is accomplished.

But only one man listens, and he finds many pretexts for preferring comfortable expedience to the discomforts of idealism. When she

---

[1] Unp. MS.
[2] Quoted by Walter E. Houghton in *The Permanence of Yeats* (New York, Macmillan, 1950), 379. James Hall and Martin Steinmann, eds. Houghton's ingenious reading of the poem assumes that it follows in the Crazy Jane series, but many of the poems in *Words for Music Perhaps* have no reference to Crazy Jane.   [3] MS. book.

repeats her appeal, he gives a further reason : there can be no dancing in a country where all things are awry, and he gives her back her own words by pointing out that there is no time to remedy these things. Yet her cry continues, as if indifferent to his prudential explanations, like the cry of all idealism and heroism.

'The Delphic Oracle upon Plotinus' (written August 19, 1931)

Plotinus's friend, Porphyry, reported the Delphic Oracle's pronouncement on Plotinus's journey to the Elysian fields,

. . . where Minos and Rhadamanthus dwell, great brethren of the golden race of mighty Zeus ; where dwells the just Aeacus, and Plato, consecrated power, and stately Pythagoras and all else that form the Choir of Immortal Love, there where the heart is ever lifted in joyous festival.[1]

But Yeats's poem is quite unlike the Oracle's ; it represents Plotinus's voyage as hazardous and troubled, with his eyes blocked by salt blood. It also represents Rhadamanthus as beckoning him.

These details are best understood if we remember that Yeats sees Plotinus and Plotinus's philosophy as heavily influenced by the early Christian period. His philosophy is less transcendent than that of the classical Greek period (Plato and Pythagoras) and closer to Christianity, which always has for Yeats an 'odour of blood'.[2] Consequently Plotinus has a hard journey to reach the transcendent isles of the blessed. Yeats may also have had in mind the famous close of Plato's Gorgias, where Rhadamanthus is charged with judging the souls that come from Asia ; Yeats thought of both Christ and Plotinus as coming out of the East.

'Ribh at the Tomb of Baile and Ailinn' (written July 24, 1934)

'I would consider Ribh, were it not for his ideas about the Trinity, an orthodox man', Yeats wrote in a note on the 'Supernatural Songs'.[3] His orthodoxy is Yeats's doxy ; he reads his holy book, to be sure, but it is more likely to be A Vision than the Bible, and he reads it by the light of the sexual intercourse of two angels, and these angels are the pagan lovers Baile and Ailinn. Ribh is one of Yeats's many

---

[1] Quoted by W. Y. Tindall in The Permanence of Yeats, 276, and by Henn, 132-3.
[2] Compare 'Two Songs from a Play' and Vision (1925), 189, where Plotinus is discussed as primary.
[3] The King of the Great Clock Tower (1935), 46.

symbolic projections of the role of the artist; like the man who in 'Vacillation' hangs Attis's image on the tree of flame and green leaf, Ribh is somewhat detached from the experience which he celebrates. Hence the light is 'somewhat broken by the leaves', as incomplete life blurs the ideal image.

The angelic union is consonant with Yeats's view of heaven as expressed in 'News for the Delphic Oracle', for the two lovers find heaven to be an intensification and completion of the physical delights they have experienced on earth. Yeats profited here from Swedenborg, who had described angelic intercourse as a union 'of the whole body' which 'seems from far off an incandescence'.[1]

The poem has the urbanity of Yeats's later manner, and states with a combination of force and wit his themes of the incompleteness of human love and life, the detachment of the artist, and the contrast and fusion of physical and spiritual elements.

'*Ribh Denounces Patrick*' (written July 1934)

The Christian Trinity of Father, Son, and Holy Ghost seems to Ribh an absurdity; St. Patrick is crazed by it. All myths of the gods, like all stories of human beings, demand a father, a mother, and a son; Mary's virginity makes the Trinity an unnatural abstraction. As the Smaragdine Tablet of Hermes Trismegistus declares, heavenly things correspond to natural ones: 'As above, so below'. Human and divine love are of the same kind; but, whereas God is only three, human beings multiply over the earth. The reason is that human love is no lasting union of body and mind, but is damped by one or the other. Human beings go on endlessly begetting in the search for a union as complete as that of a god. Yeats wrote to Mrs. Shakespear on July 24, 1934, 'The point of the poem is that we beget and bear because of the incompleteness of our love'.[2]

'*Ribh in Ecstasy*' (written 1934)

When Yeats read his poem, 'Meru', to some friends gathered at his house, and asked them whether they understood it, Frank O'Connor answered, 'No, I didn't understand a word of it'. His remark may have suggested the beginning of another poem in the

[1] *Essays*, 523. For the story of Baile and Ailinn see Yeats's poem of that title.
[2] *Letters*, 824. In 'Under Ben Bulben' only the dead complete their passions.

series. Yeats compares the perfection and unity of godhead with his own momentary sense of unity in writing the previous poem, as if he had momentarily brought into pure expression the 'unborn, undying, unbegotten soul'.[1] Then the spell was broken, the poem over.

'Ribh Considers Christian Love Insufficient' (written 1934 ?)

'All relations are possible between a man and his God',[2] even hatred; out of hatred springs the ecstasy of complete submission expressed in the last stanza. The poem probably developed out of some automatic writing of Mrs. Yeats. In a journal the poet writes of the 'communicator' whose ideas she was writing down, 'He insisted on being questioned. I asked about further multiple influx. He said "hate God", we must hate all ideas concerning God that we possess, that if we did not absorption in God would be impossible . . . always he repeated "hatred, hatred" or "hatred of God" . . . said, "I think about hatred". That seems to me the growing hatred among men [which] has long been a problem with me.' [3] The soul has to enter into a personal and individual relation with God, through enmity if necessary, to escape mere credulity or religiosity.

'He and She' (written before August 25, 1934)

'She' in the poem is the soul or humanity, which must follow the pattern of the moon's changes as set forth in *A Vision*. Yeats sent 'He and She' to Mrs. Shakespear on August 25, 1934, with the remark, 'I have written a lot of poetry of a passionate metaphysical sort. Here is one on the soul — the last written.' He adds, 'It is of course my centric myth'.[4] He was not always, however, so determinist.

'What Magic Drum?' (written 1934 ?)

In Yeats's verse new gods or heroes are frequently the issue of a human mother and a bestial or avian father, like the sphinx of 'The Second Coming' or the Helen of 'Leda and the Swan'. This poem is based on such a conjunction, although Yeats does not disclose precisely what the child is to be. But the bestial father has come to see his offspring, and there is a rather terrifying contrast between his parental love and his bestial form. The magic drum-beat increases the portentousness and gives the visit supernatural sanction.

[1] See above, p. 165.   [2] Unp. notes.   [3] Unp. MS.   [4] *Letters*, 829.

'News for the Delphic Oracle'

Yeats had kept fairly close to the Delphic Oracle's account of Plotinus's journey to the Elysian fields, as related by Porphyry, in his 'The Delphic Oracle upon Plotinus'. But in this poem he set himself to improve upon the oracle's paradise with three items of 'news'. These represent heaven in three aspects, with decreasing propriety, the first being devoted to heavenly love, the second to innocence, and the third to carnal love.

Probably in no other poem did Yeats combine mockery and seriousness more effectively. For the paradise of Pythagoras and Plotinus in the first section is one of 'golden codgers', and has two unexpected inhabitants, Oisin and Niamh, of whom the oracle had never heard. Yeats is half-satirizing his early work, *The Wanderings of Oisin*, in which Niamh is the more aggressive of the two lovers and therefore 'man-picker'. (In 'The Circus Animals' Desertion', too, Oisin is represented as 'led by the nose'.) The third book of *Oisin* is the 'island of forgetfulness', where there is much sighing and lying about; Yeats associated it at first with introspective dreaming,[1] then with 'thought for its own sake'.[2] His too pure lovers, caught up in mutual contemplation when they might have embraced, are fitting companions for the thoughtful philosophers and fitting denizens of a heaven of such rarefied love.

The finely incongruous image of the codgers as 'golden' probably derived from Diodorus Siculus's allusion to Pythagoras's golden thighs, which Yeats used in 'Among School Children'. The first few lines also allude with mild irony to Enobarbus's description of Cleopatra on her barge.

In the second section Yeats had authority for making the souls of the dead Innocents go to heaven on the backs of dolphins. He had read in Eugénie Strong's *Apotheosis and After Life* that, under the Roman empire, 'The dolphins . . . form a mystic escort of the dead to the Islands of the Blest, and at the same time carry with them an allusion to the purifying power of water and to the part assigned to the watery element in Mithraic and solar cults'.[3] He also mentioned a cast at the Victoria and Albert Museum which helped to shape the image.[4] His waters laugh at the babies' cries, as if the unhappy events which the Innocents relive are now far off, and their suffering only a

---

[1] *Man and Masks*, 52 (51).   [2] *Wheels and Butterflies*, 137 (122).
[3] P. 215.   [4] Unp. notes for *A Vision*.

part of the purifying ritual. But he does not allow us to feel much sorrow for the Church's first martyrs; 'straddling each a dolphin's back / And steadied by a fin', and at last pitched off to paradise by the dolphins, they are faintly ridiculous. For this is no more the Christian than it is the Plotinian or Delphic heaven.

The third section stamps it as a Yeatsian heaven, by adding an element which the first two sections lacked, sensuality. T. R. Henn has discovered that Peleus and Thetis are taken from Poussin's 'The Marriage of Peleus and Thetis', which Yeats had seen in Dublin's National Gallery.[1] But Poussin was not describing heaven, and Yeats's use of the myth has to be taken on its own terms. He transplants Poussin's Peleus and Thetis, his dolphins, nymphs, and satyrs, to another sphere; they help to complete the picture of a heaven which, like his poetry, must satisfy the whole man. Neither the pagans of the first section nor the Christians of the second fulfil this need, although their aspirations can be included, along with a more sensual ideal, in Yeats's more ample paradise.[2]

[1] Henn, 235-6.

[2] Yeats has also modified Poussin's details; for example, he separates the hero and heroine so that they can stare at one another, something which their propinquity in Poussin's picture precluded. The result is to throw into even stronger relief the pagan sensuality of the last four lines of the poem.

A CHRONOLOGY OF THE COMPOSITION
OF THE POEMS[1]

The following titles are arranged in the order of their appearance in
Collected Poems. Where poems are not listed, no information as to the
date of their composition was available.

CROSSWAYS (1889)

'The Song of the Happy Shepherd', 1885
'The Sad Shepherd', 1885
'Anashuya and Vijaya', 188(7 ?)
'The Indian Upon God', 1886
'The Indian to His Love', 1886
'Ephemera', 1884
'The Madness of King Goll', 1884
'The Meditation of the Old Fisherman', June 1886

THE ROSE (1893)

'The Lake Isle of Innisfree', 1890
'The Sorrow of Love', Oct. 1891
'When You Are Old', Oct. 21, 1891

THE WIND AMONG THE REEDS (1899)

'The Hosting of the Sidhe', Aug. 29, 1893
'The Everlasting Voices', Aug. 29, 1895
'The Host of the Air', 1893
'Into the Twilight', June 31, 189(3 ?)
'The Song of Wandering Aengus', Jan. 31, 189(3 ?)
'The Heart of the Woman', 1894
'He Bids His Beloved Be at Peace', Sept. 24, 1895
'A Poet to His Beloved', 1895
'He Gives His Beloved Certain Rhymes', before Aug. 1895
'The Cap and Bells', 1893
'The Lover Asks Forgiveness Because of His Many Moods', Aug. 23, 1895

[1] Not all the dates of composition of the poems are certain, but this list is reasonably
accurate.

'He Tells of the Perfect Beauty', Dec. 1895
'The Lover Speaks to the Hearers of His Songs in Coming Days', Nov. 1895
'The Fiddler of Dooney', Nov. 1892

IN THE SEVEN WOODS (1903)

'Old Memory', Nov. or Dec. 1903
'Adam's Curse', before Nov. 20, 1902
'The Old Men Admiring Themselves in the Water', before Nov. 20, 1902
'O Do Not Love Too Long', before Feb. 23, 1905
'The Players Ask for a Blessing . . .', about June 1902

From THE GREEN HELMET AND OTHER POEMS (1910)

'His Dream', July 3, 1908
'A Woman Homer Sung', April 5–15, 1910
'Words', Jan. 22, 1909
'No Second Troy', Dec. 1908
'Reconciliation', Sept. 1908
'King and No King', Dec. 7, 1909
'Peace', May 1910
'Against Unworthy Praise', May 11, 1910
'The Fascination of What's Difficult', Sept. 1909–March 1910
'A Drinking Song', Feb. 17, 1910
'The Coming of Wisdom with Time', March 1909
'On Hearing that the Students of our New University Have Joined the Agitation Against Immoral Literature', April 3, 1912
'To a Poet, Who Would Have Me Praise Certain Bad Poets, Imitators of His and Mine', April 1909
'The Mask', Aug. 1910
'Upon a House Shaken by the Land Agitation', Aug. 7, 1909
'At the Abbey Theatre', May 1911
'These Are the Clouds', May 1910
'At Galway Races', Oct. 21, 1908
'A Friend's Illness', Feb. 1909

RESPONSIBILITIES (1914)

Introductory Rhymes, Dec. 1913
'The Grey Rock', 1913
'To a Wealthy Man . . .', Dec. 24, 1912

'September 1913', Sept. 1913
'To a Friend Whose Work Has Come to Nothing', Sept. 1913
'Paudeen', Sept. 16, 1913
'To a Shade', Sept. 29, 1913
'When Helen Lived', Sept. 20–29, 1913
'On Those That Hated "The Playboy of the Western World", 1907',
    1909
'The Three Hermits', March 5, 1913
'Beggar to Beggar Cried', March 5, 1913
'Running to Paradise', Sept. 20, 1913
'The Hour Before Dawn', Oct. 19, 1913
'The Witch', May 24, 1912
'The Mountain Tomb', Aug. 1912
'To a Child Dancing in the Wind', 1912
'Two Years Later', Dec. 3, 1912 or 1913
'A Memory of Youth', Aug. 13, 1912
'Fallen Majesty', 1912
'Friends', Jan. 1911
'An Appointment', 1907
'The Magi', Sept. 20, 1913
'The Dolls', Sept. 20, 1913
'A Coat', 1912
Closing Rhyme, 1914

THE WILD SWANS AT COOLE (1919)
'The Wild Swans at Coole', Oct. 1916
'In Memory of Major Robert Gregory', June 14, 1918 (eighth stanza is May
    1918)
'An Irish Airman Foresees His Death', 1918
'Men Improve with the Years', July 19, 1916
'The Collar-Bone of a Hare', July 5, 1915
'Under the Round Tower', March 1918
'Solomon to Sheba', 1918
'The Living Beauty', 1917
'A Song', 1915
'To a Young Beauty', 1918
'To a Young Girl', 1913 or 1915
'The Scholars', 1914 and April 1915
'Tom O'Roughley', Feb. 16, 1918
'Shepherd and Goatherd', March 19, 1918

'Lines Written in Dejection', Oct. (?) 1915
'The Dawn', June 20, 1914
'On Woman', May 21 or 25, 1914
'The Fisherman', June 4, 1914
'Memory', 1915–16
'Her Praise', Jan. 27, 1915
'The People', Jan. 10, 1915
'His Phoenix', Jan. 1915
'A Thought from Propertius', by Nov. 1915
'Broken Dreams', Oct. 24, 1915
'A Deep-Sworn Vow', Oct. 17, 1915
'Presences', Nov. 1915
'To a Squirrel at Kyle-na-no', Sept. 1912
'On Being Asked for a War Poem', Feb. 6, 1915
'In Memory of Alfred Pollexfen', Aug. 1916
'Upon a Dying Lady', 1912–14 (Section I, Jan. 1913; II, Jan. 1912;
    VII, about July 14, 1914)
'Ego Dominus Tuus', Oct. 5, 1915
'A Prayer on Going into My House', 1918
'The Phases of the Moon', 1918
'The Cat and the Moon', 1917
'The Saint and the Hunchback', 1918
'Two Songs of a Fool', 1918
'The Double Vision of Michael Robartes', 1919

MICHAEL ROBARTES AND THE DANCER (1921)

'Michael Robartes and the Dancer', 1918
'Solomon and the Witch', 1918
'An Image from a Past Life', Sept. 1919
'Under Saturn', Nov. 1918
'Easter, 1916', May 11–Sept. 25, 1916
'Sixteen Dead Men', Dec. 17, 1917
'The Rose Tree', April 7, 1917
'On a Political Prisoner', Jan. 10–29, 1919
'The Leaders of the Crowd', 1918–19
'Towards Break of Day', Dec. 1918–Jan. 1919
'Demon and Beast', Nov. 23, 1918
'The Second Coming', Jan. 1919
'A Prayer for My Daughter', Feb. 26–June 1919
'A Meditation in Time of War', Nov. 9, 1914

'To be Carved on a Stone at Thoor Ballylee', 1918

THE TOWER (1928)

'Sailing to Byzantium', Sept. 26, 1926
'The Tower', Oct. 7, 1925
'Meditations in Time of Civil War', 1921–2
'Nineteen Hundred and Nineteen', 1919–22
'The Wheel', Sept. 1921
'Youth and Age', 1924
'The New Faces', Dec. 1912
'A Prayer for My Son', Dec. 1921
'Two Songs from a Play', 1926, except last stanza, 193(1 ?)
'Leda and the Swan', Sept. 18, 1923
'On a Picture of a Black Centaur by Edmund Dulac', Sept. 1920
'Among School Children', June 14, 1926
'Colonus' Praise', March 24, 1927
'Owen Aherne and His Dancers', Oct. 24–7, 1917
'A Man Young and Old', 1926–7 (Section I, May 25, 1926; IV, Jan. 31,
    1926; V, Dec. 1926; VII, July 2, 1926; X, 1926; XI, March 13, 1927)
'All Souls' Night', Nov. 2 (?), 1920

THE WINDING STAIR AND OTHER POEMS (1933)

'In Memory of Eva Gore-Booth and Con Markiewicz', Oct. 1927
'Death', Sept. 13, 1927
'A Dialogue of Self and Soul', July–Dec. 1927
'Blood and the Moon', Aug. 1927
'Oil and Blood', about Dec. 1927
'Veronica's Napkin', 1929
'Symbols', Oct. 1927
'Spilt Milk', Nov. 8, 1930
'The Nineteenth Century and After', Jan.–March 2, 1929
'Statistics', 1931
'Three Movements', Jan. 26, 1932
'The Seven Sages', Jan. 30, 1931
'The Crazed Moon', April 1923
'Coole Park, 1929', 1928–Sept. 7, 1929
'Coole Park and Ballylee, 1931', Feb. 1931
'For Anne Gregory', Sept. 1930
'Swift's Epitaph', 1929 or 1930
'At Algeciras — A Meditation Upon Death', Jan. 23, 1929

'Mohini Chatterjee', Jan. 23–Feb. 9, 1929
'Byzantium', Sept. 1930
'The Mother of God', Sept. 3, 1931
'Vacillation', 1931–2 (Section I, Dec. 1931; IV, Nov. 1931; V, 193(1 ?);
     VI, Jan.–March 5, 1932; VII, Jan. 3–4, 1932; VIII, Jan. 3, 1932)
'Quarrel in Old Age', Nov. 1931
'The Results of Thought', Aug. 18–28, 1931
'Remorse for Intemperate Speech', Aug. 28, 1931
'Stream and Sun at Glendalough', June 23, 1932

WORDS FOR MUSIC PERHAPS

'Crazy Jane and the Bishop', March 2, 1929
'Crazy Jane Reproved', March 27, 1929
'Crazy Jane on the Day of Judgment', Oct. 1930
'Crazy Jane and Jack the Journeyman', Nov. 1931
'Crazy Jane on God', July 18, 1931
'Crazy Jane Talks with the Bishop', Nov. 1931
'Crazy Jane Grown Old Looks at the Dancers', March 2, 1929
'Girl's Song', March 29, 1929
'Young Man's Song', 1929 (after March 29)
'Her Anxiety', 1929 (after April 17)
'His Confidence', 1929 (after March 29)
'Love's Loneliness', April 17, 1929
'Her Dream', 1929 (after March 29)
'His Bargain', 1929 (after March 29)
'Three Things', March 1929
'Lullaby', March 27, 1929
'After Long Silence', Nov. 1929
'Mad as the Mist and Snow', Feb. 12, 1929
'Those Dancing Days Are Gone', March 8, 1929
'I Am of Ireland', Aug. 1929
'The Dancer at Cruachan and Cro-Patrick', Aug. 1931
'Tom the Lunatic', July 27, 1931
'Tom at Cruachan', July 29, 1931
'Old Tom Again', Oct. 1931
'The Delphic Oracle upon Plotinus', Aug. 19, 1931

A WOMAN YOUNG AND OLD

'Before the World Was Made', Feb. 1928
'A First Confession', June 1927

'Her Triumph', Nov. 1929
'Consolation', June 1927
'Parting', Aug. 1926
'Her Vision in the Wood', 1926
'A Last Confession', June 1926
'From the "Antigone"', 1927–8

From A FULL MOON IN MARCH (1935)

'Parnells' Funeral', 1932–April 1933
'Three Songs to the Same Tune', Nov. 30, 1933–Feb. 27, 1934
'Church and State', Aug. 1934
'Ribh at the Tomb of Baile and Ailinn', July 24, 1934
'Ribh Denounces Patrick', July 1934
'Ribh Considers Christian Love Insufficient', 193(4 ?)
'He and She', before Aug. 25, 1934
'The Four Ages of Man', July 24–Aug. 6, 1934
'Conjunctions', a few days before Aug. 25, 1934

LAST POEMS (1936–1939)

'Lapis Lazuli', July 25, 1936
'Imitated from the Japanese', about Dec. 31, 1936
'Sweet Dancer', Jan. 8, 1937
'The Three Bushes', July 1936
'The Lady's First Song', Nov. 20, 1936
'The Lady's Second Song', July 1936
'The Lady's Third Song', July 1936
'The Lover's Song', Nov. 1936
'The Chambermaid's First Song', Nov. 1936
'The Chambermaid's Second Song', Nov. 1936
'To Dorothy Wellesley', Aug. 1, 1936
'The Curse of Cromwell', Jan. 8, 1937
'Roger Casement', Nov. 1936
'The Ghost of Roger Casement', Jan. 1937
'Come Gather Round Me, Parnellites', Sept. 8, 1936
'The Great Day', Jan. 28, 1937
'Parnell', Jan. 28, 1937
'What Was Lost', Jan. 28, 1937
'The Spur', Dec. 1936
'Colonel Martin', Aug. 10, 1937
'A Model for the Laureate', July 26, 1937

'The Old Stone Cross', June 1937

'Those Images', before Aug. 10, 1937

'The Municipal Gallery Revisited', Aug.–Sept. 5, 1937

'The Statues', June, 1938

'Three Marching Songs', rewritten Dec. 1938 from 'Three Songs to the Same Tune', Nov. 30, 1933–Feb. 27, 1934

'Long-legged Fly', Nov. 1937

'John Kinsella's Lament for Mrs. Mary Moore', about July 21–29, 1938

'The Statesman's Holiday', April 1938

'Politics', May 23, 1938

'The Man and the Echo', July–Oct. 1938

'Cuchulain Comforted', Dec. 1938–Jan. 13, 1939

'The Black Tower', Jan. 21, 1939

'Under Ben Bulben', Sept. 4, 1938

NARRATIVE AND DRAMATIC

'Baile and Ailinn', Summer 1901

'The Two Kings', Oct. 1912

NOTES

THE numerals at the left refer to page numbers in this book. The two italicized words which follow the numerals are the end of the quotation or phrase which is being annotated. A list of abbreviations and short titles used in the notes is given on page 250 above.

CHAPTER I

2. *of action.*   *Dramatis Personae* (1936), 134 (143).
3. *of Shelley.*   Ltr. of August 1892. *Man and Masks*, 97-8 (94-5).
   last romantics'.   'Coole Park and Ballylee, 1931', CP, 276 (240).
   and loveliness',   *Idem.*
4. *fixed creature'.*   T. E. Hulme, *Speculations* (London, Routledge, 1949), 117.
   a limit.'   *Ibid.* 120.
   exceedingly complex.   An unp. ltr. to Annie Horniman of about 1907 puts his position eloquently. Miss Horniman had suggested that, in view of the controversy over Synge's *Playboy of the Western World*, Yeats write for the English instead of the Irish theatre. He replied : 'I am not young enough to change my nationality — it would really amount to that. Though I wish for a universal audience, in play-writing there is always an immediate audience also. If I were to try to find this immediate audience in England I would fail through lack of understanding on my part perhaps through lack of sympathy. I understand my own race and in all my work, lyric or dramatic, I have thought of it. If the theatre fails I may or may not write plays, — there is always lyric poetry to return to — but I shall write for my own people — whether in love or hate of them matters little — probably I shall not know which it is.'

His nationalism was literary, not chauvinistic. He denied that he had written even *Cathleen Ni Houlihan* with any thought of its political implications. His unpublished notes, written for Horace Plunkett's use in the inquiry of 1904 into the Abbey Theatre's patent, asserted : 'It may be said that it is a political play of a propagandist kind. This I deny. I took a piece of human life, thoughts that men had felt, hopes they had died for, and I put this into what I believe to be a sincere dramatic form. I have never written a play to advocate any kind of opinion and I think that such a play would be necessarily bad art, or at any rate a very humble kind of art. At the same time I feel that I have no right to exclude for myself or for others, any of the passionate material of drama.'

5. *inviolate Rose*'   'The Secret Rose', CP, 77 (67).
   and 'whole'   'Crazy Jane Talks with the Bishop', CP, 295 (255).
6. *'dull decrepitude'*   'The Tower', CP, 224 (197).
7. *of excrement,*   'Crazy Jane Talks with the Bishop', CP, 295 (255).
   his grave.'   'Tom O'Roughley', CP, 159 (139); probably a reminiscence of Blake, who affirmed to Crabb Robinson 'that he had committed many murders, and repeated his doctrine, that reason is the only sin, and that careless, gay people are better than those who think, etc. etc.' *The Portable Blake* (New York, Viking, 1946), 692. Yeats quoted Blake's remarks in *Dramatis Personae* (1936), 92 (99).
   Genius unity'.   Unp. MS.
   single circle.   One of Yeats's clearest statements of this desire is an unp. MS. entitled 'The Return of the Stars', which he dictated on May 24, 1908. He says there in part : 'An old thought came back to me — we are completing in this age a work begun in the Renaissance — we are re-uniting the mind and soul and body of man, to the living world outside us. Christianity revolted against the nature-worship of the heathen, and gradually as Christianity completed itself, and especially when the Paradise it set in Nature's place began to fade, set the mind of man apart like a pebble where nothing is reflected, a hard and abstract thing, with nature for tempter or breaker. Whether you call that abstract thing the reason or the soul matters very little, for to both alike in the long run when their own sweetness is exhausted comes weariness as they look out upon a world which seems no longer a portion of themselves — what the painters and poets, who rediscovered landscape, joyous movement, the voluptuous body, began, the astrologer, who arose with the interpretation of Ptolemy by Palidus a Spanish monk, and the spiritist and the student of Eastern contemplation are carrying into the very depths of the soul, restoring to us the meaning of tonight's mystery, bringing into our houses (for the seance room has but to move into the country to discover that old world) the cloven foot of the faun, the devil who inhabits fields and hills, lucky hours that double time's mystery, and hours that measure the tides of being, setting stars to keep the bounds of pleasure and excitement.'

are wed'.   'Ribh Denounces Patrick', CP, 328 (283).

lover's night' ;   *The King of the Great Clock Tower* (1935), 13.

they bend',   'The Municipal Gallery Revisited', CP, 369 (317).

8. *more conflict* " '.   Hone, 459 (491).

my self-knowledge'.   Unp. ltr., undated ; the whole passage reads :
'I once wrote you some hurried sentences about "peace and again
peace" and I think you misunderstood me. I think that we must
for the most part choose war in the soul, peace in external circumstance or peace in the soul, war in circumstance ; or in other words
I find my peace by pitting my sole nature against something and
the greater the tension the greater my self-knowledge.'

beast underneath.'   *Letters on Poetry from W. B. Yeats to Dorothy
Wellesley* (New York, Oxford, 1940), 94.

CHAPTER II

12. *one's life.*'   Ltr. to Elizabeth White, January 30, 1889. Hone,
83 (87).

14. *and knowledge*',   Ltr. to Katharine Tynan, 1888. Tynan, *The
Middle Years* (London, Constable, 1916), 39.

Muses home'.   'Those Images', CP, 367 (316).

all possible.'   Ltr. to Tynan, 1889. Tynan, *Middle Years*, 54.

wonder at.'   Ltr. to Tynan, about 1888. Tynan, *Twenty-Five
Years : Reminiscences* (London, Constable, 1913), 262.

Moll Magee,   'The Ballad of Moll Magee', CP, 25-7 (22-4). Yeats
submitted this poem to O'Leary for the *Gael*, and when O'Leary
rejected it as morbid, replied : 'I do not think the Howth one
morbid though now on thinking it over I quite agree with you
that . . . [it is not] suitable for a newspaper'. Unp. ltr., 1888,
copy in Central Library, Belfast.

on me',   This line is from the early version of 'The Lamentation
of the Old Pensioner', *Poems* (London, Unwin, 1899), 132, and
note, 295.

to him.   'Down by the Salley Gardens', CP, 22 (20) ; see also
Poems (1899), note, 294.

15. *right through.*'   Ltr. to O'Leary, October 1890. *Irish Book
Lover* (November 1940), 247.

Peter's gate. . . .   *Mosada* (Dublin, Sealy, Bryers, & Walker,
1886), 56.

of Munster'.   *The Wanderings of Oisin and Other Poems* (London,
Kegan Paul, 1889), 98.

Irish novelist.   Ltr. of Dec. 2, 1891.   W. B. Yeats, *Letters to Katharine Tynan* (Dublin, Clonmore & Reynolds, 1953), 132. Roger McHugh, ed.

16. *little of.*   'The Poet of Ballyshannon', *Letters to the New Island* (Cambridge, Mass., Harvard, 1934), 174.   Horace Reynolds, ed.

18. *expressing ourselves.'*   Ltr. of Dec. 4, 1888.   Yeats, *Letters to Tynan*, 75-6.

'independent life'.   Elizabeth A. Sharp, *William Sharp* (New York, Duffield, 1910), 335.

living one.   Yeats, 'Introduction', in Percy Arland Ussher, *The Midnight Court* (London, Cape, 1926), 7.

all life.   *Wheels and Butterflies* (1934), 101-2 (91-2).

his own.   In a ltr. to the editor of the *Spectator*, August 3, 1889, Yeats listed his Ossianic sources and then said : 'The pages dealing with the three islands . . . are wholly my own, having no further root in tradition than the Irish peasant's notion that Tir-n-an-oge (the Country of the Young) is made up of three phantom islands'.

vain repose'.   'The Circus Animals' Desertion', CP, 391 (336).

English chains.   See also *Man and Masks*, 51-5 (50-54).

never done'   'The Rose of Battle', CP, 42 (37).

19. *'eternal pursuit'*   *Wheels and Butterflies* (1934), 101 (91).

20. *and antiquity',*   T. S. Eliot, 'Ulysses, Order, and Myth', *Dial*, 75 (Nov. 1923), 480-83.

of tapestry'.   *Dramatis Personae* (1936), 35 (37).

21. *fields of tapestry. . . .*   *The Countess Kathleen and Various Legends and Lyrics* (London, Unwin, 1892), 32.

shadowy folds'.   Programme note for *The Shadowy Waters*, *Inis Fail* (August 1905). Cf. *Early Poems and Stories* (1925), 474.

22. *wandering tress. . . .*   'He Gives His Beloved Certain Rhymes', CP, 71 (61).

a thread. . . .   'The Song of Wandering Aengus', CP, 66 (57). The second line may owe something to the opening of Arthur Symons's 'The Broken Tryst', 'That day a fire was in my blood', which Yeats would have read in *The Book of the Rhymers' Club* (London, Mathews, 1892), 19.

numberless dreams. . . .   'A Poet to His Beloved', CP, 70 (61).

23. *dim hair. . . .*   'The Lover Mourns for the Loss of Love', CP, 68 (59).

lingering hand. . . .   'He Remembers Forgotten Beauty', CP, 70 (60).

pearl-pale hand. . . .   'He Gives His Beloved Certain Rhymes',
CP, 71 (61).

has worn. . . .   'A Poet to His Beloved', CP, 70 (61).

dream-dimmed eyes. . . .   'He Tells of a Valley Full of Lovers',
CP, 74 (64).

24. *in dream*.   Unp. MS.

mental states.   'I sought some symbolic language reaching far
into the past and associated with familiar names and conspicuous
hills that I might not be alone amid the obscure impressions of the
senses. . . .'   'Art and Ideas' (1913), *Essays*, 433.

of them.   Yeats, 'A New Poet [AE]', *Bookman*, 6 (August 1894),
147-8.

and wind'.   AU, 112.

25. *its totality*.   Yeats and Edwin John Ellis, *The Works of William
Blake* (London, Quaritch, 1893), I, 238.

26. *and forms*.   'The Symbolism of Poetry', *Essays*, 191. As F. W.
Bateson has noted in *English Poetry* (London, Longmans, 1950),
124, the lines from Burns should read :

> The wan moon is setting ayont the white wave,
> And time is setting with me, oh !

Yeats's misquotation adds to the symbolic content of 'white'.

the results :   Unp. journal, dated October 1889.

27. *music, energy*.'   *Letters from Yeats to Wellesley*, 95. In FD Yeats
acknowledged his debt to Mathers and the Golden Dawn : 'Now,
too, I learned a practice, a form of meditation that has perhaps been
the intellectual chief influence in my life up to perhaps my fortieth
year. . . . There was nothing in the symbolism, so far as I could
judge, to have called up this result — if it was associations of ideas
they were subtle and subconscious. As I mastered the Kabbalah
I discovered that his [Mathers's] geometric symbols were a series
which I could classify according to the four elements, and what
the ancients call the fifth element, and the sub-divisions of these. . . .
I allowed my mind to drift from image to image and these images
began to affect my writing, making it more sensuous and more
vivid. I believed that with the images would come at last more
profound states of the soul, and was lost in vain hope.'

28. *in 1893*.   For the distribution of labour between Yeats and Ellis
see Yeats's note in Allan Wade, *A Bibliography of the Writings of
W. B. Yeats* (London, Hart-Davis, 1951), 217. See also AU,
199-200.

and thought.'   Yeats, *Letters to Tynan*, 142.

one another.   In an epilogue which Yeats apparently planned to include in *Per Amica Silentia Lunae*, but eventually omitted, one of the characters gives a Blake-like account of the world : 'I heard a voice talking in the hedge, and like the chirruping of a bat and it is saying that before the fall man had his head in the fire, his heart in the air, his loins in the water, and his feet on the earth, and that after Eve pulled the apple, he has had his feet on the fire, his loins in the air, his heart in the water, and his head in the earth'. Unp. MS.

The symbols for head, heart, loins, and fall appear in the diagram in *Vision* (1937), 66.

29. (*presumably seen*).   A further complication is that the talismans have different significations in the 'inner man' and the 'outer man'. So in the outer man the spear is 'fire but in the inner man it has its affinities rather with air. In the same way the passions and enthusiasms are the driving powers of the outer man and are therefore of fire but in the inner man they are driven by spiritual thought like the winds. The passions are therefore in reality of the Kingdom of the Air.' Unp. MS. In *A Vision* the four faculties and the four principles have a rough equivalence to outer man and inner man.

30. *at Peace'*,   Afterwards entitled, 'He Bids His Beloved Be at Peace', CP, 69 (59).

31. *majestical multitude*.   'To His Heart, Bidding It Have No Fear', CP, 71 (62).

dreaming things'.   The Wind Among the Reeds (London, Mathews, 1899), 90.

32. *Kathleen-Ny-Hoolihan*.   National Observer, 12 (August 4, 1894), 303-4. The poem was later much changed.

may cease. . . .   'The Poet Pleads with the Elemental Powers,' CP, 80 (69).

sighs too. . . .   'When You Are Sad', Countess Kathleen (1892), 129 ; not reprinted in CP.

33. *I love*.   Countess Kathleen (1892), 120.

lonely   mysteries.   'Michael   Robartes   Remembers   Forgotten Beauty', *Wind Among the Reeds* (1899), 28 ; altered in CP, 69-70 (60-61), where title is, 'He Remembers. . . .'

34. *of time*. . . .   'A Poet to His Beloved', CP, 70 (61).

flaming door.   'The Valley of the Black Pig', CP, 73 (63).

burn time. . . .   'He Tells of the Perfect Beauty', CP, 75 (64).

passing feet.   'He Gives His Beloved Certain Rhymes', CP, 71 (61).

of fire.   'The Blessed', CP, 77 (66).

and fro'.   'To Ireland in the Coming Times', CP, 57 (50).

the country.' Ltr. of October 8, 1890. *Irish Book Lover*
(November 1940), 246.

to each. Yeats's notes on these characters in *The Wind Among
the Reeds* (1899), 73-4, require amplification. Hanrahan is 'fire
blown by the wind' or 'the simplicity of an imagination too change-
able to gather permanent possessions'. The imagination is fire;
the emotions that besiege it, as well as its susceptibility to them, are
related to the wind or the element of air. As a description of
Hanrahan, these words apply better to the prose stories about him
in *The Secret Rose*, which Yeats was composing at the same time,
than to the poems, where he remains a shadowy figure. But the
principle of assigning to Hanrahan the three poems, 'Hanrahan
[later 'He'] Reproves the Curlew', 'Hanrahan Laments Because
of His Wanderings [later 'Maid Quiet']', and 'Hanrahan [later
'The Lover'] Speaks to the Lovers [later 'Hearers'] of his Songs
in Coming Days', must have been that they had wind, air, or flight
imagery in common to describe emotional states.

The sketch of Robartes is equally elliptical. He is 'fire reflected
in water' or 'the pride of the imagination brooding upon the
greatness of its possessions'. The association of water with dreams
has the obvious naturalistic basis that countless images of reality
form in water but remain illusive there. Yeats means more than
this. To be fire reflected in water suggests a conflict of energy
and stillness, a kind of suspended animation, and suits the Robartes
poems, where the speaker expresses a dreamy, contemplative
passion in the most elaborate and allusive way. Still water seems
to be also a means of retention, of hoarding imaginative things.
Robartes' poems were: 'Michael Robartes [later 'He'] Bids His
Beloved Be at Peace', 'Michael Robartes [later 'He'] Remembers
Forgotten Beauty', and 'Michael Robartes [later 'The Lover']
Asks Forgiveness Because of His Many Moods'.

Robartes' poems are much less immediate and intense than
those of Aedh (the Irish word for 'fire'), whom Yeats depicts as
'fire burning by itself' or 'the myrrh and frankincense that the
imagination offers continually before all that it loves'. Aedh is
more concerned with a present passion than Hanrahan or Robartes,
being neither a will-o'-the-wisp nor a hoarder of splendid images,
and less likely to ponder some memory of past frustration or of
ancient beauty than his present hapless plight. His poems were:
'Aedh Laments [later 'The Lover Mourns for'] the Loss of Love',
'Aedh [later 'The Poet'] Pleads with the Elemental Powers', and a
group in which his name later became simply 'he': 'Aedh Gives

His Beloved Certain Rhymes', 'Aedh Tells of the Perfect Beauty', 'Aedh Hears the Cry of the Sedge', 'Aedh Thinks of Those Who Have Spoken Evil of His Beloved', 'Aedh Wishes His Beloved Were Dead', 'Aedh Wishes for the Cloths of Heaven'.

The distinction between the characters is not perfect ; they are, as Yeats said, 'principles of the mind' rather than 'actual personages', and even as principles of the mind are not perfectly separated.

36. *the body.*   Jeffares, 283.
   or above.   *Ibid.* 282-4. Compare *Vision* (1937), 93.
37. *long ago.*   *Bookman*, 5 (November 1893), 76. Not reprinted.
   sisters born.   Unp. MS.

CHAPTER III

39. *our age.*   *A Packet for Ezra Pound* (Dublin, Cuala, 1929), 32-3. Compare *Vision* (1937), 24-5, and 'Introduction' to *The Resurrection* in *Wheels and Butterflies* (1934), 101 (91). In an unp. MS. for the second edition of *A Vision*, Yeats asks rhetorically : 'Who will understand if I say that I must and should believe it because it is a myth?' The words 'must' and 'should' emphasize the pragmatic approach.

40. *human survival ;*   'Preliminary Script of E.R.', unp. MS.
   the mind.   See above, pp. 239-40.
   extent unpoetic.   An unp. ltr. of J. B. Yeats to Edward Dowden, written in the year 1870, contains a passage that deserves to be known :

'I wish we knew something about the laws and nature and real essence of belief. What is the nature of the link by which Browning is attached to his peculiar ideas etc. — what is this link which constitutes his belief ? Shakespeare and the great poets seem to me always to be attached to their ideas by quite a different link from that by which such a man as Browning is attracted to his ideas. The psychological question of the nature of belief lies at the root of the whole of criticism. I strongly suspect that a man who writes much prose dims his poetic faculty (at least if the prose be of the oratorical and persuasive kind) by practising and cultivating in himself a kind of belief foreign from the whole nature of poetry.'

See also his ltr. to W. B. Yeats, written about 1915, in *Passages from the Letters of J. B. Yeats* (Dundrum, Cuala, 1917), 10.

41. *unbecome me.*   *Celtic Twilight* (London, Bullen, 1902), 1-2. See also Robert Bridges' discerning ltr. to Yeats about *The Secret Rose*

in Hone (English edition only — London, Macmillan, 1942), 136.

violent shock'.   *Wheels and Butterflies* (1934), 110 (98).

empty day'.   *Bookman*, 4 (April 1893), 21.

42. *this obvious?*   'Some Passages from the Letters of W. B. Yeats to A.E.', *Dublin Magazine*, 14 (July–September 1939), 15. Corrected by reference to copy in possession of Dr. James Starkey. Russell replied with some heat : 'I deny altogether that Beauty is the *sole* end and law of poetry. Even there you will find very few poets who declaring the law of their art will agree with you. I think the true and the Good, using them in the old Hermetic sense, are equally the subject of verse and demand an equal share in the guidance of the writer. . . . With regard to the use of words it is quite allowable to use some which express ideas with a peculiar fitness even if the word be modern or not beautiful. . . . Ideas have a beauty in themselves apart from words, and in literature or art I think the aim of the writer should be to afford an avenue to the idea, and make the reader forget the words or painting or sound which first evoked it. To quote Plato in *The Banquet*, the aim of the initiate is to lead the neophyte from the perception of the beauty of forms or sounds or colours to the beauty of laws and of ideas until at last he attains a vision which is equal to a beauty so vast. I find nothing to agree with in your letter and see clearly that in mysticism and in our ideas we have little or nothing in common.' *Some Passages from the Letters of AE to W. B. Yeats* (Dublin, Cuala, 1936), 26-7.

43. *Daimon-possessed.*   Copy of unp. ltr. dated April 20, 1929.

certain ideas'.   'A New Poet', *Bookman*, 6 (August 1894), 147-8.

emotional colours.'   Pound, *Guide to Kulchur* (London, Faber, 1938), 295.

44. *be again.'*   'The Pathway', *Collected Works* (1908), VIII, 193.

45. *ever be.*   *Wanderings of Oisin* (1889), 68.

47. *past incarnations;*   For Taliesin see Matthew Arnold, *The Study of Celtic Literature* (London, Smith, Elder, 1891), 57-8. I owe this source to John V. Kelleher. For Mongan see H. d'Arbois de Jubainville, *The Irish Mythological Cycle* (Dublin, Hodges, Figgis, 1903), 190-96 ; Yeats's Mongan only slightly resembles the legendary Mongan, himself an elusive character.

his poems,   A curious poetic example is the poem 'Ephemera'. The version published in *Wanderings of Oisin* (1889) ends on a note of scepticism about reincarnation ; but by 1895, in a new edition of his poems, Yeats removed the sceptical lines.

48. *Buddhist Nirvana.*   A description of heaven that recurs in Yeats

owes much to a vision of one of his friends, Mrs. Dorothea Hunter, early in the 'nineties. Once, when she was in a sort of trance, he asked her, 'What is the nature of the Music of Heaven?' to which she at once replied, 'The continuous clashing of earth's swords'. When in the nineteen-thirties she wrote to remind him of it, he replied, 'Yes, of course I remember. In a vision you described to me of the music of Heaven you heard as the clashing of swords. That had a great influence on my thought.' Unp. ltr. to Mrs. Hunter, in her possession.

He did, in fact, use it directly in 'To Some I Have Talked with by the Fire', where he imagines the angels

> Who rise, wing above wing, flame above flame,
> And, like a storm, cry the Ineffable Name,
> And with the clashing of their sword-blades make
> A rapturous music. . . .

In his story, 'The Death of Hanrahan the Red', Hanrahan hears 'a sound like the continuous clashing of many swords'. *Secret Rose* (1897), 186, 194-5. The hero of *Where There Is Nothing* (London, Bullen, 1903), 44, declares : 'But the music I have heard sometimes is made of the continual clashing of swords. It comes rejoicing from Paradise.' In the later version of that play, *The Unicorn from the Stars* (New York, Macmillan, 1908), 128-9, the idea is embellished : 'Father John, heaven is not what we have believed it to be. It is not quiet ; it is not singing and making music and all strife at an end. I have seen it, I have been there. The lover still loves, but with a greater passion ; and the rider still rides, but the horse goes like the wind and leaps the ridges ; and the battle goes on always, always. That is the joy of heaven, continual battle.'

Yeats probably had also in mind the ending of Blake's poem *Vala*, which he and Ellis were the first to publish ; it ends with an image of the state of perfection as 'intellectual war'.

happy townland',   'The Happy Townland', CP, 94-6 (82-4).

glittering town',   'The Players Ask for a Blessing on the Psalteries and on Themselves', CP, 93 (82).

dancing-place'.   'Upon a Dying Lady', CP, 179 (156).

for it'.   J. B. Yeats, *Letters* (London, Faber, 1944, and New York, Dutton, 1946), 123. Joseph Hone, ed.

separate feelings.'   *Ibid.* 179. Cf. *Letters* (ed. Wade), 384, 731.

49. *consuming ecstasy.* . . .   A bound proof copy of the volume, *The Countess Kathleen* (1892), is in the Sterling Memorial Library

of Yale University, which has kindly permitted me to quote
Yeats's corrections. Compare 'To Ireland in the Coming Times',
CP, 57-8 (50).

50. *and woods.* *The Shadowy Waters, North American Review*, 170
(May 1900), 729.

new cycle. Yeats's story, 'Rosa Alchemica', began in its original
publication with the story of 'a priest, unfrocked for drunkenness,
who had preached at the roadside of the secret coming of the
Antichrist'. *Savoy*, 2 (April 1896), 56.

without bristles, 'He Mourns for the Change That Has Come
Upon Him and His Beloved, and Longs for the End of the World',
CP, 68 (59).

black pig, 'The Valley of the Black Pig', CP, 73 (63), and note to
Wind Among the Reeds (1899), 95.-102.

death-pale deer. *Wind Among the Reeds* (1899), 51. In a note to
the poem he speaks of the deer as a symbol 'of night and of shadow'.
'O'Sullivan the Red upon His Wanderings', *New Review*, 17
(August 1897), 162.

51. *difficult school.* Ltr. of April 30, 1896, partly published in Hone,
153 (161). Complete text among Hone papers at National
Library, Dublin.

52. *taken place.* Unp. MS.

the gods'. 'The Tribes of Danu', *New Review*, 17 (November
1897), 550.

ampler life. In an early unp. draft of *Per Amica Silentia Lunae*,
Yeats wrote : 'After I had written "Rosa Alchemica" I became
restless. I was dissatisfied with its elaborate style where there is
little actual circumstance, nothing natural, but always an artificial
splendour. The lamp that had burned before Solomon would not
light the stars' bedroom and who knows what terrifying shadows
lay in wait. I must find a tradition, that was a part of actual history,
that had associations in the scenery of my own country, and so bring
my speech closer to that of daily life. Prompted as I believed by
certain dreams and premonitions I returned to Ireland, and with a
friend's help began a study of the supernatural belief of the Galway
and Aran cottages. Could I not found an Eleusinian Rite, which
would bind into a common symbolism, a common meditation, a
school of poets and men of letters, so that poetry and drama would
find the religious weight they have lacked since the middle ages
perhaps since ancient Greece ? I did not intend it to be a revival of
the pagan world, how could one ignore so many centuries, but a
reconciliation, where there would be no preaching, no public interest.

I could not like a Frenchman look for my tradition to the Catholic Church for in Ireland to men of my descent, organized Catholicism, with its Guido Reni, and its Manuals, does not seem traditional ; and in the cottages I found what seemed to me medieval Christianity, now that of Rome, now that of the Celtic Church, which turned rather to Byzantium, shot through as it were with perhaps the oldest faith of man.   Could not a poet believe gladly in this country Christ. . . .'

Compare AU, 313-15 ; *Per Amica Silentia Lunae* in *Essays*, 538 ; *If I Were Four-and-Twenty* (Dublin, Cuala, 1940), 1-6.

was mischievous.   *Some Passages from the Letters of AE* (1936), 39. As a young man, Yeats wrote Ethel Mannin in an unp. ltr. of December 11, 1936, he was accustomed to repeat to himself Blake's lines :

> And he his seventy disciples sent
> Against religion and government.

53. *first version.*   Compare 'O'Sullivan Rua to Mary Lavell', *Savoy*, 3 (July 1896), 67 ; 'Michael Robartes Remembers Forgotten Beauty', *Wind Among the Reeds* (1899), 28 ; 'He Remembers Forgotten Beauty', CP, 70 (60).

'Eternal Darkness',   'The Seeker', *Dublin University Review*, I (September 1885), 120-23.

'Supreme Enchanter'   'Magic' (1901), *Essays*, 63.

'Ineffable Name',   'To Some I Have Talked with by the Fire', CP, 56 (49).

of Lights',   *The Countess Cathleen*, in *Poems* (1899), 95.

flaming door'.   'The Valley of the Black Pig', CP, 73 (63).

the skies'   'The Wild Old Wicked Man', CP, 356 (307).

Thirteenth Cone'.   *Vision* (1937), 210, 301-2.

full sound'.   Unp. ltr. to Russell, in possession of Dr. James Starkey, probably written late in 1898.

54. *no mystic.*   Bose's account of Yeats's remarks is among Hone papers at National Library, Dublin.

can command.'   *Idem.*

55. *extremely wary.*   The Virgin Mary appears rather frequently in Yeats's early work, but is deprived of institutional significance. Part of the squabble over the *Countess Cathleen* in 1899 was due to his having spoken publicly 'of our apprehension of the invisible by symbol, so I must have said the Virgin Mary was a symbol'. FD.

In 'The Unappeasable Host' the Virgin serves as an opposite for the fairies, who are described tactfully not as more beautiful than she, but as comelier than the candles before her feet. She appears as intercessor in 'The Lover Speaks to the Hearers of His Songs in Coming Days', where as 'Maurya [a poor phonetic rendering of the Irish 'Máire'] of the Wounded Heart' she rescues his beloved and him from a state resembling purgatory; but Yeats eventually transformed her into 'the attorney for Lost Souls' so as to make the poem less exclusively Christian.

55. *individual's heart.*   *Secret Rose* (1897), 223-35, 257.

   a day?'   Unp. MS. An amusing letter from Yeats to his friend F. J. Gregg, written from Rosses Point about 1886, carries on his campaign against Eliot :

'MY DEAR GREGG,

   I have only read four books of George Elliot's [*sic*] — Silas Marner, Romola, Spanish Gypsy, and a volume of selections. I don't mean to read a fifth.

   Reasons why

Firstly

   Tito, her most famous character, is as interesting as a cat on the vivisection table. In him there is none of that beauty that Hugo gave to everything he touched not only to Esmeralda but to the hunchback. In literature nothing that is not beautiful has any right to exist. Tito is created out of anger not love.

Secondly—

   She understands only the conscious nature of man, his intellect, morals — she knows nothing of the dim unconscious nature, the world of instinct which (if there is any truth in Darwin) is the accumulated wisdom of all living things from the monera to man while the other is at the very most the wisdom gathered during four score years and ten.

Thirdly her beloved analysis is a scrofula of literature. All the greatest books of the world are synthetic, Homeric.

Fourthly she has morals but no religion. If she had more religion she would have less morals. The moral impulse and the religious destroy each other in most cases.

Fifthly I never met a George Elliotite who had either imagination or spirit enough for a good lie.

Sixthly In the "Spanish Gypsy" there are seven arguments of about fifty pages each. This is the way she describes passion.

Seventhly She is too reasonable. I hate reasonable people. The activity of their brains sucks up all the blood out of their hearts.

I was once afraid of turning out reasonable myself. The only buisness [*sic*] of the head in the world is to bow a ceaseless obeisance to the heart.

Yours truly,

W. B. YEATS'

Unp. ltr. in Lockwood Memorial Library of the University of Buffalo.

or good.   *Celtic Twilight* (1902), 61.

my being'.   *Early Poems and Stories* (1925), 513.

56. *the other.*   Unp. ltr. to J. B. Yeats, November 24, 1909.

complete man,   Yeats and Ellis, *Blake*, I, 241. Compare Yeats's annotations in his copy of Nietzsche, pp. 96-7 above, and his discussion of affirmative capability, pp. 238-45 above.

such knots.   Unp. MS.

at all'.   *Vision* (1925), 214-15 ; compare his statement in *Discoveries* (1906) that the morality of art 'is personal, knows little of any general law. . . .' *Essays*, 362. A somewhat different ethical scheme is implied in his ltr. to Russell of 1898: 'It is bad morals not to obey to the utmost the law of one's art for good writing is the way art has of being moral and the only way'. Unp. ltr. in possession of Dr. James Starkey.

her youth   'On Being Asked for a War Poem', CP, 175 (153).

57. *shabby penumbra'.*   'Irish Folk Tales', *National Observer*, 5 (February 28, 1891), 382.

world beyond';   *Celtic Twilight* (1902), 182. First published in *Scots Observer*, 1 (March 2, 1889), 411. He speaks of the 'independent reality of our thoughts' in *Secret Rose* (1897), 250 ; of the animating of images in 'Magic' (1901), *Essays*, 43, 49; and of the similarity of dreams and external objects in 'The Philosophy of Shelley's Poetry' (1900), *ibid.* 93.

masterful reality . . .'.   *Celtic Twilight* (1902), 93.

our feet.'   *Ibid.* 7.

58. *mortal dream'.*   'The Hosting of the Sidhe', CP, 61 (53). *Cf.* 'The Rose of the World', CP, 41 (36).

God Almighty'.   *The Writings of William Blake* (London, Nonesuch, 1925), III, 162. Geoffrey Keynes, ed.

another's truth?'   *Celtic Twilight* (1902), 10.

intellectual falsehoods ;   FD.

musical tongues.'   'The Message of the Folk-Lorist', *Speaker*, 8 (August 19, 1893), 188-9.

59. *mortal things*',   'The Wisdom of the King', *Secret Rose* (1897),
21. A poem written in 1893, 'The Moods', salutes their permanence :

> But, kindly old rout
> Of the fire-born moods,
> You pass not away.

Celtic Twilight (1902), vi ; the version in CP, 62 (54), is not so
explicit.
of leaves.   *Secret Rose* (1897), 252-3.
a means. . . .   'The Moods', *Essays*, 239-40 ; *cf. Celtic Twilight*
(1902), 6-7.
name God.   Yeats and Ellis, *Blake*, I, 239.

60. *its existence'.*   *The Hour-Glass* . . ., *Being Volume Two of Plays
for an Irish Theatre* (London, Bullen, 1904), 13.
the world.'   Unp. MS.
solipsist theory.   The similarity of Yeats's thought to his father's
is remarkably illustrated by this amusing catechism which J. B.
Yeats sent his son about 1915 :

> 'What are you ?   I am myself.
> What is your duty to your neighbour ?   To love him as myself.
> Who is your neighbour ?   Myself.
> Who is myself ?   My neighbour.
> What is necessary to salvation ?   To believe that I myself am the
> centre of the Universe for which it exists.
> What is necessary to salvation ?   That I love myself with my
> whole soul and strength.
> Can an imperfect man love himself ?   No.
> How does a man become perfect ?   By making of himself a fresh
> creation.
> Does the creation take place in the material world or in the
> immaterial world ?   In the immaterial world.
> What is the immaterial world?   The world of imagination.'

Unp. ltr.

61. *our lives'.*   Unp. ltr., February 21, 1901.   The next day he
added : 'All that we do with intensity has an origin in the hidden
world, and is the symbol, the expression of its powers, and even
the smallest detail in a professedly magical dispute may have
significance'. Unp. ltr., February 22, 1901.

A secret pamphlet he wrote for the Golden Dawn has the same
tenor : 'The central principle of all the Magic of power is that
everything we formulate in the imagination, if we formulate it

strongly enough, realises itself in the circumstances of life, acting either through our own souls, or through the spirits of nature'. *Is the Order of R.R. & A.C.* [*Rosae Rubeae et Aureae Crucis*] *to Remain a Magical Order?*' (London, Privately Printed, 1902), 21.

to enter. In an early version of 'Rosa Alchemica' he suggested that symbolism would itself become a religion. *Savoy,* 2 (April 1896), 66-7.

CHAPTER IV

62. *the 'nineties.* See, for example, *Celtic Twilight* (1902), 22. The book was first published in 1893.

visible array'. See above, p. 105.

emotional resources'. A. G. Lehmann, *The Symbolist Aesthetic in France, 1885–1895* (Oxford, Blackwell, 1950), 306.

63. *with emotions'.* 'The Symbolism of Poetry', *Essays,* 197.

the procession. Ibid. 198.

66. *the abyss. Shadowy Waters,* in *Collected Works* (1908), II, 236.

in magic'. Unp. MS.

67. *the Cross. Bookman,* 9 (October 1895), 16.

passionate dream. Christian imagery in the same symbolical, not necessarily Christian sense, occurs in the story 'Of Costello the Proud . . .', *Secret Rose* (1897), 111-12 :

'He was of those ascetics of passion who keep their hearts pure for love or for hatred as other men for God, for Mary and for the saints, and who, when the hour of their visitation arrives, come to the Divine Essence by the bitter tumult, the Garden of Gethsemane, and the desolate Rood ordained for immortal passions in mortal hearts.'

68. *into song.* . . . *Mosada* (1886), 1.

a symbol. In *Discoveries* (1906), Yeats urges that 'familiar woods and rivers should fade into symbol' with a very gradual change. *Essays,* 368. Among his early manuscripts are two poems, obviously uncompleted, which show his concentration on the rose image. In both it is on the verge of symbolism. They date from about 1885 :

Sudden as I sat in a wood
An old grey bard before me stood
His eyes were burning with molten fire
He touched the strings of a silver lyre

It was like the voice of the spring
And to it he began to sing
'Many have sung of maiden fair
Many have sung of golden hair
Many have sung of eyes of blue
I sing of highborn maiden too
Of all maidens she is the peerless
O no mortal has a face so sweet
Around each man's heart she has wrapt a tress
Of the blazing hair that rolls to her feet
Her voice is in the treacherous echo
Her eyes are the flames of yellow
That burn in flickering light
Above the marsh at night
Some she loves happy are those'
He ceased. I held a crumpled rose
I looked before the old grey man gone
This long haired scald
What was he called
Was he the mind of the rose
. . . Who knows
I heard the caw of a rook
And the gurgle of a far off brook.

The second example is from his unp. play, *The Blindness* :

There sings a rose by the rim
Of a rock in the woodways dim
  Where patter the rabbit's feet
  And the foot of the squirrel rushes
  Through the home of the babbling thrushes
A song that is giddy and sweet.

'Dear wind, I long to rest
Upon thy song-heaved breast
  If a light silt [?] over it flows
  Then ah for the ruined glow
  Of the scattered petals a-blow
Ah dead of thy love, poor rose.'

69. *the night.* . . .   *Wanderings of Oisin* (1889), 13-14.
70. *relation is.*   Compare the images in stanzas xxv-xxvi of Shelley's
    Revolt of Islam.

special birds,   'Folk-lore makes the souls of the blessed take upon themselves every evening the shape of white birds, and . . . is ever anxious to keep us from troubling their happiness with our grief.' 'The Message of the Folk-Lorist', *Speaker*, 8 (August 19, 1893), 188-9.

71. *shadowy folds'.*   Programme Note, *Inis Fail*, August 1905, in Henderson Collection.

up another',   *Poems* (London, Unwin, 1899), vii.

of Peace'. Ibid. (1895) v-vi.

my friends'.   'The High Crosses of Ireland', *Dublin Daily Express*, January 28, 1899. Yeats signs the essay 'Rosicrux'.

The rose symbol appears constantly in his short stories of this period. In 'The Binding of the Hair', the lady is 'the Rose of my Desire, the Lily of my Peace'. *Secret Rose* (1897), 6. An odour of roses is stirred up miraculously by the pagan saint in 'Where There Is Nothing, There Is God', *ibid.* 33. The Quixotic knight in 'Out of the Rose' has a small rose of rubies upon his helmet, and prays to the Divine Rose of Intellectual Flame, 53-4. In 'The Heart of the Spring' the ladies crown themselves with either roses or lilies according to whether they choose love or purity, 83. In ' Of Costello the Proud', the moon 'glimmered in the distance like a great white rose', 118, and the women of the Shee rush 'together in the shape of a great silvery rose', 123. The magical power of the rose is prominent in 'The Vision of Hanrahan the Red', 176-9. At the climax of 'Rosa Alchemica' there is a pagan ceremony at which the cross and rose are joined, 257.

72. *very obscure.*   Unp. MS. It should not be assumed from this statement that Yeats did not himself read Plato. Lionel Johnson gave him an edition of Plato early in the 'nineties and made him read it, Mrs. Yeats heard from her husband. The conception of art in 'The Tables of the Law' as 'sowing everywhere unlimited desires, like torches thrown into a burning city', suggests the *Republic,* although its attitude towards the burning is different, and the description of Eros in 'Rosa Alchemica' surely borrows from the *Symposium.*

73. *from afar'.*   Note to CP, 524 (447).

its eternity'.   'The Rose of Battle', CP, 43 (38).

74. *the Incarnation . . .'.*   'Some Passages from the Letters of W. B. Yeats to A.E.', *Dublin Magazine,* 14 (July–September 1939), 16.

75. *in either.*   See, for example, *Secret Rose* (1897), 183.

of Life.   *Wind Among the Reeds* (1899), 75.

her soul.   Rossetti, *The House of Life*, xlv.

77. *of life,*   *Wind Among the Reeds* (1899), 77.

　　 the Bear.   *Ibid.* 78.

　　 Elemental Powers',   Afterwards entitled 'The Poet Pleads with
the Elemental Powers'.

　　 in mythology.   *Wind Among the Reeds* (1899), 77. In an early
note on the poem, Yeats spoke of 'the Tree of Life, on which is
here imagined the Rose of the Ideal Beauty growing before it was
cast into the world'. 'Aodh Pleads with the Elemental Powers',
Dome, 1 (December 1898), 238. Compare the serpents in 'The
Curse of the Fires and of the Shadows', *Secret Rose* (1897), 72 ;
'The Twisting of the Rope', *ibid.* 154 ; and the serpent dance in
the latter story, *ibid.* 148-9.

78. *the Sedge',*   Afterwards entitled 'He Hears the Cry of the Sedge'.

79. *to do.*   Unp. ltr., May 18, 1898.

80. *in symbol'.*   Unp. ltr. to Russell, August 27 [1899], in possession
of Dr. James Starkey.

　　 may become'.   'Mr. Rhys' Welsh Ballads', *Bookman,* 14 (August 27,
1899), 14-15.

　　 general hints.   Clipping in a Yeats scrapbook ; the name of the
newspaper is not given.

　　 more communicative.   About this time Yeats devised a prologue
to be spoken by an old juggler who is a representation of the
dramatist. He decided to omit it, but it is helpful in illuminatin
the workings of the symbolist mind :

　　 'The stage manager says I've got to juggle for you. That I'm
to cause a vision to come before your eyes, but he doesn't want to
let me please myself. He says it must be simple, easy to understand, all about real human beings, but I am going to please myself
this time. It's no use shaking your head at me there. I am going
to do just as I like. What is the use of getting the black jester out
of the waste places if he is not to do what he likes ? These are my
friends that I have here hung round my neck. Some of them I
picked up on the wayside, some of them I made with a jackknife.
[In unsymbolic speech, some come from tradition, and some are
invented ; a similar distinction is made in Yeats's poem, 'A Prayer
on Going into My House'.] I am going to make you dream about
them and about me. I am going to wave my fingers and you will
begin to dream.

　　 'These two are Aengus and Edaine. They are spirits and
whenever I am in love it is not I that am in love but Aengus who is
always looking for Edaine through somebody's eyes. [One of the
uses of mythology is to merge individual feelings into universal

ones ; thus the lover becomes the god Aengus.] You will find all about them in the old Irish books. She was the wife of Midher, another spirit in the hill, but he grew jealous of her and he put her out of doors, and Aengus hid her in a tower of glass. That is why I carry the two of them in a glass bottle. O Aengus ! O Edaine ! be kind to me when I am in love and make us all believe that it is not you but us ourselves they love. [The juggler longs to keep his personality instead of merely serving as a vehicle for an archetype. Compare 'Cuchulain, the Girl, and the Fool', a poem printed only in limited edition of *Collected Poems* (London, Macmillan, 1949), II, 110.]

'These others — the black dog, the red dog, and the white dog — I am always afraid of them. Sometimes the black dog gets on my back, though I have not been juggling, but I will not talk about him for he was very wicked. I do not know the red dog from myself whenever I am angry or excited or running about. And it is only when I escape from him and the black dog, that the pale dog leads me when I would go, go to everything impossible and lasting, to the place where these poor flowers that I have round my head can never die because they are made out of precious stones. [For these symbols see pp. 81-3 above.] They too are myself but that is a great mystery. The dogs and the little king and queen in the bottle and the flowers, they are all going to be in the dream that you are going to dream presently, but they will be great and terrible and my birds will be there too. These sea birds that I shall be like when I get out of the body [as in 'The White Birds'] and this eagle [inspiration, as in 'Those Images'] that carries me messages from beyond the body and this harp [inspired poetry] that I play on when my birds and my beasts won't talk to me and I too shall be there, there in the dream and all that I did long ago or that I would like to do [for no powerful images ever fade].' Unp. MS.

81. *lover's dream.*   *The Arrow*, November 24, 1906, in Henderson Collection, National Library, Dublin.

the body.   Programme note, *Inis Fail*, August 1905, in Henderson Collection.

the Alchemists'.   *Idem.*

final rest'.   The three qualities are the *Gunas*. Müller, *The Six Systems of Indian Philosophy* (New York, Longmans, 1899), 147.

82. *and wisdom.*   'Introduction to "Mandukya Upanishad"', *Essays 1931 to 1936* (Dublin, Cuala, 1937), 127-8.

the man" '.   Note to *Wind Among the Reeds* (1899), 92-3. Vivian
Mercier informs me that Yeats is quoting Coleridge's *Table
Talk*.

of him.   This unp. correspondence is summarized obliquely in
'The Queen and the Fool' (1901), *Celtic Twilight* (1902), 186-94.

the stars'.   *Shadowy Waters*, in *North American Review*, 170
(May 1900), 724.

83. *the poem'*.   Unp. diary, July 13, 1899.

own perfection';   *Arrow*, November 24, 1906, in Henderson
Collection, National Library, Dublin.

love symbol',   Programme note, *Inis Fail*, August 1905, in Henderson Collection.

CHAPTER V

85. *new material'*.   *The Bounty of Sweden* (Dublin, Cuala, 1925), 1.
He used almost the same words in his *Speech to the British Association*, 1908.

88. *as theirs*.   R. Ellmann, 'Joyce and Yeats', *Kenyon Review*, 12
(Autumn 1950), 624-6.

89. *of images. . . .*   AU, 205.

90. *one body'*.   *The Unicorn from the Stars* (New York, Macmillan,
1908), viii-ix.

the gutter'.   *Dramatis Personae* (1936), 28 (30).

green ground'.   Undated ltr. in Florence Farr, Bernard Shaw,
W. B. Yeats, *Letters* (New York, Dodd, Mead, 1942), 58. Clifford
Bax, ed.

folk tradition.   'The Happiest of the Poets', 'Edmund Spenser',
and *passim* in *Essays* and AU.

vague regret.   *Poems, 1899-1905* (London, Bullen, 1906), xii-xiii ;
compare 'Preface', *Plays and Controversies* (London, Macmillan,
1923, and New York, Macmillan, 1924), v-vi.

91. *unruly soul*.   Farr, Shaw, Yeats, *Letters* (1942), 78. Compare
Essays, 336.

92. *astringent joy*.   Unp. ltr.

run out.'   Friedrich Nietzsche, *Thus Spake Zarathustra*, in *The
Philosophy of Nietzsche* (New York, Modern Library Giant, no
date), 247.

93. *tragic realities.'*   Ibid. 165.

'*a mirror*',   *Beyond Good and Evil*, ibid. 504.

God's mask'.   *Thus Spake Zarathustra*, ibid. 134.

94. *of Galiani*) . . .'.   *Beyond Good and Evil, ibid.* 597.
    own ideal.'   *Ibid.* 457.
    the better'.   *Ibid.* 406.
    illusoire, insaisissable.'   A. G. Lehmann, *The Symbolist Esthetic in France,* 43.

95. *my reasons?'*   *Thus Spake Zarathustra, ibid.* 138.   Yeats altered the phrasing a little. 'Bishop Berkeley', *Essays* (1937), 41.
    of laughter;   *Where There Is Nothing* (London, Bullen, 1903), 46.
    and ease',   'Upon a House Shaken by the Land Agitation' (August 7, 1909), CP, 107 (93).
    of Death'.   'Upon a Dying Lady' (written 1912–13), CP, 179 (157).
    to come'.   Hone, 187 (197).
    self sufficient.   'Some Passages from the Letters of W. B. Yeats to A.E.', *Dublin Magazine,* 14 (July–September 1939), 15.

96. *German philosopher.*   This volume, borrowed by Yeats from Quinn and returned to him, is now in the possession of Deering Library, Northwestern University ; Jens Nyholm, Librarian, has kindly permitted me to quote from Yeats's annotations.

98. *'wild thought'*   'In the Seven Woods', CP, 85 (75).

99. *at me.*   Unp. MS.
    apple-blossom.   'The Arrow', CP, 85 (75).

100. *thy destiny'.*   *Wanderings of Oisin* (1889), 125.
     my heart.   *Secret Rose* (1897), 145.

101. *their glory'.*   'The Song of the Happy Shepherd', CP, 7 (7).

102. *King George.*   Unp. MS.

104. *colouring idiosyncrasy'.*   1896 entry, *Journals of André Gide* (New York, Knopf, 1947), I, 77.   Justin O'Brien, ed.
     and Change.   *Collected Works* (1908), II, 7.
     and actions.   A more sophisticated treatment of the theme was a poem he planned in 1915 about the duellist and the gambler. Unp. ltr. to J. B. Yeats, January 18, 1915.
     of life'.   *Wheels and Butterflies* (1934), 103 (92-3).

106. *those images.*   Unp. MS. Compare his remark, dated October [1913], in an unp. notebook : 'Great art, great poetical drama is the utmost of nobility and the utmost of reality comportable with it. The persons of a drama fall into two groups commonly : the group where nobility predominates and the group where reality predominates. If there is too much of the first, all become sentimental, too much of the second, all become sordid. Nobility struggles with reality, the eagle and the snake.'

108. *an image'.*   *The Player Queen* (London, Macmillan, 1922), 46.
     to be.'   1892 entry, *Journals of Gide,* I, 18-19.

109. *ephemeral life.'* Unp. MS.
it choose. Unp. ltr. in possession of James A. Healy.
110. *about me'.* *Where There Is Nothing* (London, Bullen, 1903), 24.
'her boy'. 'When Helen Lived', CP, 124 (109).
112. *present personality.* *Dramatis Personae* (1936), 74 (79).
unmixed wine. 'A Thought from Propertius', CP, 172 (150).
113. *unchristened heart'.* 'Vacillation', CP, 286 (247).
115. *and Donne.* 'To a Young Beauty', CP, 157 (138).

CHAPTER VI

116. *in life;* *Dramatis Personae* (1936), 133 (143).
117. *'self-conquest'.* *Idem.*
of everybody'. 'Introduction', *Oxford Book of Modern Verse* (1936), ix. Compare 'Art and Ideas', *Essays*, 431-3.
of poetry', AU, 180.
118. *of delight. . . .* *Wanderings of Oisin* (1889), 8-9.
119. *'Dawn passioned'*, *Ibid.* 28.
any other. Unp. ltr., February 3, 1889, in National Library, Dublin.
than another'. *Vision* (1925), 176.
wooded earth'. Copy in Mrs. Yeats's possession.
120. *made conventional.* *Essays*, 370; AU, 91; *Early Poems and Stories* (1925), v.
a board. AU, 456.
in verse. *Letters to the New Island*, ix, and FD.
calamitous times. *Countess Kathleen* (1892), 16.
with her. *Ibid.* 89.
121. *falls forgetting.* *Ibid.* 84.
early verse. *Early Poems and Stories* (1925), v.
loose feeling. *Idem* ; AU, 234. See also the MS. note Yeats wrote in his copy of *Poems* (London, Ernest Benn, 1929), printed in Wade, *A Bibliography of Yeats*, 154-5.
romantic movement', AU, 91.
painter's business. *Essays*, 432.
is finer'. Ltr. from Keats to Benjamin Bailey, March 13, 1818.
122. *weary cry.* An earlier draft of this poem, dated Oct. 1891, at Dublin, has the following variations : lines 3-4, 'The song of the ever-singing leaves, / Had hushed away . . .'; line 8, 'her million years' ; lines 9-10, 'And now the angry sparrows in the eaves, / The withered moon . . .'; line 11, 'The wearisome loud chanting of the leaves'.

its character.   MacNeice, *The Poetry of W. B. Yeats* (Oxford, 1941), 69-72. See also Thomas Parkinson, *W. B. Yeats, Self-Critic* (Univ. of California Press, 1951), 165-72.

123. *the window'.*   *Essays,* 201.
    and body'.   *Ibid.* 336.

124. *dim hair'.*   'The Lover Mourns for the Loss of Love', CP, 68 (59).
    'still life'.   *Essays,* 336.
    being 'cold'.   AU, 255, 91.
    'symbolic language'   *Essays,* 433.
    in it.   AU, 189.
    linnet's wings.   Yeats, *Letters to Tynan,* 77-8.

125. *some beauty. . . .*   *Essays,* 201.
    dream-dimmed eyes. . . .   'He Tells of a Valley Full of Lovers', CP, 74 (64).

126. *other stanzas'.*   Unp. ltr., September 24, 1901, from Hearn to Yeats, quoting a ltr. of Yeats.
    the words'.   *Man and Masks,* 154 (151).

127. *head before.*   Pound, *Personae* (New York, Liveright, 1926), 3.

128. *earlier work.*   Interview with Yeats reported in *San Francisco Examiner,* January 31, 1904.
    of life'.   *Discoveries,* in *Essays,* 336.
    'personal utterance'.   AU, 127.
    the 'Spectator'.   Unp. ltr., 1910.

129. *brief lives.'*   Clipping in Henderson Collection, National Library, Dublin.
    own lives.   Hone, 270 (288-9).

130. *numb ones.*   *Dramatis Personae* (1936), 53 (56).
    'climbing moon'.   *Idem.* Parkinson, *Yeats,* 192.
    to stray   Unp. MS.
    my bed'.   Unp. MS.

131. *it were'.*   The typescript, with Pound's corrections, is in the Harriet Monroe Collection at the University of Chicago Library, which has kindly authorized my use of it.

132. *tenth line.*   A MS. of this poem among Yeats's papers contains these corrections in Pound's hand.
    'theatrical element'   *Essays,* 497; *Dramatis Personae* (1936), 87 (94).
    of words'.   *Essays,* 331-2.
    long-mounting thought'.   AU, 123.

133. *his 'dignity'.*   *Essays,* 335.
    learned language.'   AU, 270; *cf.* Walter Pater, *Essays* from *The Guardian* (London, Macmillan, 1901), 15.
    'common syntax'.   AU, 374, 190.

134. *the south.*   'The Hour Before Dawn', CP, 130-34 (114-17).
      formula helps'.   Ltr. of April 6, 1936, in *Letters from Yeats to Wellesley*, 62.
135. *body was.'*   'A Woman Homer Sung', CP, 100 (88).
      most defamed. . . .   'The People', CP, 169 (148).
      long ago. . . .   'Reconciliation', CP, 102 (89).
      twelvemonth since. . . .   'The Fisherman', CP, 167 (146).
      merely voice!'   'King and No King', CP, 102 (90).
      of stone. . . .   'The Three Beggars', CP, 126 (111).
      had dreamed. . . .   'Against Unworthy Praise', CP, 103 (91).
      can break. . . .   *Idem.*
      a form. . . .   'Peace', CP, 103 (90).
      for companions. . . .   'At Galway Races', CP, 108 (95).
      greasy till. . . .   'September 1913', CP, 120 (106).
      nine centuries. . . .   'The Hour Before Dawn', CP, 132 (116).
      the form. . . .   'Memory', CP, 168 (147).
136. *and wrought.* . . .   'A Woman Homer Sung', CP, 100 (88).
      the altar. . . .   'A Thought from Propertius', CP, 172 (150).
      a tale. . . .   'King and No King', CP, 102 (90).
137. *or write.* . . .   'Ego Dominus Tuus', CP, 181 (158).
      years again. . . .   'September 1913', CP, 121 (106).
      he lies. . . .   'To a Friend Whose Work Has Come to Nothing', CP, 122 (107).
      topless towers. . . .   'When Helen Lived', CP, 124 (109).
      to prolong. . . .   'The Living Beauty', CP, 156 (137).
      the crane. . . .   'The Three Beggars', CP, 126 (111).
      growing old. . . .   'On Woman', CP, 165 (145).
      had come. . . .   'In Memory of Alfred Pollexfen', CP, 176 (154).
      a jest.   'When Helen Lived', CP, 124 (109).
      could say. . . .   'A Memory of Youth', CP, 137 (121).
138. *are gone.* . . .   'Lines Written in Dejection', CP, 164 (143).
      the roads. . . .   'The Cold Heaven', CP, 140 (123).
      single soul. . . .   'Paudeen', CP, 122 (107).
      Spanish politics?   'Politics', CP, 392-3 (337).
      of his. . . .   'A Friend's Illness', CP, 109 (95).
      not come. . . .   'To a Shade', CP, 123 (108).
      at need. . . .   'Closing Rhyme' of *Responsibilities*, CP, 143 (126).
      their tears. . . .   'Lines Written in Dejection', CP, 164 (143).
139. *of Death.*   'Upon a Dying Lady', CP, 179 (157). (Barhaim in this poem is probably Bahram, that 'great hunter' and warrior of whom Omar wrote.)
      to mind. . . .   'An Irish Airman Foresees His Death', CP, 152 (133).

140. *morning light.* . . .   'Paudeen', CP, 122 (107).

    was cast. . . .   'Introductory Rhymes' of *Responsibilities*, CP, 113 (99).

    draughty seas?   'At the Abbey Theatre', CP, 107 (94).

    his eye?   'The Peacock', CP, 135 (119).

    crystalline cry.   'Paudeen', CP, 122 (107).

    appointed him.   'An Appointment', CP, 141 (123).

    omits it.   W. A. M. Peters, *Gerard Manley Hopkins* (Oxford, 1948), 125-31.

141. *this place.* . . .   'The Dolls', CP, 142 (124).

    me friend. . . .   'To a Young Beauty', CP, 157 (138).

    wild tears.   'The Living Beauty', CP, 156 (137).

    been crossed.   'King and No King', CP, 103 (90).

    the dawn.   'The Dawn', CP, 164 (144).

143. *still madness.*   Henn, 89-90, recognizes the word's ambivalence.

145. *the affections'*   A ltr. from Ezra Pound to Kate Buss, March 9, 1916, says Yeats had complained that Pound's verse gave him 'no asylum for the affections'. Pound, *Letters* (New York, Harcourt, 1950), 73. D. D. Paige, ed. Yeats was quoting a sentence of Tulka, 'Give me the world if Thou wilt, but grant me an asylum for my affections', which he used as an epigraph. *Early Poems and Stories* (1925), xii.

CHAPTER VII

146. *is changed.*   J. W. N. Sullivan, *Beethoven* (New York, Knopf, 1927), 261.

    blasted oak,   'Crazy Jane and the Bishop', CP, 290 (251).

    poet's house.   See, for example, 'Coole Park and Ballylee, 1931', CP, 275 (239).

147. *the earth.*   Unp. ltr., September 21 [1926].

    Scott designed.   Unp. ltr., copy of which is in John Quinn Collection at New York Public Library.

149. *perfectly explicit.*   'Meditations in Time of Civil War', CP, 225 (198).

152. *the rose.*   I am indebted here to a brilliant article of Northrop Frye, 'Yeats and the Language of Symbolism', *University of Toronto Quarterly*, 17 (Oct. 1947), 1-17.

153. *is conflict'.*   See p. 8 above. Cf. *Vision* (1937), 214.

154. *the rock,*   Mrs. Yeats tells me he was studying this point.

155. *in comprehension.*   Henry More, *Complete Poems* (Edinburgh University Press, 1878), 108. A. B. Grosart, ed. Yeats says he read More's verse in Lady Gregory, *Visions and Beliefs*, II, 328-9.

or vortexes.   In a private diary kept at the end of the nineteenth century, Yeats relates a 'vision' of a vortex, which came to him as 'a form of the cauldron', one of his four talismans.

156. *and emotion'.*   Pound, *Letters*, 74 (March 10, 1916).

name 'Vorticism'.   Pound, *Gaudier-Brzeska* (London, John Lane, 1916), 106. This book is in Yeats's library.

a 'top',   'The Double Vision of Michael Robartes', CP, 193 (169).

'Plato's spindle',   'His Bargain', CP, 299 (258).

157. *and wound';*   *The King of the Great Clock Tower* (1935), 4.

lunar mansions';   Unp. MS., dated 1919. He added a Buddhist touch, 'I say typal man for sins may increase or virtue decrease the number of incarnations'. *A Vision* is much less explicit about the number of cycles and the influence of sin or virtue.

158. *the dark.*   'The Phases of the Moon', CP, 184-5 (161).

of itself!'   *Ibid.* 185 (162).

the gyres.   Some of the blood and moon imagery of the later poems unconsciously suggests the menstrual cycle.

159. *traditional, emotional.'*   AU, 456.

160. *every saint.*   'The Saint and the Hunchback', CP, 189 (165).

162. *his soul';*   *Man and Masks*, 19 (18).

sudden blazed',   'Vacillation', CP, 284 (246).

exultation almost'.   *Vision* (1925), xiii.

163. *automatic writing.*   *Vision* (1937), 8-25 and *passim.*

psychological classification.   *Ibid.* 78, 187 ; *Man and Masks*, 238 (234).

a language.   He customarily refers to it in this way in his correspondence with Mrs. Shakespear. See also *Vision* (1925), 214-15, where he probably has his own work in mind.

to reality';   Unp. notes for *A Vision.*

'lunar parable';   *Idem.*

or mythology;   *Vision* (1925), 252.

of metaphors;   *Vision* (1937), 8.

of experience';   *Ibid.* 25.

of experience'   Unp. MS. Among Yeats's papers is an unp. account ostensibly written by one of his characters, Aherne, to describe the way *A Vision* came to be published. The poet was at pains to surround his book with legendary trappings :

'It was only, however, on our return to London, on the eve of his [Robartes'] final departure, that I understood that he was the same passionate, capricious man I had known in my youth. At the time of our old theological difference I had repudiated his whole view of life with vehemence, and because I could now consider any point of view dispassionately, and could even explain it to others without insisting upon my own, he seemed to think I was no longer a Catholic. I had given much time and thought to his rambling notes and ill-drawn diagrams, and had shown that they interested me as a contribution to religious history, and he had come to consider me, it seems, as his disciple.   I was discussing the general arrangement of the proposed book, when I used these words, "In the introduction I will of course explain my own point of view : that I concede to this Arabian system exactly the same measure of belief that an intelligent reader concedes to a Platonic myth".

'He flared up into a rage and said that I had led him to believe that I was convinced, that I had been convinced until my Catholicism gripped me by the throat, and he even asked me if [I] had not taken the advice of some confessor and before the evening was out we had our old quarrel over again. He called upon me the next day, made some kind of an apology, and said that I must come to see Mr. Yeats and that he had made an appointment for us. At Woburn Buildings he told of his Arabian discoveries and spread out upon the table his diagrams, his notes, my written commentary without even explaining that it was mine ; and after a couple of hours' exposition, and answering many questions, asked Mr. Yeats to undertake the editorship.

'Mr. Yeats opened a large gilded Moorish wedding chest, took out a number of copy-books full of notes and diagrams ; showed that our diagrams and his were almost exactly the same ; that our notes only differed from his because our examples and our general atmosphere were Arabian whereas his were drawn from European history and literature.

'"You can only have found that all out", said Robartes, who was pale and excited, "through the inspiration of God."

'"Is not that a rather obsolete term ?" said Mr. Yeats. "It came in the first instance quite suddenly. I was looking at my canary, which was darting about the cage in rather brilliant light, when I found myself in a strangely still and silent state and in that state I saw with the mind's eye symbols streaming before me. That still and silent state always recurs in some degree when I fix my mind upon the canary."

'He then suggested that I should publish my book upon the philosophy of the Judwalis at the same date as that upon which his book should appear. Michael Robartes seemed ready to forgive my unbelief, but I would not have his forgiveness, for I knew now that he would not accept any exposition of mine as adequate.

'Then Mr. Yeats suggested that I should write the preface to his book and annotate his text here and there. "That", he said, "will show that Robartes was the first discoverer and it will be of great value to the exposition. I will explain this philosophy in its isolated abstract form, you in its concrete form as a part of history. Certain French and English poems which seemed vague and faint when first written have grown precise and solid now that they have influenced thought and literature."

'I accepted this proposal but when we were out in the street once more I said, "I do not believe that story of the canary, he is keeping something back ; these notes of his have had a much more humdrum origin. Are you quite sure that no other traveller has met the Judwalis or found the *Speculum* of Giraldus?" Robartes would have none of my suggestions and pointed out that Boehme had passed into what he called his walking trance while contemplating a gleam of sunlight upon a brazen pot and so found philosophy.   OWEN AHERNE
                                                December 1922'

Later in the same notes, Yeats, still struggling to define *A Vision* more precisely and to establish the attitude it was intended to elicit, wrote : 'For the present I but ask my reader to accept my dream as he would accept the play of Hamlet when the curtain is up'.

164. *bursting pod'*.   *Vision* (1937), 141.
     one destiny.   Unp. MS. Compare the line in 'The Statues', 'Mirror on mirror mirrored is all the show'.
165. *unbegotten soul*.   Unp. MS.
166. *of history*.   Unp. MS.
168. *boiling point. . . .'*   Arthur Symons, 'Ballet, Pantomime, and Poetic Drama', *Dome*, 1 (October 1898), 66.
170. *trunk), well.'*   Unp. ltr., written about 1921 in connection with the cover of *Four Plays for Dancers*.
     of trance', —— 'Byzantium', CP, 281 (244).
171. *the Mabinogion*.   John V. Kelleher has pointed out that Yeats quotes it from Matthew Arnold's *On the Study of Celtic Literature* rather than from Lady Guest.
173. *was conceived?*   'Whence Had They Come?' CP, 332 (286).
178. *hovering still. . . .*   Unp. MS.
     her drop?   *To-morrow*, 1 (August 1924), 4.
179. *lost faith'*.   Unp. ltr., August 31 [1929 ?].

CHAPTER VIII

180. *and fly'.*   Conversation with Mrs. Francis Stuart. The butterfly is first used by Yeats as a symbol of the soul in *The Hour-Glass* (London, Bullen, 1904), 32.

181. *by religion'.*   T. S. Eliot, 'The Poetry of W. B. Yeats', in *The Permanence of Yeats* (1950), 338.

 the past,   I am indebted to an unp. essay of Julian Moynihan for a brilliant interpretation of this poem.

183. *as well'.*   Yeats, 'Introduction', in Tagore, *Gitanjali* (London, Macmillan, 1913, and New York, Macmillan, 1916), vii-xxii.

184. *formless matrix'*   On the Boiler (1939), 28.

 has come'.   'Introduction' to *An Indian Monk*, in *Essays* (1937), 77.

 whole man'.   'Introduction' to *The Ten Principal Upanishads*, translated by Shri Purohit Swami and Yeats (London, Faber, and New York, Macmillan, 1937), 11.

185. *heroic cry.'*   *Letters from Yeats to Wellesley*, 8-9.

186. *of joy',*   *On the Boiler* (1939), 35.

 to himself,   *Wheels and Butterflies* (1934), 75 (67).

 usual posture.'   Gide, *Journals*, I, 18.

187. *the poets',*   'Introduction' to *Ten Principal Upanishads* (1937), 10.

 half-Asiatic.   Idem.

 is nothing.   'Introduction' to *Fighting the Waves*, in *Wheels and Butterflies* (1934), 73 (65).

188. *rich experience.'*   *On the Boiler* (1939), 27.

 the bowels',   Idem.

189. *faery tale'.*   Unp. ltr., October 20, 1938.

 fixed type.   *On the Boiler* (1939), 37. '. . . The human norm, discovered from the measurement of ancient statues, was God's first handiwork, that "perfectly proportioned human body" which had seemed to Dante Unity of Being symbolised.' *Vision* (1937), 291.

190. *gone before.*   The marriage of Europe and Asia would be a reflection of the timeless, spaceless sphere. *Vision* (1937), 205.

 and periods.   *Letters from Yeats to Wellesley*, 149.

 in argument',   'Poetry and Tradition', *Essays*, 313.

191. *in heat.* . . .   'Under Ben Bulben', CP, 399 (342).

 look forth. . . .   'The Gyres', CP, 337 (291).

 of Spring. . . .   'Imitated from the Japanese', CP, 340 (293).

 you please!   'The Statesman's Holiday', CP, 389 (334).

 than Pythagoras. . . .   'The Statues', CP, 375 (322).

thirty years. . . .   'The Municipal Gallery Revisited', CP, 368
(316).

tomb-haunter once. . . .   'A Bronze Head', CP, 382 (328).

it all.   'Under Ben Bulben', CP, 398 (341).

193. *have lied.*   'He Thinks of Those Who Have Spoken Evil of His
Beloved', CP, 75 (65). The phrase, 'a mouthful of air', was first
used by Yeats in describing the fairies : 'Nations of gay creatures,
having no souls ; nothing in their bright bodies but a mouthful of
sweet air'. 'Tales from the Twilight', *Scots Observer*, 3 (March 1,
1890), 409. Cf. *Collected Plays* (New York. 1953), 403.

194. *driving force',*   *Letters from Yeats to Wellesley,* 47.

the clay. . . .   'The Curse of Cromwell', CP, 350 (302).

heroic centuries,   'Under Ben Bulben', CP, 400 (343).

was crucified.   'The Curse of Cromwell', CP, 350 (302).

200. *of Kings !*   O'Connor's translations were published as *The Fountain
of Magic* (London, Macmillan, 1939) ;   he has graciously lent me
his MS. with Yeats's corrections.

201. *of sound'.*   'Edmund Spenser', *Essays,* 472. Compare his remark
to Dorothy Wellesley about the need for 'vast sentiments, generalizations supported by tradition'. *Letters from Yeats to Wellesley,*
64-5. He repeats it in 'Introduction' to *Ten Principal Upanishads*
(1937), 10.

him understand'.   Conversation with O'Connor.

to say?   'The Curse of Cromwell', CP, 350 (302).

204. *a coat-hanger.*   Henn, 140, relates the refrain to some dreams of
his own death which Yeats experienced about the time of writing
the poem.

of desire.   'Prometheus Unbound', *Essays* (1937), 55-7, 62.

a bird'   'Among School Children', CP, 244 (214).

205. *common people'.*   A quotation from Aristotle of which Lady
Gregory was also fond. *Dramatis Personae* (1936), 14.

206. *artistic movement.*   Henderson Collection, National Library,
Dublin.

in mind.   Stephen Spender, *World within World* (London, Hamish
Hamilton, and New York, Harcourt Brace, 1951), 150.

public man',   'Among School Children', CP, 243 (213).

wicked man'.   CP, 356 (307).

207. *woman's breast'.*   *Ibid.* 358 (309).

211. *Dec. 27 [1934].*   Unp. MS.

and heads'   'Under Ben Bulben', CP, 400 (343).

man's revery',   'Introduction' to Patanjali, *Aphorisms of Yoga*
(London, Faber, 1938), 11.

through contradictions'.   *Ibid.* 16.

too false.'   *On the Boiler* (1939), 36.

staring eyes'.   *Idem.*

ivory balls'.   *Ibid.* 25.

212. *become beliefs.*   Graham Hough, *The Last Romantics* (London, Duckworth, 1949), 251.

      our solitude.   *Wheels and Butterflies* (1934), 20 (18).

      the dice.   *Ibid.* 108 (97).

      to confusion.   *Ibid.* 106 (96).

      human mind'.   *On the Boiler,* 26.

213. *possible wisdom.*   Unp. ltr.

214. *my life'.*   *Man and Masks,* 289 (285).

215. *this place?*   'The Man and the Echo', CP, 394 (338).

CHAPTER IX

216. *'Southern Californian',*   *The Permanence of Yeats* (1950), 345.

217. *great artist . . .'.*   Unp. notes for *A Vision.*

      artistic life.   Unp. ltr.

219. *finest poems.*   His first important statement about the image was probably a review written in 1896 :

      ' "The word image", says "The Way of Christ", a compilation from Boehme and Law's interpretation of Boehme, published at Bath when Blake was eighteen, "meaneth not only a creaturely resemblance, in which sense man is said to be the Image of God ; but it signifieth also a spiritual substance, a birth or effect of a will, wrought in and by a spiritual being or power. And imagination, which we are apt erroneously to consider an airy, idle, and impotent faculty of the human mind, dealing in fiction and roving in phantasy or idea without producing any powerful or permanent [effects], is the magia or power of raising and forming such images or substances, and the greatest power in nature." ' 'William Blake', *Bookman* (April 1896), 21.

220. *unwinding thread.*   ' "We clothe ourselves to descend, and unclothe ourselves to ascend", says the occult aphorism.' Yeats and Ellis, *Blake,* I, 272-3.

      Roman tombstones.   Eugénie Strong, *Apotheosis and After Life* (New York, Dutton, 1915), 136, 161. Yeats first admired mechanical birds in 1899 in Beerbohm Tree's stage sets. *Letters* (ed. Wade), 309.

221. *full sail.*[2]   Unp. MS.

      nature's spite',   'Coole Park, 1929', CP, 274 (238).

222. *work began :* Compare 'Those images that waken in the blood', 'Hound Voice', CP, 385 (330).

I dream" '. Unp. ltr. He was quoting an early version of 'Fergus and the Druid'.

Katharine Tynan. Yeats, *Letters to Tynan*, 64.

223. *the work'.* 'The Choice', CP, 278 (242). Yeats's MS. shows that this poem was originally the next to last stanza of 'Coole Park and Ballylee, 1931'; he wisely removed it.

'The Tower'. It is interesting to compare the first stanza of this poem with the prose version which preceded it : 'What shall I do with this absurd toy which they have given me, this grotesque rattle. O heart & nerves, you are as vigorous as ever, you still hunger for the whole world, & they have given you this toy.' MS. book, 1921.

224. *of existence ;* So he writes in AU, 143, 'I had even created a dogma : "Because those imaginary people are created out of the deepest instinct of man, to be his measure and his norm, whatever I can imagine those mouths speaking may be the nearest I can go to truth" '.

this designation, Note to CP, 533 (454).

225. *a vision'.* MS. notes ; *cf.* Lady Gregory, *Journals*, 265.

seventh day. Unp. MS.

232. *cheated dead.*[1] *Rann, An Ulster Quarterly of Poetry*, Autumn 1948, 3.

thought away. . . . Unp. MS.

233. *human life?* 'Preliminary Script of E.R.', unp. MS. Compare *Wheels and Butterflies* (1934), 20 (18).

234. *the void.* Hone, 405 (433-4).

the head'. 'Lapis Lazuli', CP, 338 (292).

235. *of contradictions.* Unp. MS.

of souls', Unp. MS. Compare *Wheels and Butterflies* (1934), 107-8 (97).

other's universe.' Jeffares, 237.

237. *abstracts are'.* *A Full Moon in March* (London, Macmillan, 1935), 38.

or states. Unp. MS.

238. *be truth'.* Keats, ltr. to Benjamin Bailey, November 22, 1817.

and reason'. Ltr. to George and Thomas Keats, December 28, 1817.

of Thoughts', Ltr. to Bailey, November 22, 1817.

240. *our scepticism.*[1] Unp. journal.

242. *complete man'*,   Yeats and Ellis, *Blake*, I, 241.
   into it.'   Unp. MS.
   or another'.   'Estrangement', *Dramatis Personae*, 86 (93).
   those desires.   Unp. ltr. In a diary of 1930 he elaborated : 'I must
   not talk to myself about "the truth" nor call myself "teacher" nor
   another "pupil" — these things are abstract — but see myself set
   in a drama where I struggle to exalt and overcome concrete realities
   perceived not with mind only but as with the roots of my hair'.
   Pages from a Diary Written in Nineteen Hundred and Thirty (Dublin,
   Cuala, 1944), 15.

243. *clipped enough ?*   Unp. MS.

244. *in symbols*.   Yeats wrote in *A Vision* (New York, Macmillan, 1956),
   p. 193, 'Reality can be symbolized but cannot be known.'

245. *be possible*.   Henderson Collection, National Library, Dublin.
   in marmalade'.   'Ego Dominus Tuus', CP, 181 (159).

247. *the streams'*.   'Men Improve with the Years', CP, 153 (134).

INDEX